Mexploitation Cinema

Mexploitation Cinema

A Critical History of Mexican Vampire, Wrestler, Ape-Man and Similar Films, 1957–1977

DOYLE GREENE

McFarland & Company, Inc., Publishers
Jefferson, North Carolina, and London

LIBRARY OF CONGRESS CATALOGUING-IN-PUBLICATION DATA

Greene, Doyle, 1962–
Mexploitation cinema : a critical history of Mexican vampire, wrestler,
ape-man and similar films, 1957–1977 / Doyle Greene.
p.   cm.
Includes bibliographical references and index.

ISBN 0-7864-2201-7 (softcover : 50# alkaline paper)

1. Exploitation films — Mexico — History and criticism.
2. Sensationalism in motion pictures.   I. Title
PN1995.9.S284G74   2005   791.43'653 — dc22   2005011057

British Library cataloguing data are available

On the cover: Promotional artwork from the
1957 film *El Tesoro de Pancho Villa*

Manufactured in the United States of America

*McFarland & Company, Inc., Publishers
Box 611, Jefferson, North Carolina 28640
www.mcfarlandpub.com*

For Kathleen Newman,
whose enthusiasm for a paper on El Santo
in a course on Mexican cinema at the
University of Iowa made this project possible

Acknowledgments

I owe an enormous debt of thanks to Rob Craig, whose "Wonder World of K. Gordon Murray" website provided invaluable historical material regarding Murray's illustrious career and Mexican horror cinema. Additionally, Rob contributed numerous insightful comments throughout the course of this project and generously provided several illustrations. Another substantial debt is owed to David Wilt, as my numerous citations to his work indicate. His "Films of El Santo" website and myriad other sources pertaining to Mexican cinema supplied an indispensable wealth of material, and he also generously provided many illuminating comments and suggestions. Simply put, without the efforts, research, and contributions of Rob Craig and David Wilt, I shudder to speculate to what extent, or even *if*, my own work on Mexican horror cinema could have developed. Thanks also to Brian Moran at the "Santo Street" website for his assistance in compiling my own collection of Mexican cinema and Azteca Studios lobby cards.

Thanks to the following academic programs: The Master of Liberal Studies Program and the Department of Cultural Studies and Comparative Literature at the University of Minnesota, and the Film Studies Program and Department of Cinema and Comparative Literature at the University of Iowa. My work in these settings provided both the intellectual inspiration and the opportunity to explore trash cinema in a serious context. Finally, thanks to my family and friends for their support, above all to my late parents, Earl and Laura Greene.

Table of Contents

Table of Contents

Introduction:
Why Mexploitation?

From approximately 1957 to 1977, one of the more popular genres in Mexican cinema consisted of horror films featuring an array of vampires, Aztec mummies, mad scientists, ape-men, and various other macabre menaces. However, the most striking and famous aspect of these horror films was their incorporation of *lucha libre* (Mexican professional wrestling), resulting in numerous movies that starred not only fiendish monsters but a variety of popular *luchadores* (wrestlers), including one of the most important figures in Mexican popular culture: *El Santo, el Enmascarado de Plata* ("The Saint, the Silver-Masked Man") — universally known simply as "Santo." It is this collection of horror and horror-wrestling movies that have been termed *mexploitation* by both cult-film fans and, more recently, Latin American film scholars.

Certainly, much of mexploitation's notoriety in America has so far centered on its cult-film credentials: the limited budgets born out of the conditions of the Mexican film industry; the surreal qualities generated by their eclectic merging of disparate film genres and other elements of Mexican popular culture; and the enigmatic dubbing of the films provided by exploitation entrepreneur K. Gordon Murray, who single-handedly introduced mexploitation cinema to America via late-night television and drive-ins during the 1960s. Unfortunately, in the United States mexploitation films have been widely ridiculed; at best they are granted a "so bad they're good" status.

My own intention in exploring mexploitation cinema is to move beyond the debate of whether, or to what degree, these films have any sort of artistic integrity or legitimacy. Rather, this project will focus on how mexploitation films, as products of a specific time and place, are entertaining, insightful, and, yes, *important* cultural documents that address the conditions, contradictions, and visions of contemporary Mexican society, politics, and culture. It is my contention that any discussion of the historical and cultural importance of "Mexican national cinema" could, and *should*, include the mexploitation era as well as the Golden Age of Mexican cinema or the films of Luis Buñuel.

1

In pursuing this critical history, I have adopted an interdisciplinary approach, combining research in cultural theory, film studies, and Mexican history and popular culture. I pay specific attention to the historical and cultural context in which these films were produced; close textual analysis of specific films; and, perhaps most importantly, the consistent ideological messages these films offer. In keeping with these areas of emphasis, this book is roughly divided into three sections, each focusing on a crucial facet of mexploitation.

The first section, composed of the first three chapters, might be said to spotlight early mexploitation. Chapter One provides an historical overview of Mexico's political situation and the economic conditions of the Mexican film industry in the late 1950s, which laid the foundation for the development of mexploitation; a brief overview of some of the key films and figures in mexploitation cinema; and the subsequent introduction of these films to America. Chapter Two argues that mexploitation can be viewed as far more than camp oddities, but instead forms a strange "counter-cinema" that addresses key issues in Mexican society: the valorization of *mexicanidad* (Mexican national identity), the cultural conflict between modernity and tradition, and issues of gender politics. Chapter Three employs what is probably Murray's most famous mexploitation import, *The Brainiac*, as a specific case study the issues outlined in the previous chapters.

Chapter Four constitutes the second section of this project and is devoted to a historical and critical discussion of the lucha libre films (focusing, perhaps inevitably, on the legendary El Santo). A short history of the lucha libre genre, an analysis of the cultural significance of lucha libre in Mexican society, and an overview of the iconic status of Santo in Mexico provides the contextual framework for a discussion of three seminal Santo films (all of which also address the issues of mexicanidad, modernity, and gender): the Murray import *Santo vs. the Vampire Women* (retitled *Samson vs. the Vampire Women* in America), *Santo, el Enmascarado de Plata vs. la invasión de los marcianos* (*Santo, the Silver-Masked Man vs. the Invasion of the Martians*), and *Santo y Blue Demon contra Drácula y el Hombre Lobo* (*Santo and Blue Demon vs. Dracula and the Wolf Man*).

The third section consists of Chapters Five and Six, which will concentrate on legendary Mexican director René Cardona's *Luchadoras* ("Wrestling Women") films from 1962 to 1968. Chapter Five provides an examination of Cardona's first two "Wrestling Women" entries, the Murray imports *Doctor of Doom* and *Wrestling Women vs. the Aztec Mummy*. Chapter Six focuses on the final film of the "Wrestling Women" cycle, the horror-exploitation classic *Night of the Bloody Apes*. Once again, critical inquiry will center on how Cardona's films address the social and cultural issues of mexicanidad, modernity, and especially gender and sexual politics in highly problematic and often hilarious ways.

Ultimately, this project is not intended to argue that one day mexploitation directors such as René Cardona and Chano Urueta will be considered as cinematically influential or artistically accomplished as Luis Buñuel or Paul Leduc. However, it will argue that mexploitation films, while certainly provoking more than their share of ironic amusement and amazement, also provide perceptive studies of Mexican society; and, as such, merit serious critical attention. Perhaps, as absurd as it may initially sound, it is possible to posit that *The Brainiac* or *Night of the Bloody Apes* might one day be mentioned in the same breath as *Bride of Frankenstein* or *Psycho*.

1

Mexploitation: Horror, Mexican Style

Mexican Horror Cinema in Social Context

Throughout the twentieth century, the two primary and inherently related political projects designed to create a *modern* Mexico were the establishment of a Mexican national identity and the development of an industrial-consumer economy. However, by the 1950s, the political and cultural efforts to instill a sense of *mexicanidad* were demonstrating signs of serious disarray. As described by Carlos Monsiváis, the construction of a modern Mexican nationalism proved to be an utter failure by ignoring and even denying Mexico's history and cultural heritage:

> The 1950s were a decade in which a struggle was lost. During the Ruiz Cortines period [the presidential administration from 1952 to 1958] the concept of nationalism is irreversibly ruined, to be replaced with another kind of mentality — not devotedly colonial, *still linked to very deep national ideas, but indifferent to tradition, unable to facilitate coherent visions of the national past and future.*[1]

It can be said that an *ahistorical* nationalism was fomented in Mexico, one which viewed the past as an obsolete liability and envisioned the future through the vague and idealized possibilities of modern progress — a consistent ideological position ultimately taken by numerous mexploitation films. Latin American film scholars such as Carl J. Mora contend that one specific area of Mexican popular culture where this crucial loss of direction in Mexican politics during the 1950s seemed to be especially evident and debilitating was in Mexican cinema:

> In 1958, Aldofo López Mateos was designated candidate for president. During his administration (1958–64), the film industry was to enter its darkest days…. Producers of nonexistent social vision in combination with nervously conservative officials were to render the film industry *almost totally unreflective of the problems and conditions of Mexican society.*[2]

5

Along with this failure of Mexican politics to manufacture "coherent visions of the national past and future" and its perceived effect on the Mexican cinema (i.e., causing it to abandon any sense of "social vision"), the Mexican film industry faced its own serious internal crises by the late 1950s. Foremost was the economic collapse of the film industry itself, which led to its virtual nationalization by the early 1960s. Churubusco-Azteca, the studio which produced numerous Mexican horror films in the late 1950s and throughout the 1960s, had the majority of its stock bought by the Mexican government in 1957 and by 1960 was completely nationalized. One immediate effect of a government-controlled film industry was that all films were required to pass censor boards. As a result, the final film product was not necessarily determined by the director or producer but by government officials who could excise any objectionable scenes for moral, political, or other arbitrary reasons. This subsequently generated a pattern of self-censorship in the Mexican film industry, a great reluctance to engage in any social or political controversy, and certainly precluded any overt criticism of the government. Moreover, with the state apparatus actively supporting the film industry, the benefits of government-subsidized film production were offset by demanding production and distribution quotas which strained the already-limited financial and logistical resources of the studios. Furthermore, the Mexican film industry was in direct competition with a much larger Hollywood studio system and its imports, and in order to optimize commercial appeal and revenue, Mexican film studios increasingly relied on popular and predictable genre films — the goal being to satisfy audience expectations and generate box-office profits rather than to promote an artistically innovative and socially conscious national cinema. Mora argued:

> As films became costlier and had to be produced on an assembly-line basis, there was an ever-greater reliance on "formulas"—*comedias rancheras*; films based on dance fads ... melodramas; horror vehicles à la Hollywood; American-style Westerns; and "super-hero" adventures in which masked cowboys or wrestlers took on a variety of evil-doers or monsters. *Quality plummeted but production increased.*[3]

A second major factor in the perceived decline of the Mexican film industry was the rise of television as a popular medium competing with the film industry for audiences. Hollywood responded to the threat of television by creating film products that promised the audience a viewing experience attainable only in movie theaters: Cinemascope, 3-D films, big-budget spectaculars, and, of course, racier content. However, the common and somewhat inaccurate view of Mexican cinema is that the emergence of television, coupled with the film industry's own economic condition, state influence, and product conformity, led to the development of what might be called a "B-Movie" film industry that hastily produced shoddy and irrelevant movies targeted for television as much as theaters. Indeed, Mora described many films of the era as being

> ostensibly serials designed for television; however, their marketability on that medium was so restricted that producers turned to combining the separate serials into one or more full-length features that were released to neighborhood theaters. One of these, which spawned a never-ending series ... was *Santo contra el cerebro diabólico* (1961) [*Santo vs. the Diabolical Brain*] (Santo was a popular wrestler); it made 125,000 pesos at its premiere despite its atrocious quality.[4]

Thus, the late 1950s and into the 1960s might be considered the lowest point of Mexican cinema, a period where it arguably became little more than a national "Culture Industry."[5] Much like the Hollywood studio system, the Mexican film industry's structure came to resemble the structure of industrial monopolies, and its production practices mirrored the principles of assembly lines — its methods and goals designed to expedite the mass production of standardized, predictable cultural-consumer commodities bereft of any social conscience. For Mora, the many films of Santo painfully epitomized the decline in *both* the artistic quality and the social relevance of Mexican cinema. However, such a blanket condemnation of these films completely ignores any cultural function these films may have served. Rather than categorically dismissing them as "atrocious" products of a Mexican culture industry, "totally unreflective of the problems and conditions of Mexican society," one should consider that Mexican horror films *very much* reflected the concerns and problems of contemporary Mexican society in highly complex ways. As Eric Zolov noted, "What Mora misses ... is an understanding that the new characters and themes — such as 'El Santo' and the young rebel — served popular interests, especially among the growing youth population, in ways which the older films could not."[6]

The Birth of Mexploitation

The lineage between the Hollywood horror film and Mexican horror film dates back to the 1930s and the origins of classic Universal Studios horror. When Tod Browning made *Dracula* in 1931, a Spanish version was produced simultaneously for the Latin American market. Directed by George Medford, the Spanish-language *Dracula* featured Mexican actors and crews who used Browning's sets at night. Horror films were also made in Mexico throughout the 1930s and 1940s, and film historian Gary D. Rhodes suggested these films not only reflected the deep influence of the Hollywood horrors, but their emphasis on monsters and mad scientists depicted a cultural conflict between *science* and *religion* in a predominantly Catholic country undergoing considerable social change in the wake of industrialization and modernization.[7]

As noted, the 1950s were a decade marked by growing political uncertainty in the Mexican public sphere and various crises within the Mexican film industry, leading to the production of quickly-made, low-budget genre films that seemed to emphasize rank commercialism over meaningful social commentary. While horror film production steadily increased throughout the decade, in the late 1950s the horror genre experienced a sudden and unprecedented proliferation that heralded the mexploitation era. In 1957, the seminal *El vampiro* (*The Vampire*) was made. Produced by Abel Salazar, written by Ramón Obón, and directed by Fernando Méndez, it starred Germán Robles in the title role. All would become important figures in mexploitation cinema. *El vampiro*'s commercial and critical success in Mexico not only provided the impetus for the increased production of Mexican horror films throughout the next two decades, but Christopher Lee reportedly stated that *El vampiro*, a popular and critical success in Europe as well as Mexico at the time of its original release, was a major source of inspiration for Hammer Studios' glossier *Horror of Dracula* (1958, made one year after *El vampiro*)—a film instrumental in launching the Hammer dynasty of horror films. Unfortunately, *El vampiro* would not be released in the United States (in an English-dubbed version by K. Gordon Murray) until 1968, over a decade after its production. Due to the film's antique appearance, budget limitations, dubbed dialogue, and consignment to late-night television and drive-in circuits, *El vampiro* was dismissed as a cheap Mexican knock-off of the very Hammer Dracula films it actually inspired.

Despite the unfair reputation it earned in America based on Murray's dubbed version, *El vampiro* is a very effective horror film. Essentially an adaptation of *Dracula,* it is typical of mexploitation's emphasis on Gothic atmospherics, melodramatics, and long stretches of expository dialogue at the expense of taut action and consistent pacing. *El vampiro*'s success established Abel Salazar as a major force in mexploitation, and Salazar went on to produce a rapid succession of horror films after *El vampiro*: a quickly-made sequel, *El ataúd del vampiro* (*The Vampire's Coffin, 1957;* dir. Fernando Méndez); *El hombre y el monstruo* (*The Man and the Monster*, 1958; dir. Rafael Baledón); *El espejo de la bruja* (*The Witch's Mirror*, 1960; dir. Chano Urueta); the celebrated *El mundo de los vampiros* (*The World of the Vampires*, 1960; dir. Alfonso Corona Blake); the mind-boggling *El barón del terror* (*The Baron of Terror*, 1961; dir. Chano Urueta; U.S. title: *The Brainiac*); *La cabeza viviente* (*The Living Head*, 1961; dir. Chano Urueta); and *La maldición de la Llorona* (*The Curse of the Crying Woman*, 1961; dir. Rafael Baledón). In addition to his production duties, Salazar, a veteran actor as well as producer, had featured roles in most of his horror productions, most memorably as the nefarious title character in *El barón del terror*.

From left to right: Luis Meneses (René Cardona), Mrs. Meneses (Ofelia Guilmaín), and the evil Baron Vitelius (Abel Salazar) in Chano Urueta's *El barón del terror* (1961; U.S. title: *The Brainiac*). A founding father of mexploitation cinema, Salazar produced and starred in many of the seminal Mexican horror films of the late 1950s and early 1960s. Cardona was arguably the most important director in the mexploitation era. (Courtesy Rob Craig.)

Rivaling Abel Salazar, and perhaps eventually overtaking him as the premier mexploitation film producer, was Guillermo Calderón Stell, whose productions included Rafael Portillo's *Aztec Mummy* trilogy from 1957, René Cardona's *Luchadoras* ("Wrestling Women") film cycle between 1962 and 1968, and numerous Santo films in the late 1960s and early 1970s, several of which were also directed by Cardona. *La momia azteca* (*The Aztec Mummy*), *La maldición de la momia azteca* (*The Curse of the Aztec Mummy*), and *La momia azteca contra el robot humano* (*The Aztec Mummy vs. the Human Robot*; U.S. title: *The Robot vs. the Aztec Mummy*) were all made in 1957, and the *Aztec Mummy* trilogy was among the first of many mexploitation "series" horror films. Both the sequels, *La maldición de la momia azteca* and especially *La momia azteca contra el robot humano,* required recycled footage from their forerunners to extensively pad out an extremely brief running time — both last little more than one hour, which is much shorter than the standard 90 to 120 minute length of a feature film. This suggests that the three *Aztec Mummy* films may have been shot simultaneously as a television serial and later adapted for theatrical release, as Mora has claimed regarding the production of many low-budget horror and lucha libre films of the era. However, David Wilt has pointed out that Mora's contention may be somewhat erroneous. The *Aztec Mummy* series was filmed at Clasa Studios, a studio affiliated with the STPC union that had control over making feature films, thus making delving into any television production unlikely.

In contrast, the four-film *Nostradamus* series (written and directed by Mexican cinema veteran Federico Curiel in 1959) starring *El vampiro*'s Germán Robles as the title character, a criminal genius *and* vampire — *La maldición de Nostradamus* (*The Curse of Nostradamus*), *Nostradamus y el destructor de monstruos* (*Nostradamus and the Destroyer of Monsters*; U.S. title: *The Monster Demolisher*), *Nostradamus el genio de las tinieblas* (*Nostradamus, the Genius of Darkness*; U.S. title: *The Genie of Darkness*), and *La sangre de Nostradamus* (*The Blood of Nostradamus*) — is commonly considered to have been made as a 12-part television serial that was instead released theatrically (each *Nostradamus* film is itself divided into three episodes). However, Wilt noted that the *Nostradamus* films were made at Estudios América, which was affiliated with the STIC union. STIC was prohibited from making feature films as part of their agreement with SPTC, and the public perception that these films were originally made as television serials may have actually been a (convincing) subterfuge to work around the feature film production agreement between the STIC and STPC unions.[8]

While best known today for their low quality and camp appeal (issues addressed at length in the next chapter), mexploitation films were the products of major studios and the combined efforts of respectable producers, directors, screenwriters, and actors in mainstream Mexican cinema, many of them working on numerous films in a variety of roles (actors also writing screenplays, directors also acting in films, etc.). Key mexploitation directors such as René Cardona and Chano Urueta were established studio directors during the Golden Age of Mexican cinema in the 1940s. Miguel M. Delgado, who worked with Santo in the early 1970s, directed virtually *all* the films of legendary Mexican comedian Cantinflas from the early 1940s to the early 1980s, as well as many other films in a variety of genres. While often consigned to the category of bumbling amateurs (which is not meant pejoratively) like Al Adamson, Jerry Warren, or the maestro himself, Ed Wood, Jr., the great mexploitation directors are better compared to Jacques Tourneur — a director who helmed Hollywood studio films such as the *film noir* masterpiece *Out of the Past* (1947), the classic horror films *Cat People* (1942) and *I Walked with a Zombie* (1944), and, later in his career, inventive B-horror films such as *Curse of the*

Demon (1957) and *Comedy of Terrors* (1963). Similarly, mexploitation actors and actresses were not simply B-movie journeymen and cult-film icons (such as Sid Haig or wrestler-turned-actor Tor Johnson), but popular performers appearing in a variety of genre movies and even avant-garde films. Claudio Brook starred opposite Santo as mad scientist Dr. Karol in Alfonso Corona Blake's *Santo en el museo de cera* (*Santo in the Wax Museum*, 1963; U.S. title: *Samson in the Wax Museum*) as well as playing the title character in Luis Buñuel's *Simón del desierto* (*Simon of the Desert*, 1964). David Silva would appear in *El barón del terror* and Alejandro Jodorowsky's surrealist Western *El Topo* (*The Mole*, 1969). Both Brook and Silva would eventually star in Juan López Moctezuma's horror masterpieces *La mansión de la locura* (*The Mansion of Madness*, 1971) and *Alucarda, la hija de las tinieblas* (*Alucarda, Daughter of Darkness*, 1975)—appropriate casting choices for films in which horror, exploitation, and the avant-garde converge.

While many "conventional" horror and monster films (to use the description loosely) were produced in the mexploitation era, undoubtedly the most important development in mexploitation was the incorporation of lucha libre into the horror genre, with the films of Mexico's most famous luchador, El Santo, becoming virtually synonymous with mexploitation. Beyond the immediate box-office appeal of films featuring immensely popular wrestlers such as Santo, Blue Demon, or *Mil Máscaras* ("Thousand Masks") battling criminal syndicates, mad scientists, and the classic monsters, casting real-life wrestlers allowed for extended wrestling matches to be included in the films. This stratagem not only capitalized on the widespread popularity of lucha libre in Mexico, but, by placing the wrestling matches in the context of a horror or other genre film, it allowed movie producers to circumvent the television ban on lucha libre broadcasts enacted by the Mexican government in the mid—1950s and provide the Mexican public an opportunity to see Santo and other famous wrestlers in a mass-media setting (film rather than television). Occasionally the film narrative and wrestling matches would be integrated, usually via an extremely contrived or even absurd plot development in which the heroic *real-life* wrestler would battle a *fictional* villain or monster in a public wrestling match. However, in many other cases the narratives and wrestling sequences were independent and isolated from each other, specifically the straight matches between famous wrestlers included in the films, seemingly at random. Heather Levi noted:

> What distinguishes wrestling films from other movies was the insertion of one or more scenes of lucha libre into the narrative. The wrestlers would spend most of the screen time battling evil, solving mysteries, or untangling domestic complications, the plot interrupted by gratuitous lucha libre matches tucked into the narrative like awkward dance numbers. Despite (or because of) their notably low production values, the movies were wildly popular. Roughly two hundred of them were produced between 1952 and 1983, and El Santo alone acted in fifty of them.[9]

11

2

Mexploitation:
A Critical Inquiry

Camp, Cheese, and Counter-Cinema

Before beginning any critical assessment of Mexican horror cinema *ca.* 1957–1977, it is first necessary to address the question of "bad movies." Most of the films discussed in this book are often simply dismissed as examples of inept filmmaking, or, at best, appreciated for *camp* appeal as outlined by Susan Sontag in her seminal essay "Notes on Camp":

> There is camp in bad movies such as *The Prodigal* and *Sampson and Delilah*, the series of Italian color spectacles featuring the super-hero Maciste, numerous Japanese science-fiction films ... because in their relative unpretentiousness and vulgarity, they are more extreme and irresponsible in their fantasy — and therefore touching and quite enjoyable.[1]

Building on Sontag's work, Annalee Newitz utilized the basic principles of camp as a concept to enjoy and redeem "bad movies" for their wonderful limitations and excesses in order to define a more comprehensive and potentially more subversive aesthetic of *cheese*:

> Like *camp*, *cheese* describes both a parodic practice and a parodic form of textual consumption ... and like *camp*, *cheese* describes a way of remembering history, a kind of snide nostalgia, for serious cultures of the past which now seem so alien and bizarre as to be funny ... the point of cheese, whether deliberate or "read in" by the audience, is to offer criticisms of social norms, to regulate their power in the ash can of history through the "productive" use of derisive laughter.[2]

Despite the fact they both heartily champion camp or cheese, Sontag and Newitz present somewhat problematic arguments. One is their division over the issue of *intentional* versus *unintentional* camp. Sontag argued that, "Pure camp is always naive. Camp which knows itself to be camp is less satisfying."[3] For Sontag, a text is only successful camp when it is *unintentionally* camp; a text which is knowingly or self-consciously campy is inherently and necessarily doomed to a certain degree of failure. Newitz makes no such distinction, arguing that cheese can either be "deliberate or 'read in' by the audience." For Newitz, a text can be intentionally as well as unintentionally cheesy, allowing an artist to incorporate references, injokes, excess, clichés, kitsch, and bad taste — sometimes resulting in brilliant masterpieces (Russ Meyer's *Beyond the Valley of the Dolls* or John Waters' *Polyester*), and other times simply becoming self-indulgent pastiches (the work of Quentin Tarantino).[4]

Intention aside, the greatest problem for both Sontag and Newitz is assigning the reader an inherent *superiority* over a text designated as camp or cheese. For Sontag, the reader may embrace bad films as camp simply for their sheer aesthetic inferiority, for their charming naivety and vulgarity. In Sontag's aesthetic of camp, the cultural object of consideration can not be *legitimate* camp until christened as such by an outside party — one more artistically and intellectually aware and refined than the camp object itself. For Newitz, the aesthetics of cheese provide interesting possibilities of alternative modes of filmmaking, ironic reception, and even social critique — whether or not *intended* by the artist — but primarily through "snide nostalgia" and "derisive laughter." In short, both camp and cheese aesthetics imply that the *text is inevitably beneath its readers* and their own superior cultural sensibilities.

However, to merely appreciate bad films as mere objects of campy vulgarity or cheesy derision is ultimately a disservice to such texts. Indeed, many films consigned to camp or cheese status may in fact represent a form of alternative and even experimental cinema through their very disregard of conventional form, coherent narratives, and cinematic realism. In a fascinating essay entitled "'Trashing' the Academy," Jeffery Sconce used the term "paracinema" to better describe the appreciation and analysis of the lexicon of bad movies:

> At first glance, the paracinematic sensibility ... would seem to be identical to the "camp" aesthetic outlined by Susan Sontag ... without a doubt, both sensibilities are highly ironic, infatuated with the artifice and excess of obsolescent cinema. What makes paracinema unique, however, is its aspiration to the status of a "Counter-cinema...." Camp was the aesthetic of *ironic colonization and cohabitation*. Paracinema, on the other hand, is an aesthetic of *vocal confrontation.*[5]

Sconce's definition of camp as "the aesthetic of ironic colonization" bears close consideration in relation to mexploitation films. It is not that Mexican popular culture — El Santo and lucha libre, *rancheras* films, *telenovelas*, men in sombreros singing romantic ballads, velvet paintings, and, of course, mexploitation — is inherently kitsch or campy. Rather, such objects of Mexican popular culture only become camp or kitsch by virtue of having that status foisted upon them. As Ilan Stavans noted:

> A common belief is that low-brow Mexican culture is kitschy. Nothing could be further from the truth.... [It] will not become emblematic of low-brow Mexicaness until the sophisticated elite, *always an alien source*, says so — that is, until it is rescued to become a souvenir, a Mexican curiosity in the universal archives of Western Civilization.[6]

Mexploitation as Counter-Cinema

At their worst, the formal codes and conventions of Hollywood cinema and their various genres are designed to produce standardized, recognizable, and predictable patterns of aesthetic production and consumer reception. The American film spectator does not so much watch a Hollywood film as purchase a Hollywood commodity, with the ultimate evaluation of a film's quality based on whether or not it was "worth the money." However, while conforming to the general rules of classical Hollywood cinema and providing recognizable film products for its audiences (horror films, musicals, Westerns, etc.), Hollywood genres themselves become exhausted, evolving from their classical innovative state to a period of self-reflexivity and internal critique to an all-out conscious parody of the genre itself. In the case of the American horror film, one might express this lineage as the progression from the seminal work of James Whale in the 1930s (*Frankenstein*) to the wonderfully ironic and self-deprecating films of William Castle in the 1950s (*The Tingler*) to the postmodern self-consciousness of the genre demonstrated by Wes Craven (*Scream*) or Sam Raimi (*Army of Darkness*) in the 1990s. This evolutionary pattern of a genre is suggested in order to point out that the horror film is not a monolithic film form (or formula) which exists in an aesthetic and cultural vacuum. While all horror films certainly share common generic elements, horror films are constantly evolving products of a specific time and place and producers of specific social messages. In this context, one could briefly consider the wealth of films constituting the category of the *international* horror film contemporary to the mexploitation era. Each subgroup represents a tremendous variety of films that possess their own unique forms and influences, as well as distinct social-historical contexts and concerns: the stagy Hammer Studios horror films from England; the Japanese Godzilla film series; Jean Rollin's vampire film cycle from France (*ca.* 1968–71); the consistently brilliant work of Mario Bava and other Italian *giallo* directors; the almost anachronistic Spanish horror films starring Jacinto Molina (better known in America as "Paul Naschy"); the "Coffin Joe" films of Brazilian José Mojica Marins, to name but a few. As two specific examples, Rollin, whose astonishing and anarchistic work incorporates diverse influences ranging from F.W. Murnau and Jean-Luc Godard to Hammer Studios, also reflects the tumultuous political conditions in France in the wake of the May 1968 movement. Similarly, Mojica Marins, whose films bear the imprint of the violent, naturalist surrealism of Luis Buñuel as much as the classic horror of Universal, provocatively confronted Brazil's repressive military *juntas* and conventions of bourgeois morality with his startling blend of horror, sex, and violence — his stunning 1969 film *Awakening of the Beast* was banned outright by the Brazilian government.

Similarly, mexploitation films were made under specific Mexican national, cultural, and economic conditions tremendously different from Hollywood, conditions reflected in the end result: an era of intensive modernization; ideological agendas far different than American films; arduous production difficulties; pervasive government involvement in the film industry; the strained relationship between Mexican cinema and the Catholic Church. While a specific aspect of Mexican popular culture, mexploitation films also must be considered as *part* of Mexican popular culture, sharing and borrowing aspects from it, such as the importance of melodrama as a narrative (and ideological) strategy and the incorporation of lucha libre into the horror genre. All of these factors shape Mexican horror films both in terms of their formal construction and cultural discourse.

Because non–American horror films, specifically mexploitation, subscribe to their own formal codes and structures and their own national and cultural concerns, the viewing experience can be both baffling and frustrating, as challenging as any deliberately difficult "art film." Unfortunately, American film audiences tend simply to equate the foreign horror film's idiosyncrasies with incompetence. Even many who embrace "cult cinema" do so with a sense of *contempt* rather than *respect* for the product, considering them films good for a condescending, cheap laugh and a way to momentarily slum in low-brow cultural chic, but films certainly not possessing any actual cultural relevance — the epitome of camp's "ironic colonization." Rather than consigning mexploitation films to the status of bad movies and the confines of the "enjoyable vulgarity and naivety" of *camp* or the "snide nostalgia [and] derisive laughter" of *cheese*, one could interpret these films as a challenging and wonderfully perplexing *paracinema* (as suggested by Sconce): so-called bad films that through their strange and unconventional aesthetics achieve avant-garde, confrontational qualities — as *unintentional* as that effect may be. Andrew Syder and Dolores Tierney suggested:

> [In] mexploitation films ... formal construction of the texts suggests a dialog between Hollywood viewing codes and a set of disruptive, counter viewing codes. Rather than duplicating their Hollywood models, the strategies of incorporating local elements into these films have opened up a space for not only national concerns, but also for a more flexible mode of spectatorship.[7]

Without question, mexploitation films reflect the heavy influence of the classic Universal horror films to the point of outright plagiarism. Key influences on mexploitation are the films of James Whale: *Frankenstein* (1931), *The Old Dark House* (1932), and *Bride of Frankenstein* (1935). Another palpable influence would be Karl Freund's *The Mummy* (1932), the obvious basis for Portillo's *Aztec Mummy* series and Urueta's *La cabeza viviente*. Of course, *Dracula's* various elements seem to inevitably appear in virtually every mexploitation film made. Later, the Hammer Studios horror films of the late 1950s and 1960s would also prove to be a major source of inspiration for mexploitation filmmakers. However, while mexploitation films liberally borrowed the famous monsters, general plots, and even specific scenes from the Universal and Hammer horror film canon, they also freely borrowed from *each other*. Prolific mexploitation screenwriters such as Rafael García Travesí, Fernando Osés, and especially Alfredo Salazar practically redefine the term "self-reference" given the sheer volume of recycled material in their scripts. Indeed, the cynic could suggest that mexploitation films did not have "screenplays" but rather "*a* screenplay" recycled over and over with slight variations for countless films, and that mexploitation's consistent and pervasive social and cultural agendas did not stem from an ideological vision of modern Mexico but was simply the result of endless self-plagiarizing. In discussing the lucha libre genre (and his assessment could be applied to mexploitation cinema as a whole), Nelson Carro noted it was "*a parasitic genre*—of melodrama, of comedy, of horror and of science fiction. At no time did it look to be autonomous — on the contrary, in mixture, in pastiche, in anachronism, *one finds much of its power*."[8]

While mexploitation is highly reliant on familiar Hollywood genres (in most cases, the horror film), it is also utterly indifferent to the codes and conventions of classical Hollywood cinema. Mexploitation's unorthodox formal strategies force the (American) viewer to alternate between accustomed, comfortable, traditional Hollywood codes and unfamiliar, "disruptive, counter viewing codes"—codes specifically suited to a Mexican audience. The excesses and simplicity of melodrama in mexploitation often strikes the American viewer as hopelessly corny; while held in disrepute in American and European culture, melodrama is pervasive in Mexican popular culture.[9] The broad and often forced comic relief is more likely to produce groans rather than laughter. Between the reliance on outmoded genre conventions (Universal horror films of the 1930s), the fact that many of these films were shot in black and white (as much an aesthetic decision as a budgetary consideration), and the years (if not decades) between a film's actual production and its release in America, mexploitation films seem badly dated. The narratives of the films, which alternate between comic book action sequences and long, redundant plot expositions, not only reflect the structural influence of serials, but suggest that a number of mexploitation films, if not originally made as serials for television as believed,

1931 or 1960? The unmistakable influence of Universal Studios' *Dracula* appears in Alfonso Corona Blake's *El mundo de los vampiros* (*The World of the Vampires*, 1960). Guillermo Murray stars as the licentious vampire Count Subotai, appearing here with a rubber bat. (Courtesy Rob Craig.)

had to at least *appear* to be converted serials, especially films made at studios such as Estudios América which were affiliated with the STIC union (Curiel's *Nostradamus* and *Neutrón* series, for instance). To American audiences, the long wrestling sequences inserted into mexploitation films seem extraneous and even pointless; for Mexican film spectators, these would often be the highlights. The frequent use of recycled footage from previous films, incongruous stock footage, and often painfully unrealistic scenery, settings, and special effects inevitably sabotages any possibility of creating filmic verisimilitude.

Mexploitation's unfamiliar and unconventional approach to filmmaking becomes a vital component in their reception by American audiences in that it creates a distancing and disruptive effect between the viewer and the film. Becoming

Genre-bending: horror and slapstick comedy merge in *Échenme al vampiro* (*Throw Me to the Vampire*, 1961, dir. Alfredo B. Crevenna; U.S. title: *Bring Me the Vampire*). Imported by K. Gordon Murray, the film owes as much to the classic "haunted house" films *The Old Dark House* (1932, dir. James Whale) and *House on Haunted Hill* (1958, dir. William Castle) as it does to Abbott and Costello's horror-comedies. (Courtesy Rob Craig.)

almost inevitably detached from these films by their negation of any familiar or conventional film form or even "good taste," the American viewer becomes an ironic commentator rather than a passive spectator. Within the realm of camp, the viewer's detachment from a bad film is expressed by the viewer becoming an active participant in the film through the admitted great pleasure derived from directing acerbic comments at the screen.[10] However, mexploitation films are much more than camp objects of bemused consternation or, to paraphrase Stavans, "low-brow Mexican souvenirs and curiosities." By denying conventional film form and demanding an altogether different and "flexible" spectatorship, mexploitation cinema achieves an estrangement effect (comparable, perhaps, to Bertolt Brecht's theater), which denies the audience any familiar, comfortable patterns of spectatorship and promotes a strange, alienating, and actively critical relationship between the viewer and film — although it is fair to suggest that such an estrangement effect was probably not the intention of the filmmakers but rather the result of a given film's production conditions, cultural specificity, and vastly different codes of reception between Mexican and American audiences.

Nevertheless, one might say that like the mad scientists and their unholy experiments on humanity that populate mexploitation cinema, directors such as René Cardona, Alfredo B. Crevenna, Alfonso Corona Blake, Federico Curiel, Miguel M. Delgado, and Chano Urueta take the horror film and "horribly mutate" it. The easily recognizable generic formula of the Universal and Hammer horror films is taken to bizarre extremes in mexploitation, their tone and style achieving hilarious levels of parody, exaggeration and willful cliché. These effects are made all the more humorous and disorientating by the eclectic use of other genres and other elements of Mexican popular culture, the obvious budgetary and technical limitations of their production, and, in the case of the Murray imports, their highly awkward transition into American B-movie horror film fare. Mexploitation films are at once anachronistic, parodic, melodramatic, excessive, derivative, meandering, clumsy, confusing, and, not least, absolutely experimental.

Mexicanidad *and Modernity:*
Visions of Mexico in Mexploitation

Awash in their Gothic and Expressionist overtones to the point of overkill, mexploitation departed markedly from contemporary Hollywood films of the 1950s and 1960s, which were primarily horror/science-fiction hybrids (with alien invasions and mutated monsters serving as metaphors of Cold War politics and Atomic Age fears). As John Soister noted, "Hollywood ... felt that tales of science fiction — fueled by notions of the mutative propensities of atomic energy and the not-so-logical progressions concerning Sputnik — had supplanted ticket-buyers' loyalties for the 'classic' monsters."[11] However, these "classic" monsters would literally be resurrected in Mexican horror cinema, alive and well, with an ideological agenda reflecting two primary cultural concerns in Mexico in the twentieth century: *mexicanidad* and *modernity*.

Mexploitation films embody the concept of *mexicanidad*, which, as defined by Elissa J. Rashkin, "encompasses identity, culture, national sovereignty, and authenticity and is often set against a perceived encroachment by an alien (European or U.S.) value system."[12] Furthermore, as Alison Greene observed, "Mexicanidad was institutionalized as a key facet of many state-led efforts at *nation building*, including myriad development initiatives, the extension of public education, and, not least, *through state support for the development of a national(ist) cinema* and later television."[13] However, mexploitation films differ markedly from (nationalist) American horror and science-fiction films of the era, which usually depicted monsters and especially alien invaders as a thinly-disguised analogy for the Cold War and Communist infiltration. Villains in mexploitation films, such as foreign mad scientists, aliens, monsters, or other national threats to modern Mexican society, rarely serve as metaphors for the Communist menace, with the notable exception of the Asian "Black Dragon" secret society in *Las luchadoras contra la momia,* which serves as a thinly-veiled threat of Maoist Communism to mexicanidad (while Mexico was superficially "allied" with the U.S. during the Cold War, Mexico's foreign policy was ambivalent towards Communism in other countries in the 1960s, but certainly staunchly anti–Communist in *domestic* politics).

Rather than Communism, the threat to mexicanidad is often represented by *Europe*. Several mexploitation films explicitly associate the threat to mexicanidad with Fascism, specifically Nazi Germany. The use of the name "Dr. Krupp" for the evil mad scientist in the *Aztec Mummy* films is quite politically charged: not only is Krupp a Germanic rather than Hispanic name, the Krupp family's financial empire served as the backbone of Hitler's war machine. Other examples include the Nazi war victim/mad scientist Dr. Karol in *Santo en el museo de cera*; Dr. Hugo Ulrich (Jorge Radó), the Nazi war criminal/scientist seeking to either dominate or destroy the world in *Santo contra Blue Demon en la Atlántida* (*Santo vs. Blue Demon in Atlantis*, 1969; dir. Gilberto Martínez Solares); the South American Nazi organization headed by none other than John Carradine that Mil Máscaras battles in *Enigma de muerte* (*Enigma of Death*, 1967; dir. Federico Curiel); and the resurgent Nazis Santo confronts in *Anónimo mortal* (*Anonymous Death Threat*, 1972; dir. Aldo Monti). Other mexploitation films link the villain to European *antiquity*, specifically Classical Greek and Roman civilization: "Baron Vitelius of Astera" in *El barón del terror*; the witches in Grecian gowns, among them the priestess "Medusa" (Edaena Ruiz), in the Santo film *Atacan las brujas* (*The Witches Attack*, 1964; dir. José Díaz Morales); and the Martians who consciously adopt names taken from Greek mythology in *Santo, el Enmascarado de Plata vs. la invasión de los marcianos* (*Santo, the Sliver Masked Man vs. the Invasion of the Martians*, 1966; dir. Alfredo B. Crevenna). Europe also serves as the ancestral home of the vile Frankenstein family featured in *Santo contra la hija de Frankenstein* (*Santo vs. Frankenstein's Daughter*, 1971; dir. Miguel M. Delgado) and *Santo y Blue Demon contra el Dr. Frankenstein* (*Santo and Blue Demon vs. Dr. Frankenstein*, 1973; dir. Miguel M. Delgado), as well as being the continent of origin for Count Dracula and the other vampires populating mexploitation films ranging from *El vampiro* to *Santo en el tesoro de Drácula* (*Santo in the Treasure of Dracula*, 1968; dir. René Cardona). European antiquity and Fascism would even converge in *Santo contra Blue Demon en la Atlántida*: the Nazi Dr.

Ulrich renames himself "Aquilles" (Achilles) and calls his underwater headquarters "Atlantis." In short, mexploitation films offer an affirmation of mexicanidad, the concept of Mexican national identity and sovereignty, which is threatened by various monsters and villains whose dangers are often represented as decidedly "non–Mexican" (and usually *European*) opponents to the Mexican way of life.

Inherently linked to the affirmation of *mexicanidad* is the valorization of *modernity* in mexploitation films. Ultimately, many Mexican horror films express the very ideological contradiction Carlos Monsiváis asserted lay at the core of post–World War II Mexican politics: the promotion of Mexican national ideals verses the disregard for tradition. Héctor Aguilar Camín and Lorenzo Meyer described the era from the end of World War II to the political upheaval of the late 1960s as a period in which Mexico balanced "the difficult combination of economic growth and political stability."[14] Unlike many Latin American countries, a political *status quo* was maintained in Mexico, primarily through decades of rule by an autocratic, one-party political system (the *Partido Revolucionario Nacional*, or PRI). At the same time, Mexico experienced dynamic social and economic changes, and developments in the forms of urbanization, industrialization, and consumerism: in short, *modernization*. It is these tensions which form the basis of mexploitation's cultural discourse: the affirmation of a unique, unified, and stable Mexican national identity through *mexicanidad* and a celebration of social progress through the valorization of *modernity*.[15]

A pivotal conflict in mexploitation cinema is the struggle between progress and modernity, represented by the forces of *the present* (such as popular wrestlers, socially-conscious scientists, or young, virtuous *chicas modernas* ["modern girls"]) verses the supernatural evils and dangers of *the past* (a plethora of vampires, mummies, and sorcerers — appropriate villains for a country whose cultural and ideological project was one of modernization throughout the twentieth century). Numerous mexploitation films revolve around an immortal or resurrected monster wreaking havoc on, and exacting revenge from, the present, a narrative motif which also serves as an important social and political metaphor of the dangers of Mexico's past (superstition, tradition, debauchery) and its potentially debilitating effect on the present (social, cultural, and economic modernization). Syder and Tierney cite Laura Polasky's observation that "such films can be seen to be using the horror movie conventions to engage with Mexico's nationalist project of modernization by highlighting the sensationalist, unsavory, and potentially embarrassing underside of Mexico's patrimony."[16] Mexploitation villains are often resurrected or immortal supernatural monsters from Mexico's pre-modern or Colonial-era dark ages who now pose a threat to modern Mexico's present: Gothic vampires in *El mundo de los vampiros*, *Santo contra las mujeres vampiro*, and many other films; evil necromancers in *La maldición de la Llorona*, *El barón del terror*, and *Atacan las brujas*;

and Aztec ghosts in the *Aztec Mummy* films, *La cabeza viviente*, and *Las luchadoras contra la momia*. Certainly the Spanish conquerors of Mexico are vilified in both Mexican history and culture; one of many surreal moments in Alejandro Jodorowsky's *La montaña sagrada* (*The Holy Mountian*, 1972) reenacts the Spanish conquest of Mexico with large lizards dressed as Spanish conquistadors and Aztec warriors. Specific to mexploitation, films such as *El barón del terror* and the Santo vehicle *El hacha diabólica* (*The Diabolical Axe*, 1964; dir José Díaz Morales) feature resurrected, supernatural villains from the era of Spanish conquest and colonialism, specifically the period of the Inquisition. Yet the Aztecs themselves are not depicted as heroes (or stereotypical "noble savages") against the Spanish colonialists in mexploitation films. Rather, Aztec civilization *also* undergoes a process of vilification in Mexican horror cinema by virtue of being part of an obsolescent past, and for its various components of the supernatural and "primitive" unenlightened conduct that revive to threaten modern Mexico.

As Carlos Monsiváis writes, "[Mexican] cinema offers one certainty: *that to persist in traditional ways is a form of living death*."[17] Indeed, this is precisely what the myriad vampires, Aztec mummies, sorcerers, and their ilk in Mexican horror films represent: an outmoded and dangerously obsolete form of existence. They are the "living dead" who become a profound threat to a modern, and modernizing, Mexico. By expressing a strong distrust of *the past* and its traditions, mexploitation films often celebrate modernity and social progress, glorifying technology, urban life, and cultural sophistication in a country undergoing rapid economic progress and modernization in the post–WWII era. It is no coincidence that the monsters in mexploitation films inevitably are connected to the resurrection of an evil and dangerous past marked by superstition, irrationality, and ignorance — all enemies to the rationalism of modernity. The monsters in mexploitation films are first and foremost defined as enemies of *social progress*, not only through being "non–Mexican," but by being opponents of a modern Mexico through their connection to antiquated beliefs, ideals, and behaviors. In *El monstruo de los volcanes* (*The Monster of the Volcanoes*, 1962, dir. Jamie Salvador), the film's central conflict revolves around efforts to build a railroad through a mountain range; and in order for industrial progress to be achieved, an ancient, legendary monster dwelling in the mountains, "The Lord of the Volcanoes," must first be destroyed.[18]

While most consider the concepts of mexicanidad and modernity to be inseparably linked in Mexican popular culture, including mexploitation films, several Mexican historians insist the development of a Mexican national culture was not the result of post–Revolution state efforts at "nation-building" and the ideology of mexicanidad, but rather the unifying rise of an industrial economy and consumer culture which embraced and even enforced modernity over an "obsolete" peasant life.[19] Alison Greene observed, "The adoption and personal tailoring of mexicanidad

Supernatural Aztec evil in Chano Urueta's *La cabeza viviente* (*The Living Head*, 1961). Note title character on right, played by Mauricio Garcés. (Courtesy Rob Craig.)

[is] the most appropriate and easiest entrance into modernity ... *mexicanidad serves as the most desirable variety of modernity.*"[20] In short, it was not that being Mexican meant becoming modern, but that by becoming *modern* one could therefore become *Mexican*. In mexploitation, becoming modern (and therefore Mexican) required that the monsters of an antiquated past be vanquished. Several Mexican cultural critics, notably Monsiváis, contend that Mexican cinema's overall ideological project was this affirmation of modernity and progress over tradition.[21] However, in her perceptive study of Mexican comic books, Anne Rubenstein argued that the discourse of modernity was balanced by a competing, and at the same time complimentary, discourse of tradition:

> From the vantage point of consumer culture and mass media ... a new national culture did develop after the Revolution, but it had two faces; one might even say

it was comprised of two discourses. One was the set of ideas, arguments, attitudes, and metaphors related to modernity, progress, industrialization, and urbanity. The other was a discourse of tradition, conservatism, rural life, and Catholicism. Both of these discourses were equally rooted in the past, both were equally new, and both of them changed over time. Both were deployed by representatives of the government, and their opponents, at various times and for various purposes. These discourses developed in dialogue with each other over gender, work, and nation. "Tradition" did not precede "modernity" any more than modernity displaced tradition. Each required the other. And *both* were aspects of a single national culture.[22]

Rubenstein is quite correct in stating that modernity and tradition "required the other," one needing the other to compare, contrast, and even justify and elevate itself as each was voiced and manipulated in various times and places by various political interests. In this regard, one might first discuss the rather complex relationship between the Mexican government, the architect for a vision of modern Mexico; the Catholic Church, the bastion of tradition; and the Mexican film industry. David Wilt noted that while the government (grudgingly) respected the cultural influence of the Catholic Church, it also promoted a strict separation between church and state, and even led status may have tacitly encouraged a certain degree of anti-clerical sentiment.[23] Given the state-controlled status, of the Mexican film industry by the 1960s, it is hardly surprising that mexploitation films offer little criticism of the government; in many cases, their messages are quite consistent with contemporary government polices. However, there does seem to be a space within Mexican horror for elements of anti–Catholicism, such as the portrayal of the Inquisition and its legacy in *El barón del terror,* and certainly the shocking depiction of Catholicism later seen in *Alucarda.* Conversely, popular culture was one of the Church's most enduring targets, and Rubenstein notes that the Church attacked "depictions of beliefs other than Catholicism in the strictest sense, so that images of 'superstition' and 'atheism'—*along with movies that dealt with monsters, witches, or the supernatural*—were proscribed."[24] While both mexploitation films and the Catholic Church shared a strong abhorrence of the supernatural—albeit for vastly different reasons—the relationship between the two was, for the most part, antagonistic.

Nonetheless, several mexploitation films do construct a productive place for religion in modern Mexico. In *Santo contra las mujeres vampiro,* a vampire is killed when he inadvertently walks in front of a church, bursting into flames after seeing the cross atop the steeple. In *Muñecos infenales* (*Infernal Dolls,* 1960, dir. Benito Alazraki; U.S. title: *The Curse of the Doll People*), the scientist Karina (Elvira Quintana) ultimately resorts to using a crucifix against the voodoo high priest Zandor (Quintin Bulnes). Throughout *Atacan las brujas,* the symbol of the cross is a

Not a Catholic mass: striking image of occultism and voodoo in *Muñecos infernales* (*Infernal Dolls,* 1960, dir. Benito Alazraki; U.S. title: *The Curse of the Doll People*). (Courtesy Rob Craig.)

powerful, recurring force against supernatural evil. At one point, Santo assumes the shape of a cross by standing rigid with his arms outstretched, sending the witches' henchmen fleeing in fear. When witch-queen Mayra (Lorena Velázquez) hypnotizes Ofelia (María Eugenia San Martín), her first command is to remove the cross around her neck. Most overtly, at the end of the film Santo vanquishes the witches by waving a large wooden cross in front of them, causing them to burst into flames. With *Santo, el Enmascarado de Plata vs. la invasión de los marcianos,* the two major supporting characters are a noted scientist (Professor Odorica) and a respected, socially-conscious priest (Father Fuentes), suggesting that *both* science and religion play equally important roles in modern Mexican society.

Thus, it might be said that science (modernity) and religion (tradition) in mexploitation films are not placed in binary opposition to each other: one good and the other evil. Rather, these two social forces can operate independently from one another, *each* capable of promoting social good as well as provoking social disaster in various times and places. In this sense, while mexploitation often valorizes modern life and progress, it also offers warnings of the possible dangers and abuses of progress to modern Mexico, represented by the plethora of scenery-chewing mad scientists who populate mexploitation cinema. Megalomaniacal geniuses motivated by evil self-interest, these mad scientists interfere with, rather than contribute to, social progress, ranging from local criminal pursuits to all-out world domination and meddling in the classic areas best left alone by man "playing God" — achieving power over death or creating mutant species (the creation of ape-men seems to have been a required course in mexploitation medical school). As Dr. Irving Frankenstein (Jorge Russek) succinctly proclaims in *Santo y Blue Demon contra el Dr. Frankenstein*, "Imbeciles!.... They are wondering what I wish to accomplish? If they knew, they would pee their pants!" The potential dangers of scientific and technological progress, and threat it poses to Mexican society, can be seen in a variety of mexploitation films, including the *Aztec Mummy* trilogy, *El espejo de la bruja*, *Las luchadoras vs. el médico asesino*, *Santo in el museo de cera*, *Santo, el Enmascarado de Plata vs. la invasión de los marcianos*, *Santo en el tesoro de Drácula*, *Santo contra Blue Demon en la Atlántida*, *El horripilante bestia humana*, *Santo contra la hija de Frankenstein*, and *Santo y Blue Demon contra el Dr. Frankenstein*. To briefly expand on this theme, Rafael Portillo's *Aztec Mummy* films and René Cardona's *Santo en el tesoro de Drácula* serve as specific examples of how a mexploitation film (or body of films) critiques science and its proper role in modern society.

The *Aztec Mummy* films revolve around the work of Dr. Almada (Ramón Gay), experimenting with the possibilities of using hypnosis and past-life experiences as a means to learn more about Aztec civilization. While Dr. Almada is very much the hero of these films, his scientific methods are nonetheless rooted in two highly suspect and even dangerous phenomena: hypnotism and reincarnation. As seen in every subsequent mexploitation film, hypnotism is vilified as a practice associated with the supernatural, as well as brainwashing and sexual immorality, rather than scientific advancement. The flirtation with reincarnation entails the essential danger of rekindling the past and its potential threat to modern Mexican society. Thus, Dr. Almada's "scientific" work in hypnosis and reincarnation inadvertently allows the return of past monsters to threaten the present: the cursed Aztec Mummy, Popoca. It might be said that Dr. Almada is the hero by default, only because of the presence of the hilariously diabolical mad scientist and criminal mastermind Dr. Krupp (Luis Aceves Castañeda), who seeks to manipulate Dr. Almada's research in order to steal the ancient Aztec treasure.

Santo en el tesoro de Drácula is thematically quite similar to the *Aztec Mummy* trilogy, which is not surprising since screenwriter Alfredo Salazar wrote or co-wrote the screenplays for all the films and rather audaciously reworked a great deal of material from the *Aztec Mummy* entries and *Las luchadoras contra la momia* into the subsequent Santo film. In *Santo en el tesoro de Drácula,* Santo is the epitome of modernity — an accomplished scientist as well as popular wrestler and heroic crime-fighter. In fact, Santo has done nothing short of conquering time and space by inventing a time machine. Like Dr. Almada, Santo's scientific work allows a subject to go back in time and re-experience a past life, but Santo's experiments in time-travel are rooted in the hard sciences: manipulating physics and altering the material body to return an individual back to a body used in a previous life, rather than dabbling in the paranormal phenomena of hypnosis and reincarnation. Santo sends his fiancée Luisa (Noelia Noel) through his time machine, and she relives a past-life encounter with Count Dracula (Aldo Monti), revealing a vast treasure Dracula has hoarded. Despite Luisa's protests, Santo decides to pursue the treasure — not for personal gain, but for its scientific value and the public good the treasure could potentially serve. However, an evil scientist–crime boss, Black Hood, discovers the results of Santo's experiment. In order to acquire the treasure himself, Black Hood resurrects Dracula to again spread the evil of vampirism through the modern world. Fortunately, Santo defeats Black Hood and his gang with his fists, and kills Dracula through an impressive display of scientific cunning: With Santo and his colleagues hopelessly trapped in a net in Dracula's caverns, and Dracula about to sacrifice Luisa, an explosion blows a gaping hole in the roof, allowing sunlight to stream in and destroy Dracula and his vampire slaves (all attractive young women). When Luisa's scientist father labels it "a miracle," assuming they were saved by divine intervention, Santo somewhat indignantly corrects him: "No miracle. It was all my doing." Santo explains that his plan worked to perfection: the explosion was the result of his "wrestling pals" blowing up the roof with dynamite when Santo signaled them with his hi-tech "radio-watch," a device seen in numerous mexploitation films. However, despite the fact that Santo (Mexican modernity) was able to defeat Count Dracula (the supernatural past), a humbled Santo admits to Luisa that his experiment ultimately failed: not that his scientific theory is incorrect, but the consequences of disturbing and reawakening the past and its dangers exceed the potential benefits to the present.

The Chica Moderna *and the Countermacho: Sex, Gender, and Patriarchy in Mexploitation*

Anne Rubenstein notes, "In comic books, as in Mexican cinema and recorded popular music ... *the discourses of modernity and tradition primarily formed around the representation of women.*"[25] Mexploitation certainly is no exception to how modernity, tradition, and the representation of women become intertwined, especially to the degree the discourse of modernity *appropriated* traditional Catholic codes of sexual conduct and gender relationships into an overall political vision of modern Mexico. Many mexploitation films depict a struggle between modern, Mexican sexual morality and the illicit, immoral sexuality posed by supernatural forces of the past. Resurrected monsters, especially vampires, pose a distinct *sexual* danger to the present, usually centering on the seduction of virgins and married women. As Rob Craig suggests in his reading of *The World of the Vampires*, "Count Subotai is an unusually 'pretty boy' vampire, more akin to ... one of deSade's 'voluptuaries' than a gruesome undead monster. For the same reason, the Count's seduction of Leonore, a typical '60s suburban housewife, suggests garden-variety adultery ... common, yet somehow quite erotic, even 'dirty.'"[26] In most mexploitation films, sexual promiscuity is not only associated with the forces of supernatural evil, but behavior of *the past*: the illicit sexual relationship between the young Aztec couple (the virgin Xóchitl and the warrior Popoca) which leads to them being eternally cursed in the *Aztec Mummy* films; the diabolical and lecherous Baron Vitelius who brazenly "seduced married women — and maidens" in *The Brainiac*; the scores of licentious vampires seen in *El vampiro*, *El ataúd del vampiro*, *El mundo de los vampiros*, and *Santo contra las mujeres vampiros*. All these monsters return from the past to disturb the sexual *status quo* of modern Mexican virginity and monogamy.

Within this battle of modern sexual morality against past sexual licentiousness, mexploitation films often employ the stereotype of the *chica moderna*: the young, modern Mexican woman. As Rubenstein notes, "[*Cichas modernas*] were up-to-date consumers who tried to appear desirable and expected companionate marriages. They were impatient and could speak bluntly, but were honest, *chaste before marriage and faithful afterwards.*"[27] While *chicas modernas* were young, independent, sophisticated, even headstrong and "sexy," they were also expected to have and maintain sexual virtue: virgins before marriage and monogamous wives afterwards. In mexploitation films, one of the primary threats posed by the monsters of the past is their sexually corrupting influence over young *chicas modernas* via the twin threats of adultery and especially premarital sex. The sexual danger monsters pose is frequently manifest through their supernatural and seductive powers of hypnosis, which inevitably stirs irresistible, irresponsible, and immoral sexual behavior. The supernatural-seductive power of hypnosis can be seen in *El barón del terror*, *Santo contra las mujeres vampiro*, *Atacan las brujas*, and *Santo en el tesoro de Drácula*, among numerous other films.

The *chica moderna* not only embodies sexual morality, but, as Rubenstein notes, is a Mexican popular culture "stock figure ... of feminine virtue, honor, and *mexicanidad.*"[28] Thus, when the *chica moderna*'s sexual virtue is threatened, her national identity and modern status is threatened as well, and it is this conflation of sexual morality, mexicanidad, and modernity which underscores the depiction of the *chica moderna* in mexploitation films. Yet while mexploitation films often use the stereotype of the *chica moderna* in their representation of women, they also modify it in a very important way. Rubenstein notes, "The stereotypical traditional woman stayed at home, preferably in rural areas. They subjected themselves to their fathers, husbands, and sons ... *chicas modernas,* on the other hand, obeyed no one — except, perhaps, an employer."[29] Yet in mexploitation films, *chicas modernas* are frequently also docile daughters held in the sway of a powerful, patriarchal figure, and the primacy of this father-daughter relationship is all the more striking due to the conspicuous absence of mothers and sons in mexploitation films (the exception being *El horripilante bestia humana,* which focuses on a tragically doomed father-*son* relationship). This patriarchal figure may be a wise, protective father or uncle, such as Professor Rolof in *Santo vs. the Vampire Women,* Dr. Sepulveda in *Santo en el tesoro de Drácula,* or Professor Cristaldi in *Santo y Blue Demon contra Drácula y el Hombre Lobo* (*Santo and Blue Demon vs. Dracula and the Wolf Man,* 1972; dir. Miguel M. Delgado). The paternal character may also be a benevolent father-figure, such as Dr. Tracy in *Wrestling Women vs. the Aztec Mummy* and Professor Milan in *The Brainiac.* Moreover, in all these cases the father-figure is also a respected scholar and/or scientist (a doctor or professor), thus explicitly connecting the image of the father (patriarchy) with rationalism, intellectualism, and science (modernity).

Beyond the patriarchal structure of the family, mexploitation films valorize a patriarchal social order through establishing a gender politics of heroic and virile men, often a famous wrestler (usually Santo, but occasionally Blue Demon or Mil Máscaras), versus malevolent and attractive females, such as vampire women, witches, or alien invaders: *Santo contra las mujeres vampiro, Atacan las brujas, Santo, el Enmascarado de Plata vs. la invasión de los marcianos,* and *La venganza de las mujeres vampiro* (*Revenge of the Vampire Women,* 1970; dir. Federico Curiel; a remake of, as much as a sequel to, *Santo contra las mujeres vampiro*). Similarly, Mil Máscaras would be pitted against women vampires in *Las vampiras* (*The Vampire Women,* 1967). (Like *Enigma de muerte, Las vampiras* starred Mil Máscaras, was directed by Federico Curiel, and featured John Carradine, this time as Branus, an elderly vampire leading a coven of comely vampire women.) Blue Demon would fight similarly evil women in *Blue Demon contra las Diabólicas* (*Blue Demon vs. the Diabolical Women,* 1966; dir. Chano Urueta) and *Blue Demon y las invasoras* (*Blue Demon and the Women Invaders,* 1968; dir. Gilberto Martínez Solares).[30]

Perhaps the most treacherous, not to mention hilarious, of all mexploitation villains is Dr. Freda Frankenstein in *Santo contra la hija de Frankenstein.* Played by Gina Romand (who the year before battled Santo as vampire-queen Countess Mayra

Santo wrestles vampire woman Countess Mayra (Gina Romand) in *La venganza de las mujeres vampire* (*Revenge of the Vampire Women,* 1970; dir. Federico Curiel).

in *La venganza de las mujeres vampiro*), Freda Frankenstein is an utterly malevolent figure who single-handedly manages to combine the threats of the past, Europe, science run amok, and sexually perverse women into a single, despicable character. To an almost obscene degree, the film frames the struggle between two figures of modernity around gender politics: the heroic, masculine wrestler Santo versus the mad scientist and stereotypical castrating female Freda Frankenstein Throughout the film, Dr. Frankenstein does not seek to kill Santo but instead attempts to *emasculate* Santo through repeated efforts to humiliate him in acts of symbolic castration: unmasking him; arranging a vicious battle between Santo and her monstrous ape-man creation Truxon (Gerardo Zepeda)—which she watches with sadistic-voyeuristic delight and sexual arousal; hypnotizing Santo's girlfriend in an effort to make her gouge out Santo's eyes and leave him "powerless." In fact, Freda Frankenstein seeks to capture Santo alive (while neutering his masculine power) for a very important reason: she is actually well over 100 years old, but kept young, attractive, and artificially alive by an anti-aging serum that is losing its potency, requiring her to administer more frequent and heavier doses to halt the aging process until the serum itself will ultimately have no effect. Santo, whom she saw wrestle many years ago and again recently, is still the same amazingly virile man he once was, seemingly unaffected by aging. Taking the opportunity to dab Santo's bloody nose with her handkerchief after a match, Freda studied his blood and learned it contains "the TR factor a hundred times more than normal humans"—"the TR factor" being the active agent in her anti-aging formula. As a pure physical specimen of masculine virility, Freda now seeks Santo in order to drain his blood and make her youth serum much more potent, which will prevent the effects of aging that are ravaging her body and beauty. Here, one sees a variation on the mexploitation theme of the villainous "vampire-woman" who saps the blood of the virile, modern man to maintain her own existence, as well as physical beauty (*Santo contra las mujeres vampiro*). While Freda Frankenstein is not literally a blood-sucking "vampire," she is, for all intents and purposes, the scientific, *modern* equivalent of one.

However, when Freda Frankenstein coyly recalls that Santo "smiled at me" when she dabbed the blood off his mask, she betrays a strong sexual attraction to Santo that will become more overt as the film progresses. In this regard, one is tempted to consider that Freda's cleaning Santo's "masculine essence" from his mask after his virile physical exertion in the wrestling ring represents not only the loss of blood, but the discharge of *semen* as well, especially given that Santo's highly potent "blood" is both the source and external bodily manifestation of his ageless masculine prowess. It is precisely this "masculine essence" that Freda Frankenstein covets to maintain her own youthful appearance, beauty, and very existence. As she desperately tells her assistant Dr. Yanco (Roberto Cañedo), "I *need* Santo—*I need his blood!*" While Freda seeks to dominate and control Santo, to capture him and "keep him by my side forever" as a subservient husband-slave stripped of any manhood while feeding on his super-masculine fluid (blood), she is also uncontrollably attracted to the muscular wrestler, leading to a wonderful exchange after Freda has finally captured Santo midway through the film. Santo is stripped to the waist and placed with his arms chained over his head in a sado-masochistic position of subservience. His luchador mask becomes nothing short of an S & M bondage mask, and Santo's strapping body is rendered a sexual fetish-object.[31] As Santo hangs helplessly, Freda sadistically taunts him: "The indestructible hero, defeated, at the mercy of a fragile woman." Santo's classic reply: "I don't think you're fragile—*or a woman!*" Her sexual interest piqued, Freda responds, "You would like to find out? We could be friends." As she slinks towards him, she propositions Santo, explaining that between her (female) devious, scientific cunning and his (male) physical power, they could be an invincible couple. Santo utterly rejects her advances, coldly stating, "I suspect your face is a mask that hides a horrible old woman." Indeed, a stark comparison can be drawn between Santo's mask, which defines him as a symbol of social justice and male virility, and Freda's "mask," which is one of artificial, vain, female beauty hiding a withered, parasitic force of evil. Incensed and insulted by Santo's rejection, Freda does the unthinkable and removes Santo's mask — of course, Santo is not facing the camera, so the viewer only sees the back of Santo's head (or, more likely, a double for Santo), thus keeping his private identity safe except for the prying eyes of Freda Frankenstein. She brazenly kisses him on the mouth, the scene accompanied by a blast of clichéd organ music recalling both horror film and soap-opera themes — an appropriate choice for a scene that wonderfully encompasses both ghastly horror and affected melodrama.

In regards to Santo, if mexploitation films can be seen as constructing an ideal of virtuous, modern Mexican femininity, they ultimately construct an ideal of powerful modern Mexican *masculinity* as well. Throughout his film career, Santo typifies what Rubenstein terms the "countermacho," an image of political leadership manufactured in the 1950s much more suited to the needs of a modern and modernizing Mexico: an alternative to the "macho-as-charro" — the loud, drunken, hot-tempered, womanizing cowboy epitomized by the mythic legend of Pancho Villa:

> Power lay in rejecting the macho-as-charro stereotype and instead deploying a counterimage, the equally stereotypical postrevolutionary *patriarch*, the technocrat, the bureaucrat, *the modern man*. The iteration of the virtuous Mexican man is self-controlled, whereas the charro is impulsive; he is orderly, whereas the charro is unruly; he is celibate or monogamous, whereas the charro has many women (although perhaps only one true love): he is sober when the charro is drunk, and modest when the charro is boastful. The macho as technocrat, the countermacho, is also a mature man: he must rely on — and display — a certain authority that would oddly sit on the shoulders of a teenager. And this authority is both the essence and the political function of the stereotype.[32]

Like the countermacho, Santo is depicted as a humble man of the people, a conscientious citizen and model of restraint (in *Santo en el tesoro de Drácula*, Santo is offered a cocktail but answers he would "prefer coffee"). He is a moral gentleman with the opposite sex, and willing to sacrifice his personal romantic life in favor of the public good (issues that will be examined at length in a subsequent discussion of Santo's films). At times Santo even appears sexually prudish: twice in *Atacan las brujas* Santo disapprovingly clears his throat just before the film's romantic couple, Ofelia and Arturo (Ramón Bugarini), are about to kiss in his presence. Steadfastly dependable and responsible in his dedication to the protection and betterment of every individual in Mexican society, Santo "invokes the familiar symbolism of the good patriarch who intervenes personally to look after the well-being of his clients and dependents."[33] Above all, Santo is a peerless, flawless role model to young people, particularly adolescent males. In short, Santo is "the countermacho ... *perhaps a revolutionary figure of perfect justice*, perhaps a modernized future of technological progress and material abundance."[34]

In conclusion, mexploitation cinema can be seen as a strange, challenging "counter-cinema," both dependent upon and yet dialectically opposed to Hollywood conventions. Mexploitation can also be seen as a cinema that reflects "national concerns" specific to a Mexican audience and the contemporary political situation of Mexico, above all engaging and negotiating the dominant discourses shaping Mexican national identity: mexicanidad, modernity, and gender politics. While offering a critique of the past as a dangerous and literally monstrous force that could destroy the present, mexploitation variously glorifies Mexican nationalism, social and economic progress, sexual morality, and patriarchal order. In this regard, one can turn to a discussion and close textual reading of one of the more legendary (or infamous) mexploitation films: *El barón del terror.*

3

El barón del terror
(*The Brainiac*, 1961)

El barón del terror (1961) reared its ugly head, so to speak, to confront American audiences in 1969 (thanks to K. Gordon Murray) as the brilliantly-titled *The Brainiac*. Undoubtedly one of the most well-known mexploitation films, largely due to the legendary cult-film status it has attained, *The Brainiac* became a staple of late-night television, and today is an inevitable inclusion in any cult-film encyclopedia or list of "worst films ever made." Without question, *The Brainiac* epitomizes virtually everything that a bad-film connoisseur could want: ineffective special effects, glaring technical errors, histrionic acting, and obvious budget limitations, all of which are augmented (or compounded) by Murray's brand of unnatural and often unintentionally-hilarious dubbed dialogue. (Insofar as it is Murray's English-dubbed version of *El barón del terror* which will be critically discussed, the film will be referred to exclusively as *The Brainiac* for the remainder of this chapter, and all characters will be referred to by their names in Murray's version.)

Nonetheless, *The Brainiac* was made at an established studio (Churubusco-Azteca), produced by a veteran figure in Mexican cinema (Abel Salazar), co-written by a prolific screenwriter and director (Federico Curiel, along with Adolfo López Portillo and Antonio Orellana), and directed by Chano Urueta, who helmed more than 100 films over a career that spanned four decades (1933–1972). Urueta was an industrious studio director in both the Golden Age of Mexican cinema as well as the mexploitation era, directing Blue Demon's early films and the early 1960s Salazar horror productions *La cabenza viviente* and *El espejo de la bruja* (both of which were later imported by K. Gordon Murray and released as the popular double-feature *The Living Head* and *The Witch's Mirror* in 1969). A veteran actor as well, Urueta appeared in numerous Mexican films, as well as Sam Peckinpah's *The Wild Bunch* and *Bring Me the Head of Alfredo Garcia*. In addition to producing *The Brainiac*, Abel Salazar starred in the title role as the evil Baron Vitelius of Astera, a malevolent sorcerer executed by the Holy Inquisition in seventeenth century Mexico who returns from the dead after 300 years to revenge himself upon the ancestors of the inquisitors. Along with Salazar, two other stars of *El vampiro*, Germán Robles and

Ariadna Welter, appear in small roles: Robles in a dual role as Inquisition member Sebastian de Pantoja and his doomed ancestor Professor Indalecio de Pantoja; Welter in a wonderful cameo as a bar floozy who becomes one of the Baron's early victims (despite only appearing in the film a scant few minutes, Welter receives prominent billing in the credits). Additionally, legendary director René Cardona appears in *The Brainiac* in a dual role as inquisitor Balthasar Meneses and his cursed descendant Luis Meneses; while none other than Federico Curiel himself takes on the role of the bumbling cop Bennie, assistant and comic foil to the stone-faced Chief of Police, played by another famous Mexican actor, David Silva.

The Brainiac begins with the credits shown over an etching by Francisco Goya, *Se repulen* (*They Spruce Themselves Up*), number 51 in his *caprichios* series (*ca.* 1799). It is a disturbing drawing of two brutish monsters in the foreground, one trimming the other's talon-like toenails with large scissors. Behind and between them another monster stands, his bat-like wings unfurled. As the title suggests, the monsters are mockingly making themselves presentable to the modern world by performing minor cosmetic changes, but nonetheless remain unsightly monsters. The use of the Goya etching is quite appropriate to *The Brainiac* in that many of the Goya *caprichios* were brutal and satirical illustrations of the danger that ignorance and superstition poses to intellectual reason and social progress.[1] Likewise, Baron Vitelius ultimately can be seen as the equivalent of Goya's grotesque figures: a monstrous figure representing the dangerous superstitions and irrational violence of Mexico's colonial past resurrected as a force of destructive evil to the social progress of modern Mexico — a hideous monster of unreason "spruced up" as a dapper, bourgeois aristocrat.

Unlike Hollywood films, which often begin with an action sequence or tense dramatic situation, *The Brainiac* (in a narrative strategy typical of many mexploitation films) begins with an interminable opening sequence that emphasizes Gothic atmosphere and extended plot exposition rather than drama or action. Generally, mexploitation films offer pacing that might charitably be described as "ponderous," at times making Michelangelo Antonioni look like Russ Meyer. Along with this, one especially frustrating tendency in mexploitation is the constant plot exposition that frequently grinds the films to a halt. Characters will spend valuable film time explaining key plot points that will become obvious to the viewer over the course of the film. Conversely, characters will frequently reiterate and summarize the importance of key events that have already occurred, all of which the viewer is already well aware. This often happens when *new* characters are introduced: the film essentially stops in order to provide *them* with a full plot summary.

The year is 1661, and the evil Baron Vitelius is on trial for heresy, witchcraft, moral debauchery, and other crimes that have offended the Inquisition. This opening trial sequence, lasting several minutes, tests the viewer's patience, yet it also possesses a strange fascination. The on-screen depiction of the Inquisition trial is constructed out of a limited number of shots which are re-edited and recycled through the sequence. The film opens with an establishing long shot of the tribunal chamber, followed by a medium-long shot of a hooded inquisitor with his hands on his hips standing next to a large, metal crucifix. Interestingly, a black shape on the stone wall appears in the background, forming a silhouette that bears an uncanny similarity to the winged monster in the background of the Goya etching in the opening credits, suggesting that this shape is also overseeing "spruced up" monsters: the Inquisition. The third shot is simply the first shot repeated, the fourth shot the second shot repeated, and the fifth shot cuts to the seated Baron Vitelius facing the camera. The sixth shot is the first (and third) shot used yet again. Over these first six shots (or *three* shots), a voice-over provides a detailed and convoluted description of the proceedings:

> We, the grand inquisitor, protector of the faith against heretic sins of apostasy in the city of Mexico and all the states and dominions of New Spain, and its vice royalties and governing bodies, through royal audiences in all cities and states do proclaim, that the other inquisitors, and I, have attended this hearing in the secret chamber of the holy tribunal in Mexico, to do justice in the trial that has been initiated against the aforementioned Baron Vitelius of Astera, of unknown origin, who has repeatedly refused to state same, aware of the edicts and merits of this trial, and the evidence and suspicion resulting thereof.

This voice-over quickly becomes unintentionally humorous. Constructed as one massive run-on sentence, the verbose language of the tribunal's opening announcement veers hilariously between strained hyperbole and *non-sequitur*. The convoluted speech is made even more comical by the monotone of the narrator, which is better suited to accompanying classroom education films than announcing the sinister proclamations of an ominous, secret tribunal. Further adding to the unintentional humor, the voice-over narrator is forced to deliver as many words as possible before running out of breath, resulting in a rushed, rambling delivery that contains several awkward mid-sentence pauses in which one suspects the narrator was practically gasping for air. This opening monologue is especially noteworthy in that the voice-over does not emanate directly from an on-screen character. Consequently, the rather tangled syntax is *not* the result of needing the words to match the movements of a on-screen character's mouth, but rather could stem from the original Spanish screenplay and translating the material *too* literally into English.

As this introductory narration concludes, the shot of the inquisitor with his hands on his hips is shown yet again. Pausing several moments after the opening announcement ends, the inquisitor finally moves. This segues into a long shot of the tribunal from another angle, in which the inquisitor can barely be seen in the center of the frame picking up a scroll and returning to his original mark in the previous shots. The next shot shows the inquisitor holding the scroll open rather than standing akimbo, but is otherwise identical in camera angle and character position to the second, fourth, and seventh shots. Any hopes the viewer has that some sort of drama will unfold are soon dashed when the inquisitor begins to read the seemingly endless list of criminal charges against Baron Vitelius. Again, it is notable that while this speech emanates from one of the inquisitors, his face remains hidden by his black hood. In that there is no need for the dialogue to correspond to the movements of his mouth, the cumbersome monologue can not be dismissed as simply the result of haphazardly matching words to an actor's mouth. With the list of crimes constructed as yet another gigantic run-on sentence seemingly designed to make serious delivery impossible, the narrator is again forced to make awkward mid-sentence pauses and unintentionally hilarious emphases:

> Report on the sentence and the trial by torment of that this tribunal of the Holy Inquisition instituted against said Baron Vitelius for heresy and the instigation of heresy; for practicing *dogmatism*; for having used witchcraft, superstition, and conjurations for depraved and dishonest ends; for having employed the art of necromancy invoking the dead, and trying to tell the future through the use of corpses ... for having seduced married women — and *maidens*....

Once the litany of crimes is completed, the prosecuting inquisitor then proceeds to vividly describe the specifics of the "trial by torment" Baron Vitelius has undergone (the cynic might suggest that this protracted opening is itself a "trial by torment" for the viewer). During the lengthy reading of the crimes and the description of torture, various new shots are both introduced and then repeated to further extend the tribunal scene: a medium close-up of the hooded inquisitor reading the scroll while the large metal crucifix looms in the foreground on the right side of the film frame; inserts of other seated inquisitors listening to the charges; and reaction shots of Baron Vitelius staring defiantly or scoffing as he listens to the charges being read. In one important (and hilarious) shot, the Baron breaks into lewd laughter the moment the charge of "having seduced married women" is leveled against him. Recycled and re-inserted throughout the trial sequence, these shots reach a point of maddening redundancy and over-familiarity, creating a sense of relentless repetition rather than developing any sort of dramatic tension or conflict.

Though the structure of the film's opening tribunal sequence can certainly be taxing for the viewer, in a certain sense it is also hypnotic. By repeating initial shots, introducing new shots which are then repeated, and slightly varying pre-existing shots, the film eschews a linear, narrative construction in favor of a cyclical structure of repetition, monotony, and subtle variation. One is ultimately tempted to compare *The Brainiac*'s opening scenes to minimalist, experimental filmmaking or music as much as to the generic horror film.

The names "Vitelius" and "Astera" carry symbolic meaning, as both are strongly affiliated with two common nemeses in mexploitation cinema: *Europe* and *the past*. "Vitelius" was briefly the emperor of the Holy Roman Empire in AD 69, and "Astera" does not refer to a specific location (the Baron is explicitly mentioned as being "of unknown origins"), but instead can be read as a pun on "Asteria" and a reference to a figure in Greek mythology: the Titan goddess of fire whose name translates as "flaming-one."[2] In *The Brainiac*, this not only refers to the Baron, who is killed by fire (twice), but to the role of fire throughout the film as a metaphor for violent and destructive social upheaval. In Greek myth, Asteria escaped the romantic overtures of Zeus by changing into a flaming meteor and plummeting into the Mediterranean Sea, becoming the island of Delos. Similarly, Baron Vitelius returns to threaten modern Mexico in the form of a flaming comet (in one scene in *The Brainiac* the comet is actually referred to as "a meteor"). Thus, Baron Vitelius is tied to *both* Classical European civilization and Spanish colonialism. Indeed, Mexico under the Inquisition is not even "Mexico"— it is referred to as "the states and dominions of New Spain" in the opening announcement of the tribunal, coding the horrors of Mexico's past entirely in terms of European influence and colonial conquest.

To further test the viewer's endurance and seemingly pad out the opening sequence, a character witness appears before the court to testify on behalf of Baron Vitelius—Marcos ("Marcus" in *El barón del terror*) Miranda (Rubén Rojo). He immediately announces he was born in Portugal, and thus also connected to *Europe*. This fact alone makes him and his testimony suspect, and the inquisitors respond to Miranda's brief testimony before the tribunal by ordering him to be whipped for perjury. Miranda proudly proclaims that the Baron is a gentleman of "the arts and sciences" and a humanitarian to "the downtrodden." Miranda's naive words of praise depict Baron Vitelius as a scholar, scientist, and social reformer—a noble figure opposed to the religious intolerance and tyranny of the Inquisition. However, the Baron's interests are not rooted in rational science and the advancement of society, but the use of occultism and mysticism to satisfy his thirst for unlimited power and libidinal gratification.

Thankfully, this trial sequence finally concludes and the scene shifts to the public execution of the Baron, who will be burned alive while "dressed in the clothing of shame bearing symbols of fire." Strangely, and even perhaps a bit outrageously, the robes and conical hat of the "clothing of shame" bear more than a passing resemblance to the attire of the Pope; indeed, it initially appears that it is the Holy Pontiff himself who is tied to a cross and about to be burned alive. Between this rather startling shot and the generally unkind depiction of the Catholic Church during the Inquisition, one is tempted to suggest there is indeed an implicit, even subversive, anti–Catholicism sentiment present in *The Brainiac*. With the exception of one scene that takes place inside a church (or, more correctly, in front of a poorly reproduced photographic backdrop of a church interior), the Catholic Church has no presence in the modern Mexican world of *The Brainiac*: it is ultimately *scientific ingenuity* rather than *religious faith* that leads to the defeat of the evil Baron.

As the Baron prepares for his fiery demise, a comet passes overhead (a crude animation inching across a photo of the night sky). The camera shows the Baron looking up at the comet, then cuts to a shot of the comet, then back to the Baron, then again to the comet, then *back* to the Baron, and *again* to the comet, and *then again* to the Baron, and *once more* to the comet, all the while intercutting reaction shots of an amazed Marcos Miranda. Hollywood narrative economy would dictate intercutting between the Baron and the comet once or possibly even twice to establish the filmic connection between the two, yet *The Brainiac* repeats the montage of shots alternating between the Baron, Miranda, and the comet *four* times. Finally, the Baron voices his sinister warning: one by one, he identifies the four hooded inquisitors through a sort of telepathic magic (actually, the "magic" of superimposing an actor's face over the close-ups of the hooded inquisitors). As he is consumed by flames, Vitelius announces he will return in 300 years, when the comet completes its cycle, in order to exact his revenge on the Inquisitor's descendants and "expunge their foul lineage from the face of the earth." The plot device of a monstrous evil from Mexico's past returning to menace and destroy the present is a standard and often predictable narrative motif seen in numerous mexploitation films, and this collision between past and present is coded with an ideological implication. In *The Brainiac*, the past as an evil force has two components. One is Baron Vitelius himself, representing an unenlightened past in the form of its irrational superstitions, sexual immorality, and unrestrained self-interest. The second evil of the past is the allusions to European antiquity as well as the legacy of the Holy Inquisition and Spanish colonialism in "New Spain," whose atrocities inevitably taint its descendants by making them pay for the crimes of their ancestors.

Over a long shot of Baron Vitelius' execution by fire, the years "1661," then "1761," then "1861" are superimposed on the screen. The shot fades out and then quickly fades in to a shot of a nightclub as "1961" appears. While the past of Mexico, or "New Spain," is represented entirely by continuous images of destructive fire, supernatural evil, and violent religious intolerance over which the centuries literally pass (1661, 1761, 1861), the Mexico of the present (1961) is depicted by modern, sophisticated, urban nightlife — further establishing the stark dichotomy between the horrors of the past and the pleasures of the present. Ronald "Ronnie" Miranda (played by Rubén Rojo, note that the character's name changed from "Reynaldo Miranda" in *El barón del terror*) and his *chica moderna* girlfriend Victoria

"Vicki" Contreras (Rosa María Gallardo) are enjoying a night of drinks and dancing at the nightclub. However, their evening of cosmopolitan recreation soon comes to an end because Ronnie and Vicki are astronomers and are due at the observatory. In this sense, Ronnie and Vicki must sacrifice the modern passion for urban nightlife for another, perhaps more important modern pursuit: the advancement of science. Excusing himself and Vicki, Ronnie tells their companions, "Don't forget, I'm an astronomer, and I choose to work in the dark!" Vicki knowingly giggles at Ronnie's *double-entendre*.

Ronnie and Vicki arrive at the observatory, ridiculously depicted by a blown-up photograph of an observatory building. This is one of several moments throughout *The Brainiac* in which grainy, blown-up photographs serve as exterior backdrops, resulting in obviously artificial scenery that utterly destroys any possibilities of verisimilitude the film might manufacture. Apart from generating some unintentional humor, such backgrounds also serve to create a sort of surreal *mise en scène,* manifesting a sense of pure *unrealism.*

Inside the observatory, Ronnie and Vicki are greeted by Professor Milan (Luis Aragón). While not Ronnie or Vicki's actual father, the elderly Professor does assume an authoritative, paternal presence over the couple. Though Ronnie is later introduced to Baron Vitelius as "a professor" as well, it is clear that he works *for* rather than *with* the stern Professor Milan. With the *chica moderna* Vicki, the Professor assumes both the employer *and* symbolic "father-figure." In what is perhaps the most hilarious moment in the film, the Professor begins to question the young couple about their knowledge of comets as if he were a sadistic teacher or quiz-show host: Vicki's intent concentration and game-show contestant demeanor as she ponders Professor Milan's question and successfully names two comets and their orbital cycles is absolutely priceless. Ronnie, perhaps because he is a man and thus assumed to be naturally "smarter" than Vicki, is asked a far more difficult question, but also provides a correct answer, much to the Professor's satisfaction.

Following the interrogation of his apprentices, the next several minutes of the film consist of an interminable and virtually incoherent lecture by Professor Milan (filled with astronomical metalanguage which may or may not have any actual basis in scientific fact) on the science and history of comets. Much to the relief of the viewer, the Professor finally concludes his spiel by suddenly informing Ronnie and Vicki that his calculations show that on this very night they will see a comet last seen in 1661 (the comet, of course, which will herald the return of Baron Vitelius). Ronnie is unsuccessful in his attempts to locate the comet through the observatory telescope, prompting rather impatient criticism from the Professor. However, Vicki succeeds in locating the comet, although it is implied her success was the result of sheer chance rather than intellectual or scientific skill. Elated with the sighting, Professor Milan proclaims, "I, for one, feel proud my work hasn't failed!" Ronnie and

Vicki then proceed to view the comet from a smaller telescope on the terrace of the observatory, marveling at the wonder of the view (now depicted by an extremely grainy still photograph of a city skyline in a circular frame mimicking the view from a telescope). "How beautiful!" Vicki exclaims. However, Ronnie notices a "strange light" emanating from the comet, and they depart from the observatory to investigate the unusual phenomenon.

The scene shifts to a deserted field where a passing motorist also notices the comet and the "strange light" it emits. Then, in possibly the worst of the many special effects atrocities committed by *The Brainiac*, an obviously *papier mâché* prop boulder falls into the frame after being discharged by the comet. Courtesy of a superimposed dissolve, the boulder transforms into the monstrous figure of the Brainiac, who appears to be a cross between Satan with a grotesquely-swollen head and a giant lizard, clad in the scorched clothes worn by Baron Vitelius during his execution. (For clarity, Baron Vitelius will be referred to as "the Brainiac" only in the scenes in which the Baron takes on his monstrous form.) The unfortunate motorist becomes the first victim of the Brainiac, who kills him by sticking his elongated, forked, and obviously rubber tongue into the back of his head in order to devour his brain. Upon completing this evil deed, the Brainiac magically transforms into the human form of Baron Vitelius, now wearing the dead man's suit. Apparently not devoid of all human decency, the Baron spares his victim the embarrassment of being found dead *naked*; the motorist's corpse is left clad in his undergarments (a T-shirt and boxer shorts), which presumably means the Baron is "going commando" under his suit.

Ronnie and Vicki soon encounter the now-resurrected Baron in the countryside. Strangely, upon their meeting they awkwardly stare at each other for several seconds before either utters a word. Of course, when they finally begin their conversation, the exchange is indicative of the convoluted dialogue that marks Murray's Mexican imports:

> RONNIE: Oh, sir, did you see a small aerolite land near here?
> THE BARON: An ... *aerolite?*
> RONNIE: Yes.
> THE BARON: No! You appear surprised to see me, my friend. I think I should explain. You see, I always take my walk at this hour of the night.
> RONNIE: Oh, then let me explain, also. You see, sir, we're astronomers and we were observing a meteor —
> VICKI: Oh, but Ronnie, this gentleman doesn't understand a *thing* you're saying to him!
> THE BARON: Young lady, I understand much more than you could imagine. Astronomy is my weakness — as a science it is most important. And another thing, I studied it for years. I am quite proficient.
> VICKI: Oh, really?

41

THE BARON: Yes.
RONNIE: In that case, permit me to offer you my card!

Between the complete lack of any verisimilitude or narrative logic, the obvious artificiality of the almost surreal sets, the disorientating and inconsistent pacing, and the bizarre exchanges of dialogue, one is tempted to compare *The Brainiac* to a Samuel Beckett play rather than a horror film.

The scene shifts to the city, where the Baron arrives at a nightclub and encounters a drunken barfly (a cameo by Adriana Welter). As she talks to the Baron, a light flashes on his face, suggesting the hypnotic power of his stare. An extremely common motif in mexploitation, hypnotism is an act by which a monster (especially a vampire) controls its victims, frequently infusing this supernatural and seductive power with a component of sexual indecency: the Baron's ability to "seduce married women and maidens." Entranced by the Baron, Welter rather incoherently muses:

> Since you got here, you haven't said one single word to me, but that stare in your eyes says so much to me. To tell you the truth, it makes me feel afraid. Keep staring—I don't want you to stop lookin' at me.

Frustrated at the Baron's silence but somehow unable to resist his hypnotic "charms," Welter turns and walks away, awaiting the Baron's seductive advance. He transforms into the Brainiac and attacks her with his long, forked tongue, murdering her and devouring her brain — serving, perhaps, as a warning to "loose" *chicas modernas* in modern Mexican society who would spend their time picking up strange men in city bars. Not surprisingly, in the next scene the Baron promptly claims his next victim: a street-corner prostitute, another woman who is seemingly killed because she too strays outside the bounds of sexual morality.

With the advent of a possible serial murderer in the city, two police detectives are assigned to the case: the Chief of Detectives (David Silva) and his assistant Bennie (Federico Curiel). Silva's performance as the Chief is one of the highlights of the film: his stiff posture, deadpan demeanor, and hard-boiled *non-sequiturs* make Jack Webb appear positively Shakespearean (although, of course, one must remember that Silva's dialogue and voice were dubbed in *The Brainiac*). After the two initial murders, the medical examiner (Mauricio Garcés) explains how two holes have been made in the base of each victim's skull and the brain sucked out. The Chief's classic reply: "I wish they'd find some way to control the things a man studies — a maniac with a lot of knowledge is a threat!" Later, when investigating the murder of Professor de Pantoja and his daughter, the Chief declares, "These people here were burned; only that doesn't fool me — it's clear that that madman extracted their brains as well!" In fact, the Chief is often far more (unintentionally) humorous than

Death of a less-than-virtuous *chica moderna* (Ariadna Welter) in *El barón del terror* (*The Brainiac*).

Bennie, the Chief's blundering assistant and *The Brainiac*'s intended "comic relief." A fair number of mexploitation films insist on including a character to provide overt comic relief, although their efforts to provide the intended humor are inconsistent at best (the greatest offender perhaps being Alberto Rojas and his grating perform-ance as "Perico" in *Santo en el tesoro de Drácula*).[3] In one memorable scene at a diner, the Chief begins a graphic analysis of the murders and their grisly details, prompting Bennie to exclaim, "Agh, Chief—I was really enjoying this sweet roll!" Even worse, the waitress soon arrives at the table with an order of "calf brains"(!), putting Bennie off his meal altogether.

This motif of the monster eating the brains of his victims in *The Brainiac* offers an interesting and important variation on the "revenge from the past" theme of mexploitation vampire films in which the monsters drain the *blood* of modern

Mexicans in order to maintain their evil existence. In *The Brainiac*, *brains* sustain the evil Baron Vitelius — he literally feeds on the intellect, rather than the lifeblood, of the Mexican population. The Baron is a vampire of the *mind*, preying on the intelligence of Mexico's unwary citizens.[4] By feeding on *intellect* rather than *blood*, Baron Vitelius very much represents the threat to *reason*, and, as a resurrected monster of the Colonial era, serves as a symbol of Mexico's unenlightened past: the belief and power of superstition and occultism (magic, necromancy, witchcraft) and how they become the sworn enemy of reason and social progress. This theme is manifest by the use of the Goya *caprichio* and its symbolic warnings of the dangers of ignorance and unreason to progress in the film's opening credits. Moreover, the past (1661, 1761, 1861) is a period of unchanging violence rooted in irrational superstition, reflected in both Baron Vitelius' use of black magic *and* the oppressive religious dogma of the Inquisition in "New Spain." Again, the Baron's resurrection does not simply represent the dangerous return of superstition and irrationality, but carries with it the reminders of an unfortunate chapter of Mexican history: the Inquisition and Spanish colonialism and their dangerous legacy for the present.

In order to implement his plan of revenge on the present, the Baron invites all the principal members of the cast to a lavish party he is hosting. The Baron's residence is a large castle decorated in medieval decor and Gothic architecture, establishing another anachronistic relationship between the aristocratic Baron of the past and the modern world of observatories, nightclubs, and posh apartments. One by one, the Baron's butler (where did *he* come from?) introduces four new guests arriving at the party. As each guest is shown in a close-up, the faces of the four respective inquisitors who originally tried and executed the Baron are superimposed over the condemned descendants: Luis Meneses, Ana Luisa del Vivar, Indalecio de Pantoja, and, finally, Victoria Contreras. Vicki is escorted by the two important men in her life, one on each arm: Professor Milan, her boss and surrogate "father," and Ronnie Miranda, her future husband; Ronnie is revealed to be the descendant of Marcos Miranda, the Baron's former friend and character witness. Essentially, the party scene serves one primary purpose: to introduce the viewer to the future victims of the Baron one by one and clearly indicate the narrative route the film will take. However, the highlight of the party is a wonderful moment where in the Baron temporarily excuses himself from his guests on the pretext of feeling unwell. He retreats to his study, opens a locked cabinet, and removes a small silver chalice. Inside are human brains, and the Baron eats a spoonful before returning to the party, rejuvenated by his snack, or "medicine."

Having impressed his party guests, all of whom offer their future hospitality to the Baron, Vitelius now begins his mission of ruthlessly "expunging them from the face of the Earth." The first victim is Indalecio de Pantoja, a respected history professor and an authority on colonial Mexico. De Pantoja invites the Baron to his house for a discussion of Mexican history, which soon turns to the Inquisition, the professor observing, "You know, in this century to talk about the Inquisition, and the ways that they did justice, *is not what I call easy*." The Professor's daughter María enters the scene and joins in the conversation. Far more than her father's doting assistant, the film depicts María as a *chica moderna*: an independent, career-minded woman who is completing her own dissertation on Mexican history and establishing her own promising academic career. At María's introduction, it becomes readily apparent that Vitelius is equally interested in both her *body* (to seduce) and her *mind* (to eat, of course). They soon discover an account of a Baron Vitelius of Astera in the history books, an individual who was tried and executed by the Inquisition. As the Baron coldly and lecherously stares at María, he engages in a redundant plot exposition recounting the crimes for which the Baron was condemned (almost verbatim, Vitelius finds it necessary to repeat the entire list of charges originally read in the opening trial sequence as well as the subsequent details of his torture and execution). In a medium close-up, Baron Vitelius vividly describes the charges of "heresy and furthering heresy, dogmatizing, for having used sorcery, superstition, and conjuring for evil ends all men are attracted to," and finally, "for having seduced young maidens who couldn't...." He pauses, at which point the shot cuts to a matching medium close-up of María staring transfixed at the Baron: "...Who couldn't *resist*," the Baron ominously concludes.

Suddenly, the Baron reveals that he is indeed the same Baron Vitelius executed 300 years ago, and employs his supernatural powers on the de Pantojas (the bright stage light that blinks on his face). He renders Professor de Pantoja immobile; and María de Pantoja is helpless against his hypnotic power of sexual seduction over "married women and maidens." Entranced, María slowly walks over to Baron Vitelius and passionately kisses him, her father forced to watch the Baron seduce his daughter and completely unable to prevent the heinous act. As María turns away, she is visibly in a state of sexual arousal, and awaits the Baron's caresses from behind. Indeed, she might be said to be willingly "exposing herself" to the Baron, offering unrestricted access to the nape of her neck, which leads one to suspect that this may not be the first time she has offered herself to a man. While María is a *chica moderna*, she may also lack the *chica moderna*'s necessary sexual virtue ("chaste before marriage"). Building to a perverse climax, the scene alternates between reaction shots of the helpless, horrified father; his sexually-aroused daughter, who in one shot almost obscenely and defiantly smiles at her father as she awaits the Baron's approach; and the Baron himself, who finally reverts to his monstrous appearance. The Brainiac steps behind the hypnotized María, who willingly arches her head back as the monster caresses her shoulders. She emits a shriek as the Brainiac murders her, the base of her skull probed and penetrated by the monster's long, forked and, dare one say, *phallic* (albeit flaccid) rubber tongue. Again, her father is completely

45

unable to intervene, and can do nothing but pathetically watch the utterly sordid violation of his daughter by the Brainiac. After killing María, the Brainiac pounces on Professor de Pantoja and viciously murders him, eating his brain as well. Given that both Indalecio and María de Pantoja are historians and scholars, they symbolize modern intellectual enlightenment, and it is significant that the Baron, representing the dangers of the unenlightened past, destroys them by devouring their brains. Following the murders, the monster goes on a rampage, ripping apart history books and throwing papers about the room before setting fire to the Professor's study. As the room bursts into flames, the scene fades out on a close-up of the flames, inevitably recalling not only the execution of Baron Vitelius by fire, but the continuous images of fire that symbolized the years "1661, 1761, 1861" as an unending past period of irrational violence. Now, in the modern era of "1961," fire once again appears as a force signifying social upheaval and destruction.

If the first step of the Baron's diabolical plan has been the eradication of "intellectualism," the next phase is the destruction of "industry" — the economic progress of Mexico. The Baron's next victim is Luis Meneses, a wealthy industrialist. As Meneses and Meneses' wife give the Baron a tour of Meneses' highly successful and productive foundry, the Baron compliments him: "Now I know why people are starting to say your business is helping to build the economy." A highly topical comment clearly referencing the current state of Mexican political life, *The Brainiac* (or, more correctly, *El barón del terror*) was made during the López Mateos administration, which made economic development its primary political objective. Luis Meneses is not simply a successful capitalist, he is a socially-conscious one, actively involved in the economic growth and prosperity of Mexican society as a whole rather than simply being motivated by individual profit. However, the Baron tempts Meneses by informing him he has knowledge that will help Meneses develop new and potentially lucrative alloys (presumably alloys which would be created through *alchemy*, not *industry*). Meneses welcomes the idea, excited that such new alloys could make both men rich. In effect, this temptation proves to be his undoing: Meneses seemingly forgets his important public role in "helping to build the economy" in favor of private ambition and personal wealth. At this point, the Baron effortlessly places Mr. Meneses into a state of immobility, and then hypnotizes and seduces Mrs. Meneses, who slinks toward the Baron and plants warm kisses on his lips in full view of her helpless husband. When Mrs. Meneses suddenly backs away in horror after kissing the Baron, Vitelius transforms into the Brainiac and cruelly murders her. Like María de Pantoja, she is not simply an object of desire and seduction, but of murder and destruction. After disposing of Mrs. Meneses, the Brainiac turns to the spellbound Luis Meneses and pronounces his condemnation — he will pay for his ancestor's actions from three centuries ago. Unable to control himself, Meneses opens the door of the blast furnace in the foundry laboratory, which cuts to a close-up of flames from inside the furnace, the camera itself seemingly engulfed in flames. As with the murder of the de Pantoja family, the scene fades out on flames filling the film frame; and much like the de Pantoja's body of intellectual scholarship was incinerated, Meneses and his economically important and productive industrial empire are obliterated by raging fire as well — the element that has underscored Mexico's turbulent history prior to the present (1961).

Having attacked and destroyed the modern Mexican institutions of intellectualism and industry, brazenly stopping to "seduce married women ... and maidens" along the way, the Baron next goes after another social construct of modern Mexican life — holy matrimony itself. The Baron arrives at the wedding of Ana Luisa del Vivar to extend his blessings. The scene plays out in front of another extremely unconvincing enlarged photo background, in this case the interior of a Catholic church. As suggested, this appearance of the Church in the film is not so much to convey the power of religious faith over supernatural evil, but rather to give "social legitimacy" to the marriage of Ana Luisa and her new husband, a sacred union the Baron will soon defile and destroy. Defined by her Catholic faith and (obedient) relationship to her new husband, Ana Luisa becomes the film's "'traditional woman,' who exists in relation to her family ... and for whom self-abnegation is the only possible route to power."[5] The scene cuts to the newlywed Ana Luisa preparing herself for her wedding night in the bedroom mirror; of course, the implication is that Ana Luisa will lose her virginity. When the Baron unexpectedly appears in their honeymoon suite and attempts to use his hypnotic-seductive powers on her, she reacts not with sexually arousal, but instead with pure fright. Whereas the independent, intellectual career woman María de Pantoja and the cosmopolitan socialite Mrs. Meneses succumb, however briefly, to the hypnotic seductions of Baron Vitelius, Ana Luisa, as the epitome of *traditional* sexual virtue, is aghast at the Baron's seduction effort (here it should be noted *traditional* sexual virtue ultimately bears little difference to *modern* sexual virtue). Frantically, she attempts to summon her husband out of the bathroom, but when the door finally swings open, she recoils in horror. Her spouse hangs dead, upside down, from the shower nozzle, his head submerged in the bath water (it is one of the most effective, even chilling, moments in the film, a scene that would certainly be appropriate to the *giallo* horror stylings of Mario Bava or Dario Argento). Literally powerless against the Baron, especially with her husband now dead, Ana Luisa helplessly faints on her bed. The ominous, oversized shadow of the Brainiac appears on the wall next to her, with the monster hovering over the bed, preparing to murder and eat the brain of the virgin Ana Luisa as the scene fades out.

After the newlyweds depart for their honeymoon, and prior to their murder, the film pauses to allow Baron Vitelius, Ronnie, and Vicki to engage in a plodding expository conversation in front of the excessively artificial church interior background.

Ronnie recounts the events surrounding the previous two murders, implying that the arrival of the Baron, the party, and subsequent murders of those on his guest list may be more than coincidence. The Baron asks Ronnie, "Just a minute, you mean to say a brilliant scientist like you is *superstitious*?" Ronnie retorts, "It's not superstition, really — it's only *curiosity*." Indeed, Ronnie's suspicions about the Baron are not simply the products of irrational superstitions, but logical, deductive reasoning and *scientific* curiosity. In this way, the distinction is further established between the intellectual capacity of Ronnie and Vicki. In a previous scene, when Ronnie initially voiced his logical suspicions to Vicki, she dismissed his concerns outright. While Ronnie is an actual professor, Vicki has no known academic credentials, and it is implied that her scientific success is the result of dumb luck rather than intellectual prowess. In this regard, Vicki is completely unable to fathom the possibility that Baron Vitelius is a murderer, perhaps because she is both a victim of his wily, masculine charms and relies on "female intuition" rather than logic.

With suspicion and evidence mounting against the Baron, and with Vicki Contreras the only remaining ancestor of the inquisitors still alive, *The Brainiac* reaches its climactic encounter when Vicki and Ronnie join the Baron at his castle for dinner. Once again the Baron excuses himself to partake of his "medicine," and steals away for a quick spoonful of brains. Returning to the couple, the Baron suddenly recalls that Ronnie and Vicki are to be married soon, and invites Vicki to select one of the jewels from his personal collection as a wedding present. The Baron leads Vicki to another part of the mansion to display his "jewels" for her (pun intended), and he soon makes amorous overtures towards her: "They're lovely, aren't they — ah, but you, none can compare to your tender gaze" (a pick-up line recalling surrealist prose rather than romantic verse). Despite actress Rosa María Gallardo's low-cut black evening dress and ample bosom, it is her *neck* that becomes the erotic fetish-object of the camera, signifying *this* area of Vicki's body as the region the Baron longs to violate with his phallus: his long, pointed (but limp) tongue. Baron Vitelius confesses to Vicki that he has fallen madly in love with her, but nonetheless must kill her because she is the last remaining descendant of the inquisitors who executed him three centuries ago (again the Baron offers another redundant plot exposition of already known events because Vicki is unaware of them).

Meanwhile, left alone by the Baron and driven by his scientific curiosity, Ronnie investigates the Baron's study and discovers the ghastly secret of Baron Vitelius and his medicine. Suddenly, a horrifying scream is heard off-screen, and the camera pans to the lobby of the castle. Vicki practically careens into the shot, the camera tracking her as she races across the set and into Ronnie's arms. Importantly, Vicki overcomes the Baron's evil, seductive-hypnotic advances because she is the classic *chica moderna* of the film, possessing *both* the *sexual virtue* Maria de Pantoja and

Mrs. Meneses apparently lacked and the *modern independence* the film's traditional woman, Ana Luisa del Vivar, was unable to express. Ronnie intercedes in the Brainiac's pursuit of Vicki, but is unable to overcome the monster's supernatural powers. With Vicki cornered and about to be killed by the Brainiac, the Chief and Bennie fortuitously arrive on the scene with flamethrowers in hand. In one almost slapstick moment, Bennie bashes the Baron's butler on the head with the elongated barrel of the flamethrower as they rush into the castle. The police confront the Brainiac and unleash their flamethrowers on him. Whether for reasons of comic relief or the failure of the special effects department, it is apparent that Bennie is unable to fire his flamethrower, resulting in (unintentionally) hilarious shots in which he can clearly be seen pathetically wrestling with the weapon, completely baffled as to why it refuses to operate. Nevertheless, the Chief dispatches the Brainiac with a torrent of flames. Point-of-view shots from both the Brainiac's and the Chief's perspective depict the monster's destruction. From the monster's point of view, the policemen are seen in the background, their flamethrowers pointed directly at the viewer, as flames engulf the frame (and the audience). From the perspective of the police, the Brainiac can be seen cowering, attempting to shield itself from the flames that pour into the foreground of the frame. Throughout *The Brainiac*, fire is a thematic metaphor of violent social change and transformation: the initial burning of the Baron that purges any elements of heresy and immorality from Orthodox Catholicism; the burning of Professor de Pantoja's study and his wealth of historical and intellectual knowledge; the burning of the Meneses' industrial empire. At the conclusion of *The Brainiac*, fire ultimately has a productive, transforming effect on social change: purging the monster that is Mexico's colonial and irrational past from the modern, rational present. As Ronnie and Vicki embrace and look on in horrified awe, the camera cuts to a shot of the charred, smoking body of the Brainiac, which dissolves to the body of Baron Vitelius in his original medieval garb, which then dissolves, finally, to a smoldering skeleton. With the destruction of the Brainiac, the evil fiend from the past that literally preys on the intellect of modern Mexico, the present is once again safe.

4

El Santo,
el Enmascarado de Plata

Santo and the Lucha Libre Film: A Brief History

One of the more intriguing genres in the history of Mexican cinema is the lucha libre film, typified by those starring Rodolfo Guzmán Huerta, better-known as the Mexican wrestling legend "Santo."[1] Excluding the seven years he wrestled in various "pre–Santo" identities (1935–42), Santo's illustrious career spanned four decades in which he wrestled in over 5,000 matches, won numerous wrestling championship titles, and undoubtedly became Mexico's most famous luchador. At the mere age of 16, Santo began wrestling professionally in 1935 under his own name, Rudy Guzmán, and the following year he donned a red costume and wrestled under the name *Hombre Rojo* ("Red Man"). Hombre Rojo was a classic *rudo*, a "bad-guy" wrestler who wins matches through brute strength and illegal tactics (one of Hombre Rojo's more notorious tricks was his frequent kicks to the groin). Other identities Guzmán Hureta wrestled under during his early career included *Enmascarado* ("The Masked Man"), *Demonio Negro* ("Black Demon"), and *Murciélago II* ("The Bat II"). This last persona proved to be a source of contention when the original *Murciélago* (Jesús Velázquez), a famous rudo in his own right, objected to the use of his name and image and complained to the wrestling commission, forcing Guzmán Huerta to abandon his "Murciélago II" persona (the dispute also served to fuel a brief but intense rivalry between Santo and "Murciélago" Velázquez in the early 1940s).[2]

In 1942, Guzmán Huerta settled on his trademark silver mask, tights, and cape, and officially began wrestling as *El Santo, el Enmascarado de Plata*. However, it would be some time before Santo made the transition from a dastardly but popular rudo to a beloved and heroic *técnico*, a "good-guy" wrestler who achieves victory through athleticism, skill, and a strict adherence to the rules of the wrestling ring: a stark contrast to the rudo's malicious tactics and underhanded methods.[3] Santo maintained his rudo role in the ring until the early 1960s, with his transformation from rudo to técnico primarily occurring to provide consistency between

Santo's ring persona and the heroic image of Santo developed in his popular *historietas graphicas* (comic books) and his burgeoning film career.[4] Fernando Rivera Calderón specifically noted, "20 years after he was born a bestial 'rudo,' 5 July 1962 El Santo wrestled for the first time as a técnico."[5] Santo's popularity in the wrestling ring first spawned a highly successful line of Santo comics, created by well-known comic book publisher José G. Cruz. Running from approximately 1951 to 1980, they manufactured the popular image of Santo as a superhero fighting the forces of crime and evil threatening Mexican society, and also served as a basis for the Santo movie formula. [6] However, Santo's fabled film career itself would take almost another decade to fully materialize. In 1952, Santo was offered the title role in *El Enmascarado de Plata*, obviously designed as a film vehicle for the Silver-Masked Man. In the finished film directed by René Cardona, and written by José G. Cruz and Ramón Obón, however, Santo was conspicuous solely by his own absence. Unconvinced about the film's commercial potential, Santo turned down the project and was replaced in the title role by another well-known wrestler, *El Médico Asesino* ("The Murderous Doctor"—not to be confused with the title villain in *Las luchadoras vs. el médico asesino,* a mad scientist played by Roberto Cañedo). Nineteen fifty-two also saw the release of three other major wrestling movies: the comedy *El luchador fenómeno* (*The Phenomenal Wrestler,* dir. Fernando Cortés), the drama *La bestia magnifica* (*The Magnificent Beast,* dir. Chano Urueta), and the melodramatic *Hurácan Ramírez,* the saga of a young man pursuing a career as a lounge singer—much to the displeasure of his wrestler father—who also moonlights as a masked luchador (a lucha libre version of *The Jazz Singer?*). The film's popularity led to several more films featuring Hurácan Ramírez, and in 1953 promoters created an "actual" Hurácan Ramirez to participate in the lucha libre arena proper. [7] However, these early lucha libre films betrayed a certain degree of "inauthenticity" to dedicated lucha libre fans. As noted, Hurácan Ramirez was a fictional film character who would only later be portrayed as a real wrestler. Médico Asesino, arguably the first wrestler-actor in Mexican cinema (he appeared in all of the 1952 lucha libre films except *La bestia magnifica*), was commonly perceived as a mass-media creation of the brief television age of lucha libre in the early 1950s, an attempt to manufacture and popularize a wrestler specifically designed to play for the television camera and broadcast audience rather than live spectators.[8]

Not until the latter half of the 1950s would "authentic" lucha libre and the horror genre to converge. In 1956, Fernando Méndez directed an early horror-wrestling hybrid, *Ladrón de cadáveres* (*The Body Snatcher,* or, more literally, *Thief of Corpses*). The following year, Portillo's *La maldición de la momia azteca* not only included several well-known wrestlers in supporting roles (Jesús "Murciélago" Velázquez, Guillermo Hernández "Lobo Negro"), but featured *El Ángel* (the Angel), a masked muscleman who periodically intervenes throughout the film to battle the

Prototype wrestler-superhero El Ángel puts a sleeper-hold on crime in *La maldición de la momia azeca* (*The Curse of the Aztec Mummy,* 1957; dir. Rafael Portillo). (Courtesy Rob Craig.)

evil Dr. Krupp and his henchmen. The focus on the interaction between the hilariously diabolical Dr. Krupp and heroically daring Angel shifts *La maldición de la momia azteca* toward a combination of episodic serial action and Gothic horror film atmospherics: two integral components of the later lucha libre films of Santo and other masked wrestlers. While certainly not a lucha libre film as such, *La maldición de la momia azteca* can nonetheless be seen as a formative film in the lucha libre genre.[9]

In 1958, Santo belatedly began his film career by appearing in *Cerebro del mal* (*Brain of Evil*) and *Santo contra hombres infernales* (*Santo vs. the Infernal Men*). Both films were directed by *Hurácan Ramírez* creator Joselito Rodriguez and simultaneously shot in Cuba on an extremely tight budget. However, both films regulate Santo to a supporting role as a masked secret agent, neither referring to him as "Santo" nor even recognizing him as a luchador. In *Cerebro del mal*, Santo is kidnapped at the beginning of the film and brainwashed by the title villain, subsequently spending much of his time battling the film's real hero, another masked secret agent known as *El Incógnito* (played by former wrestler Fernando Osés, who, not surprisingly, also co-wrote the film). Perhaps dismayed by the results of these films, it would be another three years before the Sliver-Masked Man returned to the silver screen, during which time an important development took place in mexploitation cinema: the advent of the *Neutrón* series. In 1960, three *Neutrón* films were made: *Neutrón, el enmascarado negro* (*Neutron, the Black-Masked Man;* U.S. title: *Neutron vs. the Black Mask*); *Los autómatas de la muerte* (*The Automatons of Death;* U.S. title: *Neutron the Atomic Superman vs. the Death Robots*), and *Neutrón contra el doctor Caronte* (*Neutron vs. Dr. Caronte*).[10] Directed by Federico Curiel, the *Neutrón* films were made at Estudios América, with each film (necessarily?) divided into three serial-style episodes, much like his *Nostradamus* film series. Incorporating elements of serials, comic books, horror, and science fiction, Neutrón is a classic superhero cast within the lucha libre mold (with his mask and wrestling tights, and portrayed by yet another wrestler-turned-actor, Wolf Ruvinskis).[11]

In 1961, Santo would finally return to Mexican cinema in four movies arguably highly influenced by Federico Curiel's *Neutrón* film series. Indeed, three of these Santo films were directed by Curiel himself, including the extremely popular *Santo contra el cerebro diabólico*. The fourth Santo film from 1961, *Santo contra los zombies* (*Santo vs. the Zombies*, dir. Benito Alazraki; U.S. title: *Invasion of the Zombies*), is arguably the first to fully construct the patented Santo film formula, combining horror, serial sensibilities, comic books, action adventure, melodrama, comedy, and wrestling matches. It would be this formula that would be refined — or, more cynically, endlessly repeated — in the seminal Santo films of the 1960s and 1970s: *Santo contra las mujeres vampiro, Santo en el museo de cera, Atacan las brujas, Santo, el Enmascarado de Plata vs. los invasión de los marcianos, Santo en el tesoro de Drácula, La venganza de las mujeres vampiro, Santo contra la hija de Frankenstein, Santo y Blue Demon contra Drácula y el Hombre Lobo*, and *Santo y Blue Demon contra el Dr. Frankenstein*. While his films were not considered "artistic" successes (recalling Carl J. Mora's highly negative assessment of the Santo films), Santo was one of Latin America's most popular box-office attractions throughout the 1960s, eventually starring in over fifty films from the late 1950s until the early 1980s, as well as inspiring a host of films which blatantly imitated the Santo formula (the films of fellow wrestlers Blue Demon and Mil Máscaras). By the time of his death in 1984, Santo achieved nothing short of an iconic status in Mexican society, as important to Mexican athletics and popular culture as Babe Ruth is to Americana.

Lucha Libre and the Semiotics of Wrestling

Before approaching the lucha libre films of Santo, it is necessary to discuss the cultural implications of lucha libre itself. Roland Barthes' essay "The World of Wrestling" (*ca.* 1957) remains one of the most insightful studies of the pervasive ideological meanings behind what is considered "low-brow" entertainment. For Barthes, wrestling is not "sport" in the sense of athletic competition (as opposed to boxing), but "theater," a melodramatic spectacle of excess rich in ethical, national, and ideological meanings:

> In America, wrestling represents a sort of mythological fight between Good and Evil (of a quasi-political nature, the "bad" wrestler always appears to be a Red). The process of creating heroes in French wrestling is very different, being based on ethics and not politics. What the public is looking for here is the gradual construction of a highly moral image: that of the perfect "bastard."[12]

Lucha libre has consistently been a highly popular form of Mexican entertainment since the 1930s, when lucha libre matches were first organized by promoter Salvador Lutterroth Gonzalez. By the 1950s, lucha libre was among the most popular spectator pastimes in Mexico, its popularity primarily provided by Mexico's lower-and working-class families. Lucha libre and its clearly delineated battle lines of técnicos and rudos "developed its own nationally specific myths and conventions ... providing inexpensive catharsis for the stresses and strains of urban life."[13] Dan Murphy notes, "Like super-heros, most *luchadores* wear masks and never reveal their identities. The mystique of the mask transforms many into icons of justice, virtual opponents of the corrupt cops and street toughs that many poor Mexicans have to deal with."[14] Indeed, wrestling serves a very specific cultural function in Mexico, just as it does in France (ethical drama) or America (international political metaphors). As Heather Levi observes:

> In the interactions between apparently suffering técnicos and apparently underhanded rudos, lucha libre demonstrated and parodied a common understanding of the post-revolutionary system, and [the peoples] place within it. It reflected a political system in which people who appear to be opponents are really working together. It paralleled an electoral system in which electioneering took place behind closed doors and elections ratified decisions that had already been made. Ongoing dramas in the ring demonstrated that loyalty to kin and friends is more important than ideology, and that the arbitrators of authority are not necessarily on the side of the honest and the honorable. By its very name (which not only means "free wrestling" but "free struggle"), lucha libre resonated with the widely held and fundamental philosophy of the Mexican popular classes: life is struggle. This struggle was ritually enacted every week in the ring.[15]

Unlike professional wrestling in America, lucha libre was not closely affiliated with the rise of television as a popular medium: lucha libre was *banned* from Mexican television in the mid–1950s and would not reappear on television until the early 1990s. Officially, the reason for the ban was lucha libre's alleged influence on impressionable male adolescents, especially the potential impact of the rudo as a negative role model — Santo himself was a highly-popular rudo at the time. However, Levi and others argue that the government ban on televised lucha libre was largely designed to keep the event confined to local working-class entertainment and out of middle-class homes.[16] Moreover, the television ban also inadvertently created a new cinematic genre: the lucha libre film. As Syder and Tierney note:

> It does not seem coincidental that the first horror/wrestling films should happen to emerge in the mid–1950s, at the same time as the ban on television.... [W]hat the fusion of wrestling and horror achieved was to enable the mexploitation film to direct its attention away from the rudo and onto clashes outside the ring with vampires, mummies and mad scientists.... [T]his kind of iconographic coding should be clear to fans of horror and science-fiction cinema ... during the same period in the United States, giant insects and alien invasions served as metaphors about atomic energy and Communist infiltration. By borrowing from Hollywood horror conventions and iconography, mexploitation films were able to carry on, in a coded fashion, the social functions of lucha libre.[17]

Thus, the traditional battles between técnicos and rudos could be played out for the public in a cinematic form, where the spectacle of lucha libre, along with its political and cultural subtext, was disguised within the framework of a horror film or some other genre: the técnico being an actual popular wrestler and the rudo taking the form of a fictional villain or monster. Santo, perpetually clad in his silver mask, fought evil and injustice, struggling on behalf of the Mexican popular classes, whether in the private sector (typified by haunted houses and secret laboratories) or in the public sphere of the wrestling arena.

Santo as "National Allegory"

While Santo is the epitome of virile masculinity, his image is also very much consistent with that of the "countermacho" political stereotype: the modern, patriarchal technocrat who is morally respectable, socially responsible, and selflessly dedicated to serving and bettering the lot of the Mexican public. In this regard, Levi argues that the conflicts between ethical técnicos and cheating rudos could also be expressed as técnicos (technocrats) verses *politicos* (politicians): "It is a split between a politics based (in theory) on rational management, and one based on negotiation of personal loyalties ... support for the técnico wrestler could be seen as a kind of support for the government, or at least a vision of modernization that the Mexican state has endorsed."[18] The various roles Santo adopts as popular superhero, societal role model, and political ideal can be seen in relation to the concept of "national allegory," a term taken from Fredric Jameson's essay "Third-World Literature in the Era of Multinational Capitalism" (1986). Jameson wrote, "Third world texts, even those which are seemingly private and invested with a properly libidinal dynamic — necessarily project a political dimension in the form of national allegory: *the story of the private individual destiny is always an allegory of the embattled situation of the public third-world culture and society*."[19] Santo, as a nationally-famous luchador fighting for ethical order in the wrestling ring and portraying himself as a superhero protecting the Mexican public, not only dismantles the barriers between reality and fiction but also eliminates any separation of the private and the public role of the character in his society. David Wilt notes:

> Santo is shown to be *both* a wrestler and famous crime fighter ... he literally interrupts his crime-fighting to rush of to a scheduled wrestling bout, and vice versa.... In its purest form, [lucha libre] films feature a protagonist who is both a masked wrestler *and* a crime-fighting super hero.... Playboy Bruce Wayne has to become Batman to fight crime, but El Santo is always El Santo. In his films, in his comic books, and in his wrestling career his true identity is a closely guarded secret. Thus the duality of most masked heroes (hero versus "normal" person) does not exist in the lucha libre films, where the hero's double life is split between his career as a professional wrestler and his crime-fighting duties.[20]

In the American "superhero" tradition, this separation or distinction between the private life of the individual and the public role of crime-fighter is essential. Clark Kent and Peter Parker assume the private identities of milquetoast journalists, which must remain distinct from their roles as Superman and Spiderman, just as Bruce Wayne's millionaire playboy image must remain divorced from his life as Batman. Unlike American superheroes, who possess this "split personality" or dichotomy of personal identity (private life) and superhero identity (public life), the lucha libre icon, while his personal identity must remain similarly hidden, has his private identity completely *subsumed* by his public persona. The cinematic depiction of Santo as a figure whose private and public persona are inseparable strongly parallels Jameson's conception of "national allegory." Santo, as a real-life luchador and a mythic superhero in a horror film, occupies two thoroughly *public* roles in Mexican society. Santo is not simply an iconic public figure in both the wrestling ring and popular cinema, but can indeed be considered a form of "national allegory." Santo is the powerful, heroic, masculine embodiment of modernity and mexicanidad—the countermacho defending Mexico from internal and external threats that would jeopardize national identity, sovereignty, and progress. There is no distinction between Santo's "individual destiny" and Mexico's "embattled situation," represented by the multitudes of villains and monsters that threaten the Mexican *status quo,* and which Santo must defeat in film after film.

Santo contra las mujeres vampiro (Santo vs. the Vampire Women, *1962)*

Only *four* of Santo's fifty-plus films were dubbed into English and released in America — of those, only *two* were officially dubbed and released by K. Gordon Murray: *Santo contra las mujeres vampiro* and *Santo en el museo de cera.*[21] Presumably to give American audiences a symbolic reference point, Murray changed Santo's name to "Samson" in both films (obviously referencing the Biblical strongman) and released the films as *Samson vs. the Vampire Women* and *Samson in the Wax Museum.* As *Samson vs. the Vampire Women, Santo contra las mujeres vampiro* became a fixture on American late-night television under Murray's "World of Terror" syndication efforts and, like many other Murray imports, eventually garnered a celebrated cult-film prestige. In addition to being the only two Santo films imported by Murray, *Santo contra las mujeres vampiro* and *Santo en el museo de cera* have the distinction of being the only two Santo films directed by Alfonso Corona Blake. Like many other mexploitation directors (René Cardona, Federico Curiel, Chano Urueta), Corona Blake was an experienced director who helmed a number of successful films, including the critically and commercially successful religious melodrama *Yo pecador* (*I, Sinner,* 1959). In addition to his two Santo films, Corona Blake directed the mexploitation horror classic *El mundo de los vampiros,* a film that *Santo vs. las mujeres vampiro* strongly echoes. As in *El mundo de los vampiros, Santo contra las mujeres vampiro* revolves around vampires resurrected in present-day Mexico, and especially focuses on the evil *sexual* threat they pose. However, the primary and obvious difference is that *El mundo de los vampiros* centers on the libidinal, licentious dangers of a *man* (Count Subotai), whereas in *Santo contra las mujeres vampiro* the threat of sexual immorality is the domain of evil, attractive, irresistible *women.*[22] Ultimately, while *Santo contra los zombies* may be credited with establishing the Santo film formula, *Santo contra las mujeres vampiro* perfected it and remains the seminal Santo film, perhaps even the archetypical mexploitation film. *Santo contra las mujeres vampiro* combines an exaggerated use of horror film clichés; the excesses of melodrama; episodic narrative construction; comic book action; a pivotal battle between Santo and a supernatural villain in the wrestling ring; a straight lucha libre sequence inserted into the film almost at random; and, not least, a valorization of modernity framed through the representation of women.

In that Murray's version of *Santo contra las mujeres vampiro* will be critically discussed, for this section the film will be referred to as *Santo vs. the Vampire Women* (rather than *Samson vs. the Vampire Women*). Typical of mexploitation's simultaneous reliance on and borrowing from classic Hollywood horror films, as well as its disregard for cinematic convention, *Santo vs. the Vampire Women*'s first shot lasts *twenty-two* seconds, consisting of a long opening left-to-right pan from of the interior of a Gothic haunted mansion, replete with cobwebs, *chiaroscuro* lighting, thunder and lightning, and ominous music: in short, every possible horror film cliché. (With *Santo en el museo de cera*, Corona Blake would not be content with merely parodying generic horror film conventions, but would freely incorporate key elements from a number of specific classic horror films, including *Mystery of the Wax Museum* [1933, dir. Michael Curtiz] and *Island of Lost Souls* [1933, dir. Erle C. Kenton], as well as *Frankenstein* and *Dracula*.) As a bat flies across the screen, the camera stops its leisurely pan and abruptly shifts back to the right to follow the bat's path. The film then cuts to an incongruous close-up of an owl scanning the room, followed by another abrupt edit in which the bat is shown flying out the window.[23] Following these confusing and extraneous inserts, the camera then resumes its leisurely pan from the point it was interrupted, again moving from right to left for another *fifteen* seconds, before eventually focusing on a painting of a young woman hanging on the wall. This cuts to a brief close-up revealing the name "Rebeca" under the painting. The film then cuts back to *another* pan across the room of the mansion, this time moving from left to right for *another ten seconds* while a disembodied scream is heard. In effect, the first minute of the film is consists of three establishing shots depicting the same scene, interrupted only by jarring and disorientating inserts.

The pan finally cuts to a shot of a coffin and the emergence of one of the vampire women, Tundra (Ofelia Montesco); all decomposed flesh and rotted clothing. Tundra begins a long, ponderous, and sometimes unintentionally hilarious monologue consisting mostly of plot exposition that becomes evident as the film progresses. The vampire women have returned from the dead after 200 years to fulfill the prophecy of replacing the current vampire queen with a new one. They also seek revenge on the man whose ancestor originally thwarted the vampire women and banished them to the slumber from which they have now awakened. This man, of course, turns out to be Santo. Santo's historic, heroic, vampire-slaying ancestor, while referenced but neither actually named nor seen in *Santo vs. the Vampire Women*, would eventually be introduced to the Mexican film public in the subsequent Santo film *El barón Brákola* (*Baron Brákola*, 1965; dir. José Díaz Morales) as el Caballero Enmascarado de Plata ("The Knight in the Silver Mask"). The Caballero defeats the vampire Baron Brákola (Fernando Osés) in the year 1765, and when Baron Brákola reawakens two hundred years later to exact his revenge on the

Caballero's descendants, Santo himself must defeat the revived, vampirical threat to Mexico (two hundred years seems to be the standard hibernation period for revenge-driven vampires in mexploitation cinema). Presuming Santo's ancestor in *Santo vs. the Vampire Women* was indeed the Caballero, he would have defeated the vampire women in 1762: an important time frame because it suggests that the supernatural danger of vampirism originated and thrived during the era of Spanish colonialism in Mexico (or "New Spain"), a period in which the Spanish conquerors existed in a "vampirical" relationship with the native Mexicans they exploited. Also, the threat of vampirism is combated by a legendary fighter of the supernatural whose lineage leads directly to the modern countermacho: Santo.

However, Tundra also pointedly explains that circumstances surrounding the vampire women's resurrection are very much related to the current conditions of the *modern* world. At one point in her monologue, Tundra proclaims, "All men are addicted to corruption and obligated to self-destruction. They have permitted us to awaken and call out all the monsters that rule the earth." Given that the film was made in 1962, the volatile conditions of then-current Cold War politics and the threat of nuclear war have set the stage for the monsters from the past to reappear and threaten the present, an idea explicitly articulated later in the film by Santo himself, and a theme integral to the subsequent *Santo, el Enmascaraso de Plata vs. la invasión de los marcianos*.

Continuing her long explanation of the plot disguised as a dramatic monologue, Tundra summons other vampire women from their coffins and then proceeds to the mansion's dungeon. Through invoking the forces of evil, she is transformed into a figure of stunning beauty in a burst of smoke and sparks. A product of the film's limited budget, many of the special effects are accomplished via dated procedures. Tundra's supernatural transformation does not so much resemble the special effects of the Universal horror films, but instead mimics the techniques of silent film pioneer and fantasist Georges Méliès, who combined primitive photographic effects with stage-magic trickery; such primitive special effects render *Santo vs. the Vampire Women* even more anachronistic and "low-budget." Her tattered robes become a silky, white evening gown (the gowns worn by both the vampire women in this film and the witches in *Atacan las brujas* strongly recall the attire of the ancient Greeks). Tundra then revives the vampire women's musclebound, monstrous henchmen, who are chained to concrete slabs in the dungeon: Marcus (Guillermo Hernández "Lobo Negro"), Taras (Nathanael León "Frankenstein"), and the most powerful of all the henchmen, Igor (the ever-present Fernando Osés). Through a series of disorientating jump-cuts worthy of Jean-Luc Godard that alternate from one henchman to the next, they transform from beastly monsters into imposing Gothic he-men. One of the more obvious ironies of the film is that Hernández, León, and Osés were all famous wrestlers, and are obviously powerful, muscular specimens of masculinity who are nonetheless ruthlessly bullied and ordered around by the diminutive and sultry Tundra. The status of men in the perversely evil world of the vampire women is one entirely of submission and enslavement, and this subjection of masculinity by the vampire women is an important component in their vilification as dangerous threats to modern Mexican society: dominators of men and threats to a strong, masculine, and patriarchal order embodied by Santo. (However, at the point in the monologue when Tundra invoked the forces of evil, the shadowy silhouette of Satan appeared behind her, suggesting that even the world of supernatural evil is ultimately governed by "a patriarch" after all.)

Tundra and her beefy henchmen make their way upstairs to the setting depicted in the opening shots of the film. The camera focuses on the painting of "Rebeca" on the wall of the haunted mansion of the vampire women and then jump-cuts to with a shot of a nearly identical painting on the wall of an upper-class home, providing a stark contrast between the interior of the dilapidated haunted house, decorated in horror film clichés, and the modern interior of this new setting: a juxtaposition between the ominous, obsolescent past and the ornate, orderly present. The viewer is introduced to Professor Rolof (Augusto Benedico, whose character is called "Professor Orlof" in *Santo contra las mujeres vampiro*), George ("Jorge" in *Santo contra las mujeres vampiro,* played by Xavier Loyá), and Diana (María Duval), the professor's daughter, George's fiancée, and the woman in the painting(s).[24] Tundra appears in the picture window, watching the idyllic bourgeois family scene with sinister intent (a standard moment in numerous mexploitation-vampire films derived from *Dracula*). Her ominous presence produces an immediate negative effect on Diana, who faints while playing the piano for her father and fiancé, forcing her to retire for the evening. Soon after, as Diana prepares for bed, she notices Tundra spying on her through the bedroom window. Diana screams in terror and pleads with her father for an explanation of these unsettling occurrences (although the bat-shaped birthmark on Diana's arm would seem to provide a clue). He convinces her that there is nothing wrong, but the viewer obviously knows otherwise, especially given the long plot exposition Tundra already provided. It is clear that Diana is desired to be the next queen of the vampire women.

Thus, the first twenty-five minutes of *Santo vs. the Vampire Women* not only creates a cliché horror film scenario (albeit at an excruciatingly slow pace), but also serves to establish the status of women in the film. Carlos Monsiváis notes that Mexican cinema "underscores the brutal sexism of Mexican society and considers the function of women in a different way, by emphasizing, through a series of close-ups, their sanctity or perversity, and by praising, of necessity, modern young people."[25] The characters of Tundra and Diana serve as binary oppositions of both

60

perversity-versus-*sanctity* and *obsolete past*-versus-*modern youth*. Tundra is a symbol of sexual *perversity*, a woman who simultaneously seduces and bends the will of men through her powerful, hypnotic eyes, expressed in a relentless "series of close-ups." One of *Santo vs. the Vampire Women*'s most obvious and redundant motif is the oft-repeated extreme close-up of Tundra's eyes when she is in the act of hypnotizing her victims; and this one shot of Tundra's eyes is recycled numerous times throughout the film (this use, and overuse, of the extreme close-up of eyes signifying hypnotic seduction is certainly one of the most common traits of mexploitation cinema as a whole). Ideologically, the "series of close-ups" becomes a filmic device that equates the female gaze with both hypnotic evil and irresistible allure: seduction, destruction and domination of men by women. As noted, Tundra and the other vampire women are literally "undead," figures of Mexico's past. To again quote Monsiváis, "[Mexican] cinema offers one certainty: that *to persist in traditional ways is a form of living death.*"[26] The vampire women typify the threat of an outmoded past returning to disturb and eventually destroy the modern present. "Traditional ways" and "living death" are literally one and the same, embodied by dead monsters returning to life to exact their revenge from the living — a standard narrative device and cultural metaphor common to mexploitation films.

While Tundra is characterized by sexual perversity and the threat of the past, Diana is a figure embodying *both* sexual sanctity and Mexican modernity. She is awaiting her birthday, which will not only mark her achieving adulthood, but her coming marriage to George. In short, it is all but explicitly stated that Diana is a virgin, a symbol of sexual *sanctity*, the *chica moderna* who is "chaste before marriage and monogamous afterward." Furthermore, Diana is indicative of Monsiváis' observation that Mexican cinema engages in a project of "praising ... modern young people." While certainly invested with elements of the traditional woman through her status in the family (obedient daughter and, eventually, wife), Diana is also a young, urban *chica moderna* whose sexual virtue and Mexican national virtue is one and the same. The conflict of an evil past impinging on the present is played out through sexual politics: the sexually alluring, "living dead" vampire women (sexual perversity/the past) seeking to transform the young, pure, modern Mexican woman Diana (sexual sanctity/the present) into one of their dangerous own. Diana's "private destiny" is one of a happy marriage, her "embattled situation" is the threat of resurrected vampire women seeking to convert her into an evil bloodsucking figure of destructive seduction. In this way, Diana serves a national allegory for the status of modern Mexican women as much as Santo serves as a national allegory for the myths and responsibilities of Mexican masculinity and patriarchy. And it is Santo, the heroic, modern, masculine, patriarchal figure — the countermacho — who must triumphantly emerge to save modern Mexican femininity (Diana) from the corrupting power of the vampire women.

Visibly unnerved by these mysterious events, the frantic Professor Rolof calls Santo for help on his television-radio communicator, but to no avail. The TV screen shows that Santo's high-tech crime lab is empty, and the Professor leaves an urgent message on Santo's tape recorder (Santo's futuristic, crime-fighting secret headquarters also connects him with ultra-modern technology). The scene changes from Santo's empty crime lab on Professor Rolof's TV screen to a brief shot of a lucha libre match about to begin. The wrestling ring is first seen *within* the confines of the TV screen, as though the match was actually televised but a jump-cut offers the same shot from a further distance minus the TV screen that formerly outlined the frame. The sequence not only offers a transition from fictional horror narrative to the reality of lucha libre, but offers a brief but blatant commentary on the banning of lucha libre from television — when the viewer first sees lucha libre, it is literally seen *on* a television screen. It is as though the film flaunts the fact that it is a means of broadcasting lucha libre matches that could not be shown on television at the time. The horror film cuts to a nine-minute wrestling match featuring Santo that has absolutely nothing to do with the narrative. As noted, several lucha libre films utilize various plot contrivances to merge the horror narrative with wrestling action (including *Santo vs. the Vampire Women* for its second wrestling match); in other films, these lucha libre sequences have virtually no relation to the film narrative proper and completely interrupt any sort of narrative continuity. As Syder and Tierney observes:

> [R]ather than adhering to Hollywood conventions, such sequences frustrate desires for narrative economy and demand the viewer alternate between the fictional/narrative and the non-fictional/non-narrative passages. Indeed, the wrestling sequences demand that the audience "unsuture" themselves from the horror narrative, thus encouraging a more flexible reading protocol than that promoted by the Hollywood cinema on which they drew.[27]

All narrative convention and continuity is broken by the lucha libre sequences, necessitating an alternative kind of spectatorship opposed to Hollywood's codes of narrative economy and continuity. Their inclusion serves no purpose other than to strategically insert a wrestling match into a film, a match which otherwise only could be seen by actually attending a wrestling event (given that lucha libre was banned from television): thus, the subversive importance of the transitional shot when the lucha libre ring briefly appears on the television screen of Professor Rolof's futuristic TV-radio-phone. The insertion of lucha libre not only forces the viewer to delay expectations of narrative development, but encourages a different, more active mode of spectatorship towards the film, encouraging direct engagement with the film's wrestling action rather than passively watching narrative events unfold. Monsiváis recalled that Mexican film audiences behave like lucha libre fans rather than movie audiences during these on-screen wrestling sequences, shouting encouragement or insults at the on-screen *técnicos* and *rudos*.[28] To an American audience, it seems the matches are included for no logical reason other than to pad out the film to an acceptable running time. However, for the Mexican audience, and especially the lucha libre fan, these wrestling sequences are far from padding, but are an essential part of the film. One might even suggest that the horror narrative is the actual padding for the film, which exists primarily to bring lucha libre to the public in a broadcast form.[29]

Following this wrestling sequence, the film abruptly shifts back to the horror narrative for another ten minutes. Tundra and her henchmen prowl the streets of the city, and the viewer is struck by the incongruity of the monsters in the settings of urban Mexico, stressing the vast difference between their anachronistic Grecian-Gothic appearance and their modern surroundings. The vampires soon come across a young couple and assault them, killing the woman and abducting the man for future nefarious purposes. A male police officer witnesses the crime and is about to intervene, but is hypnotized by Tundra's gaze (the recycled extreme close-up of her eyes): he can do nothing but passively watch as the vampire woman and her henchmen-slaves attack the young couple. One sees a social danger in the form of an attractive woman whose seductive-hypnotic stare is capable of rendering even "the law" itself helpless and ineffective. Returning to the catacombs of the vampire women's haunted castle, Tundra drains the captured man's blood into a goblet which the vampire women ritualistically pass around and partake from. Again one sees how the discourse of modernity and the representation of women is manifest in mexploitation. The "lifeblood" of a Mexican young person, and specifically a *man*, is literally drained and consumed by the evil resurrected vampire women, signifying both that the past exists in a parasitical relationship with the present, and that evil women outside of Mexican codes of sexual morality feed off the blood and youthful virility of men (issues central to the later *Santo vs. la hija de Frankenstein*). With the female vampires transformed one by one from hideous living corpses into beautiful women in Grecian gowns, the blood drinking concludes with the resurrection and transformation of the current vampire queen, Zorina (Lorena Velázquez). The film then grinds to a halt as the now-revived Zorina explains already-established plot points previously expressed by Tundra and depicted by actual events in the film.

For the first forty-five minutes of the film, or roughly the first half of *Santo vs. the Vampire Women*, the two major elements, horror and wrestling, are not at all integrated, but remain unrelated counterpoints, which with neither affecting the other. Only during the second half of the film does the presence of Santo and the horror narrative merge into an altogether surreal assemblage. Standing outside the window of Professor Rolof's study, Tundra attempts to hypnotize him, the shots

Evil vampire women feast on male blood in *Santo vs. the Vampire Women.*

alternating between the extreme close-ups of Diana's eyes and close-ups of a grimacing Professor Rolof. Invoking the name of God, Rolof succeeds in dispelling her. The scene then shifts to a shot of the Professor's study where, right on cue, Santo, replete in his mask, sequined cape, and bare chest, walks through the door and into the film frame, obviously connecting the invocation of God and the arrival of Santo himself (or "Himself"). Offering more plot exposition, Professor Rolof recounts the events of the film thus far to Santo. While the expository summary Professor Rolof provides to Santo has already been made clear to the viewer by Tundra and Zorina's speeches (and subsequent events in the film itself), as a new character entering the narrative, Santo is provided with information *he* would not be aware of (a stark contrast to the narrative economy of Hollywood). Professor Rolof reiterates that the current state of the world has allowed monsters of the past to be resurrected and threaten the present; the dangerous threat the vampire women pose to Diana; and how "ancient prophecy" tells that Santo is the only man who can stop them. Indeed, Tundra's claim that "all men are ... committed to destruction" is illustrated in a wonderful exchange between the two men:

> PROFESSOR ROLOF: We're living in a time where things are perfect for the resurrection of monsters here on earth. Since men are bent on wreaking destruction on the world today, they'll heed to their selfish desires and use the tremendous power that nature has given us.
> SANTO: Yes — *nuclear energy!*

Once again, the film clearly states that the resurrection of the vampire women and the danger they represent is the result of the contemporary situation of the world — specifically, the threat of nuclear war, a cultural context most important for a film done in 1962, the height of Cold War tensions and the year of the Cuban Missile Crisis: an event that thrust Latin America into the spotlight of Cold War politics.

Professor Rolof pleads with Santo to come to the masquerade ball that evening to protect Diana. Santo, however, must decline, explaining he "has other plans" (presumably a wrestling bout). Of course, Tundra and her henchmen manage to infiltrate the masquerade party; this time their anachronistic appearance is relatively inconspicuous, with the individuals at the masquerade ball dressed in Victorian and other period costumes of the past. The vampires abduct Diana, but Santo arrives at the last minute to single-handedly fend off the vampire women and their henchmen; throughout Santo's film career he demonstrates a sort of virtual omnipresence in Mexican society — ever vigilant and personally interceding during times of narrative and social crisis. Defeated by Santo, Tundra sheepishly returns to the vampire women's lair. Zorina, livid with Tundra's failure to capture Diana, destroys two of Tundra's accomplices in a flurry of sparks and smoke. Following her supernatural tantrum, Zorina delivers a histrionic warning regarding the dire nature of their situation and explains what must be done: capture Diana and destroy of Santo (yet again, the viewer must patiently wait while she explains obvious narrative events).

At this point in *Santo vs. the Vampire Women* the allegorical struggle fully emerges along gender lines: Santo, representing Mexican national values and myths (justice, patriarchy, social and economic progress), versus the vampire women, representing both sexually perverse, dangerous women and obsolete, debilitating ways of the past. In the final third of the film, the narrative conflict abruptly shifts from Diana's plight to the vampire women's attempts to destroy Santo. In the film's most pivotal conflict, the two relatively unrelated strains of horror and wrestling are combined when Santo is scheduled to wrestle a match against the Black Mask. The vampire henchman Igor kills the actual Black Mask and assumes his identity in order to defeat and unmask Santo in the ring. The classic lucha libre confrontation between técnico and rudo merges with the horror film narrative: the battle between modern Mexico (Santo-técnico) and evil forces that seek to destroy the values and future of Mexican society (monster-rudo). As the match builds in intensity, it becomes apparent that Santo is overmatched by the supernatural power of Igor. Nonetheless, Santo struggles manfully to overcome his opponent — a common trope in the melodramatics of professional wrestling as a whole, where the good guy (técnico, face) is pushed to the brink of utter defeat several times before miraculously overcoming the bad guy (rudo, heel). At the height of the battle, Igor looms over the prone Santo and attempts to remove his mask; a close-up of Santo's face as the mask is pulled up over his chin fills the screen. A fate worse than death, the public unmasking of Santo would be tantamount to killing Santo, or, in more vulgar psychoanalytic terms, "castrating" Santo as a powerful public icon or national allegory by revealing the mortal man underneath the mask — the mask that serves to make the luchador a public symbol of social, cultural, and political modes of conduct rather than a mere private individual with moral weaknesses.[30] With almost superhuman effort, Santo reverses the situation by placing Igor in the "Horse Lock" — Santo's signature submission hold in which he sits on his opponent's back and lifts him by the chin with both arms. With Igor immobilized by the Horse Lock, Santo unmasks Igor, who is rather inexplicably revealed to now be a grotesque werewolf rather than a vampire. By unmasking his own enemy, Santo is able to reveal the rudo as not simply a private individual or mere mortal, but literally a subhuman thing — a force of pure, primitive evil pitted against Mexican society. His true identity — and nature — revealed, Igor transforms into a bat and flies from the ring.

With Santo preoccupied in the wrestling ring battling Igor, Diana, along with her fiancé and a police detective, seeks safety in a nightclub. They are followed by Zorina and Tundra, the pair again appearing completely incongruous within the modern urban milieu of the nightclub by virtue of their Grecian gowns and Gothic demeanor. Despite another last-minute rescue attempt by Santo, the vampires finally succeed in abducting Diana and spirit her away to the haunted castle to complete her coronation as their new queen. Santo follows the vampire women, but is captured. However, the vampire women, specifically Tundra, ultimately succumb to, for lack of a better term, "mask envy" (and if the vampire women suffer from "mask envy," it can certainly be said that Freda Frankenstein in *Santo contra la hija de Frankenstein* demonstrates considerable "blood envy" toward Santo). Despite Zorina's insistent warnings that the ritual transferring of the throne to Diana must be completed before sunrise, Santo is tied to a concrete slab and mercilessly beaten

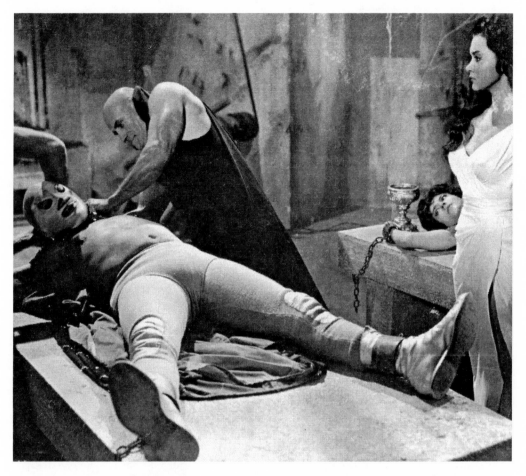

Santo placed in a compromising position by vampire women in *Santo vs. the Vampire Women.*

by Taras as Tundra looks on with sexually perverse pleasure, delighting in torment-ing, emasculating, and ultimately unmasking/castrating the virile Santo (again fore-shadowing the outrageously sexually-charged antagonism between Santo and Freda Frankenstein in *Santo contra la hija de Frankenstein*). Unfortunately for the vam-pire women, Tundra wastes valuable time torturing Santo in preparation for unmasking him — again, a trope borrowed from the melodramatics of lucha libre rather than the horror genre. When Taras finally attempts to undo the mask, sun-light begins to stream through the window of the dungeon. The decision (or rather the pathological desire of Tundra) to humiliate, punish, unmask, symbolically cas-trate, and ultimately destroy Santo becomes the fatal flaw in the vampire women's evil plans. Having failed to complete the occult ceremony that would return them to eternal youth through the enslavement and coronation of Diana as their new queen, the vampire women transform back to their original hideous state of decomposition and flee to their coffins. Those who are caught in the sunlight burst into flames, including Tundra. With his mask and power retained, Santo is able to free himself and destroy the remaining vampire women by brutally jabbing a flaming torch into each of the coffins, incinerating them. Certainly, in a vulgar Freudian sense, one can read Santo's destruction of the vampire women as the violently thrusting of his flaming, phallic torch into the vaginal coffins of the female vampires. The act of cleansing the modern world of the past, in the form of monstrous females, is depicted through a brutal metaphor of sexual intercourse or even rape.

Recalling the corny, clichéd endings of American B-movie Westerns rather than the classic horror film, the triumphant Santo rides off alone in his sports car, giving only a wave of silent acknowledgment from the grateful Rolof family and police. As Santo speeds away, the film closes on a hilarious exchange between Professor Rolof and Diana, one ripe with irony:

> PROFESSOR ROLOF: God bless Samson [Santo].
> DIANA: Who is he, papa?
> PROFESSOR ROLOF: That's his secret — I don't think you'll ever know. But I'll say this much, my dear, in this age where there are certain evil men who propose to destroy us, Samson [Santo] is an example of good will to men who serve justice.

Indeed, despite having been saved from the horrific fate of becoming queen of the vampire women, Diana demonstrates that she shares their same "female" weakness: the potentially dangerous desire to know who is behind the mask, which would be the very undoing of the luchador as an icon of social justice or even national allegory. Diana's father gently but firmly reminds her that *who* he is remains far less important than *what* he is: a symbol of the values of Mexican culture embodied in an iconic, masculine, and modern superhero — the good patriarch, the countermacho political stereotype, the técnico-as-technocrat who selflessly intercedes on behalf of the Mexican public. Thus, as Santo drives off into the distance, perhaps to another wrestling match, the security of the Mexican present, and the promise of its future, is once again established.

Santo, el Enmascarado de Plata vs. la invasión de los marcianos *(Santo, the Silver–Masked Man vs. the Invasion of the Martians, 1966)*

In 1963, Santo starred in *Santo contra el estrangulador* (*Santo vs. the Strangler*) and its sequel, *El espectro del estrangulador* (*Ghost of the Strangler*), the final two

Santo films produced by Alberto López, who oversaw the seminal Santo trilogy *Santo contra los zombies, Santo contra las mujeres vampiro,* and *Santo en el museo de cera.* Both *Estrangulador* films were directed by René Cardona, and filmed simultaneously and as quickly as possible before Santo's contract with López expired; several musical numbers were eventually included in both films to lengthen them to an acceptable running time.[31] Santo then collaborated with Luis Enrique Vergara, who produced four Santo films between 1964 and 1965: *Atacan las brujas, El hacha diabólica, Profanadores de tumbas* (*Grave Robbers,* 1965), and *El barón Brákola.* All four films were directed by José Díaz Morales, and primarily written by the team of Rafael García Travesí and Fernando Osés. Continuing the Santo formula combining horror, action, melodrama, and lucha libre, Santo battled evil witches (*Atacan las brujas*); the axe-wielding "Black Hood" (Fernando Osés), an evil figure resurrected from seventeenth century Inquisition-era Mexico (*El hacha diabólica*); a mad scientist (*Profanadores de tumbas*); and a resurrected, burly vampire (*El barón Brákola*— also played by Fernando Osés). While *Atacan las brujas* is essentially a remake of *Santo contra las mujeres vampiros,* substituting witches for vampire women, it is also one of the more visually interesting Santo films, in particular its long, pre-credit dream sequence which offers a wonderfully overwrought and ominous narration over a flurry of images; it might be described as mexploitation as done by Eisenstein. Constructed around a series of last-minute rescues of Ofelia from the witches by Santo, *Atacan las brujas* features several extended battles between Santo and black-clad witch henchmen devoid of any dialogue; in this way, the film not only strongly echoes Universal horror but low-budget serials and even silent cinema.

However, Santo's business relationship with Vergara quickly soured and they severed their ties after two brief years (an issue that will be explored at length in the context of *Santo y Blue Demon contra Drácula y el Hombre Lobo*). In 1966, Santo appeared in *Santo, el Enmascarado de Plata vs. la invasión de los marcianos* (for purposes of brevity, the film will be referred to as *Santo vs. la invasión de los marcianos*). Produced by Alfonso Rosas Priego, and featuring the almost-obligatory Rafael García Travesí screenplay, the film was one of a number of Santo projects directed by Alfredo B. Crevenna, a veteran of Mexican cinema who directed approximately 150 films in various genres from 1944 to 1993, including numerous mexploitation films.[32] Based on the most generic of science-fiction plot devices, an invasion of Earth by inhabitants of the planet Mars, *Santo vs. la invasión de los marcianos* better compares to Hollywood horror/science fiction films of the 1950s rather than the classic Universal Studios horror films of the 1930s, which served as the primary influence on the earlier Santo films. More specifically, given that the goal of the Martian invasion is to force the respective governments of Earth to disarm their military/nuclear capabilities and renounce war, the obvious Hollywood counterpart to *Santo vs. la invasión de los marcianos* would be *The Day the Earth Stood Still*

(1951, dir. Robert Wise), a science-fiction film whose anti–war sentiments profoundly clashed with Korean War patriotism, the anti-Communist hysteria of McCarthyism, and the standard metaphor of alien invasion with Communist infiltration constructed in numerous Cold War science-fiction films, such as *The Thing from Another World* (1951. dir. Christian Nyby and [uncredited] Howard Hawks), *Invaders from Mars* (1953, dir. William Cameron Menzies), and *It Conquered the World* (1956, dir. Roger Corman). However, an important distinction must be drawn between *The Day the Earth Stood Still* and *Santo vs. la invasión de los marcianos*. Wise's film depicts the alien Klaatu (Michael Rennie) as a paternally strict but nonetheless properly concerned and even noble character, a "father-knows-best" figure guiding Earth away from its political immaturity and eventual self-destruction. In contrast, the Martians in Crevenna's film are arrogant (or, pardon the pun, "bigheaded"), brutal, and ruthless, as intent on molding Earth into a planet that suits Martian purposes as on saving Earthlings from themselves. In fact, *Santo vs. la invasión de los marcianos* is probably the most overtly political of the Santo films, not only in its explicit commentary on international relations and threat of atomic warfare, but in its construction of Santo as a "national allegory" embodying principles of justice, decency, and mexicanidad.

Beginning with the credits shown over a montage of stock footage of NASA rocket launches and aerial photography of the planet Earth, *Santo vs. la invasión de los marcianos* sets the proper tone of science and the advent of the Space Age, reminding the audience of the new realities and possibilities of space exploration that only occurred within the last decade. Following the credits, stock footage of an astronaut performing a space walk is shown while an off-camera narrator poses the following rhetorical questions to the viewer: "*With the advance of science comes new mysteries. Is our planet the only one inhabited by rational beings? If so, will we conquer these other worlds?*" The stock footage cuts to a studio special effects shot of outer space as a model flying saucer on a string slowly moves into the foreground. The narrator ominously concludes: "*Or, on the contrary, will their inhabitants come to rule us?*" The scene shifts to the interior of this spaceship, where several muscular men and attractive women are gathered. All wear soft helmets over what appear to be enlarged heads, with some sort of jewel fixed in their foreheads between their eyes. This object, whether organic or implanted, is an "Astral Eye" and the source of the Martians' advanced powers. Each Martian wears a silky cape and cowls, with the bare-chested men sporting wrestling tights and the women clad in form-fitting one-piece swimsuits. The Martians also possess long blonde hair, which prompted David Wilt to wryly comment that "perhaps screenwriter Rafael García Travesí had been reading some George Adamski."[33] In fact, *Santo vs. la invasión de los marcianos* does express a certain familiarity with some of the best-known UFO mythology of the era concerning flying saucers and alien contact. In 1952, Adamski became famous after claiming he encountered a visitor from Venus in the Mojave Desert, describing the Venusian as having long hair and features of extraordinary beauty, and relaying that the alien expressed strong concerns over the dangers of potential atomic warfare.[34] Similarly, the Martians in *Santo vs. invasión de los marcianos* have luxurious blonde locks, are specimens of physical beauty (the male Martians are very muscular and the Martian women quite shapely), and, as the viewer soon learns, intend to prevent an inevitable nuclear war on Earth and its potential damage to the solar system as a whole — by any means necessary.

Interrupting the Mexican populace watching television — depicted by a middle-class family enjoying a *rancheras* musical comedy in their living room, and men watching sports at a local bar — the Martian leader, Argos (Wolf Ruvinskis, star of the *Neutrón* film series), appears on Mexican TV screens throughout the nation and solemnly announces that, "We are not just actors in a scary movie ... this is our actual appearance. We are from the planet you call Mars." A drunk watching the TV in the bar sardonically comments, "Yeah, right!" Determinedly informing the citizens of Earth of the dire predicament Earth has put itself in, Argos' introduction and the drunk's reaction becomes an ironic comment on the film itself: Ruvinskis and the other Martians are indeed "actors in a scary movie." Argos explains that the Martian rationale for coming to Earth is not simply conquest and domination, but to save the Earthlings from themselves. His pronouncement (intercut with reaction shots of skeptical and dismissive Earthlings watching the television broadcast — or "scary movie"):

> Instead of using your scientific advancements to better humanity, you Earthlings use them for your own destruction. When you wage war with your conventional weapons, you are the only victims of your destructiveness and selfishness. But with the discovery of nuclear energy, and your mad experiments with the atomic bomb, you are on the verge of destroying the entire planetary system. Before this happens, we warn you that we are prepared to disintegrate all of the inhabitants of the Earth.

Argos explains that Mexico will be the site of the alien invasion and the potential disastrous consequences should Earth not obey the edicts of the Martians. In a second televised announcement to the Earthlings, Argos elaborates on why Mexico has been chosen as the site for the Martian invasion: "We chose Mexico because it is a country dedicated to pacifism, committed to disarming its territory. We hope that its voice will be heard by other nations." Mexico is the standard of excellence by which the Martians measure world politics: a paradigm of international relations and world peace. By 1966, the U.S.A. and the U.S.S.R. were pursuing an illogical arms race predicated on the idea of "mutual assured destruction," a result that would not only end each other's existence, but that of neutral counties such as Mexico which would be caught in an atomic crossfire. Throughout the Cold War, while superficially allied with the United States, Mexico actually maintained a high degree of neutrality in international politics: "[Mexico] simply stated its traditional principle of nonintervention, and avoided taking its domestic anticommunist policy to the international arena. In order for Mexican nationalism to survive, it was necessary to keep a distance, at least minimal, from the United States."[35] Given that Mexican studio filmmakers often avoided making "political films" due to the strong government influence within the film industry, one might suggest that *Santo vs. la invasión de los marcianos* allows itself to make such explicit political statements because of the film's ideological consistency with the goals of the then-current presidential administration of Gustavo Díaz Ordaz (1964–70), which stressed a combination of international neutrality, mexicanidad and "democracy." However, this is not to say that Díaz Ordaz was left-wing — his was one of the more right-wing presidencies in twentieth century Mexico.

As Argos issues his warning, the reaction shots of smirking ordinary citizens watching TV are soon replaced by the more serious, concerned responses of two pillars of the Mexican community: Father Fuentes (Nicolás Rodríguez), a noted "priest and philanthropist," and the highly respected scientist Professor Odorica (Manuel Zozaya). They, of course, represent the twin poles of *religion* and *science* in Mexican society. In *Santo vs. la invasión de los marcianos,* modern science and religious faith are not depicted as adversaries; instead *both* are considered important and integral parts of Mexican society. Finally, the viewer sees Santo himself, who intently watches the broadcast from his office, sitting behind a desk in his silver mask, cape, tights, and bare chest. Ominously, Argos finally lists his demands: "All governments of Earth shall accept total disarmament, eliminate all borders, and unify your language, and establish a global government that does not discriminate by race or creed, and give up war forever. If not, it will be necessary for us to annihilate you."

The status of the Martians in the film is one of the more politically important aspects of *Santo vs. la invasión de los marcianos.* In one sense, the goals of the Martians seem consistent with the vision of international politics and world peace the Martians purportedly admire in the country of Mexico. Their concerns about modern civilization and the danger it presents to itself, especially in the Atomic Age, are similarly voiced by the heroes (Santo, Professor Rolof) and villains (Tundra) in *Santo vs. the Vampire Women.* However, one is certainly struck by the Martian's drastic "peace through genocide" methods, a kind of variation on U.S. foreign policy in Vietnam ("We had to destroy the village in order to save it"). It is this Draconian threat of force and authoritarianism which Santo finds so repugnant: the *ends* of the Martians are not objectionable, but the *means* they will employ to achieve their goals are — the attractive goals of eliminating war and prejudice attained by the unattractive methods of eliminating Mexican national sovereignty and individual liberty. In short, the Martians represent a threat to mexicanidad, which, to reiterate Elissa J. Rashkin, "encompasses identity, culture, national sovereignty, and authenticity and is often set against a perceived encroachment by an *alien (European* or U.S.) *value system.*"[36] Indeed, the Martians possess an "alien (extraterrestrial) value system," but also an "*alien European value system.*" Despite their futuristic demeanor, the Martians are strongly affiliated with European antiquity. At one point in the film, Professor Odorica posits a theory to Santo that the Martians are actually descendants of the inhabitants of the fabled island of Atlantis, the technologically-advanced race of ancient beings whose island continent sank into the ocean. However, before Santo can further pursue Odorica's highly provocative theory, a phone call interrupts them and the issue is summarily dropped for the remainder of the film.) While the connection between extraterrestrial life and Atlantis is another important theory in contemporary UFO lore, it also connects the Martians to ancient Greek thought and mythology. The fable of the island of Atlantis, the ancestral home of the Martians, was conceived by the Greek philosopher Plato; from the perspective of political theory, it might be said that the Martians intend to construct on Earth a political order analogous to Plato's *Republic*: a strict autocratic order (which the most mentally and physically gifted rule over the obedient masses. In this context, the connection between the Martians and both ancient Greece and totalitarian politics foreshadows *Santo contra Blue Demon en la Atlántida* (also by Rafael García Travesí): the evil Nazi mad scientist Dr. Ulrich rechristens himself Aquilles (Achilles); his attractive female operatives have names derived from Greek myth (Circe, Afrodita, Juno); and his underwater lair is called Atlantis. *Santo vs. la invasión de los marcianos* similarly combines Greek antiquity and Nazism in the form of Martians. With their impressive physiques and luxurious blond locks, the Martians are the embodiment of the *Aryan race*: Hitler's mythic master race that must be defeated by Mexico's national allegory — Santo. Indeed, one delicious irony found in the film is the fact that the actor who portrays the Martian "Kronos" is a former luchador known as *El Nazi*!

This relationship between the Martians and ancient Greeks becomes quite obvious when Argos decides that the natural appearance of the Martians is too frightening to the Earthlings, and the Martians will alter their natural appearance to human form via "the Transformation Chamber" (which suspiciously looks like an empty office space filled with smoke). The Martians emerge from the Transformation Chamber minus their long hair and Astral Eyes; the men now wear sashes and skirts, the women (of course) white gowns — attire that seems directly borrowed from an Italian "Sword and Sandal" film's wardrobe department. To make their connection to ancient Europe even more obvious, each Martian takes a name from Greek or Roman mythology. As captain of the ship, the Martian leader is

"Argos," presumably in reference to the "Argo," the ship Jason and the Argonauts sailed to seek out the Golden Fleece.[37] The Martian who possesses vast scientific knowledge is now called "Kronos," after "Cronus," the Greek god of time. A Martian (Ham Lee) with the power to hypnotize is named "Morfeo," after "Morpheus," the Greek god of dreams; and the strongest of the male Martians (Beni Galán) receives the name "Hercules" (no explanation necessary). Likewise, the most seductive and beautiful of the Martian women (Maura Monti) is named "Afrodita," after "Aphrodite," the Greek goddess of love. Another (Eva Norvind), who has "the serene beauty of the moon," is named "Selena," after "Selene," the Greek goddess of the moon. The remaining two Martian women (Gilda Mirós and Belinda Corell) are christened "Artemisa," after "Artesmis," the Greek goddess of nature and fertility, and "Diana," the Roman goddess of nature and fertility. In this context, one might briefly compare *Santo vs. la invasión de los marcianos* to the contemporary Italian "Sword and Sandal" film *Hercules Against the Moon Men* (1964, dir. Giacomo Gentilomo), a similar tale in which a culturally mythic muscleman battles an invasion from outer space. However, Santo is a iconic figure of the Mexican present, wrestling (literally) with evil forces representing *the past;* and despite the fact that the Martians belong to a technologically-advanced future, they are very much connected to *the past* by being descendants of the lost continent of Atlantis, and through the ancient Greek and Roman names and costumes they adopt when transforming into Earthlings. Conversely, the Hercules of *Hercules Against the Moon Men* is an archetypal figure from Roman mythology, firmly entrenched in the past: a powerful, superhuman male representing the greatness and tradition of Classical civilization (the ancient Greeks, the Holy Roman Empire) fighting the evil forces of *the future*, exemplified by space travel and alien invasion. Of course, in *Santo vs. la invasión de los marcianos*, Hercules himself becomes one of the very Martian invaders intent on imposing their "alien value system" on Mexico.

Learning that their message to the Earthlings was generally received as no more than "a comedy skit," the Martians land their flying saucer in a desolate field and take more drastic measures in their quest to disarm Earth. The scene cuts to several minutes of stock footage of Mexican citizens engaged in one of the more important social activities in the Mexican public sphere: sports. Over a montage of track meets, bicycle races, soccer matches, and cheering fans, an off-screen narrator delivers a stern political analysis of the situation and the Martian goals (seemingly included so the film's ideological position will in no way be misinterpreted by the film audience):

> And the Martians, who claim to come from a world much more civilized than our own and whose scientific advancements surpass the Earth by more than 500 years, nonetheless make the same fatal error of which they accuse us, attempting to

impose brotherhood through fear and force, forgetting that violence only promotes destruction and hate.

The scene shifts to a number of young boys in a park, playfully wrestling under the watchful eye of Santo, who has taken time from his busy schedule of pro-wrestling and crime-fighting to instruct the youth of Mexico in both lucha libre and Mexican civics. When one boy's headlock on another lad appears a bit too strident, Santo breaks them up and scolds the boy: "Luis, how many times have I told you not to cause deliberate harm? Your skill should only be used to counter aggression or —." Luis enthusiastically interrupts and finishes Santo's sentence, "— or to defend the weak and defenseless. Isn't that right, Santo?" Satisfied that Luis has demonstrated an awareness of his skills and how to use them responsibly, Santo pats him on the back and urges the boys to continue "wrestling like good sports."

Unfortunately, this idyllic scene of athletic competition and good citizenship in the public sphere of the park is shattered by the appearance of Hercules, who begins to indiscriminately disintegrate adults and children alike with the blinking Astral Eye in his forehead, the victims simply fading away on-screen.[38] Santo quickly intervenes, and the first of several lucha libre–style confrontations between Santo and a muscular Martian ensues. Despite its other cinematic faults, *Santo vs. la invasión de los marcianos* does stress extended action sequences over long plot exposition, and features many lengthy confrontations between Santo and the Martians interspersed throughout the film. As Santo and Hercules struggle on the soccer field, it becomes a sort of open wrestling ring, with Santo and the Martian demonstrating a number of lucha libre holds and throws during the course of their battle. Inside their spaceship, the Martians watch the events unfold on a large, circular monitor screen that functions as a sort of "all-seeing eye" and affords the Martians an omnipresent ability to see any event at any time. At the same time, the Martians seemingly become a film audience, silently and attentively watching a "scary movie" as it unfolds on a circular theatrical screen. In this regard, the Martians' technologically-advanced ability to monitor any space at any given time on Earth suggests Michel Foucault's famous concept of "Panopticonism," the basis of modern societies of surveillance in which power is exercised through the ability *to observe without being observed*.[39] Foucault wrote, "Our society is not one of spectacle, but of surveillance ... *We are much less Greeks than we believe*. We are not in the amphitheater, nor on the stage, but in the panoptic machine."[40] Through this all-seeing "panoptic machine," the Martian power of surveillance, the ability to observe and monitor any moment of any activity on Earth, is panopticonism taken to the point of omnipresence through technology. However, given the already-explicit relationship established between ancient Greece and the futuristic Martians, it could also be said that the Martians are much more Greeks than Foucault believes. The Martian "panoptic machine" not only provides them unlimited *surveillance*, but also unlimited *spectacle*.[41] As observed by the Martians on their immense circular screen, Earth (and specifically Mexico) becomes an inexhaustible theater of fantastic cinema and the athletic melodrama of lucha libre—in short, a mexploitation film starring Santo.

Unable to defeat Santo "man to Martian," Hercules attempts to disintegrate Santo. In a highly comic moment, Santo places Hercules in a submission hold from behind while Hercules frantically twists his head from side to side in order to use the blinking Astral Eye in his forehead. As he slumps into unconsciousness courtesy of Santo's choke-hold, Hercules vanishes, his fade-out accompanied by strange electronic sound effects. The frequent teleportations of the Martians become a source of unintentional comedy throughout the film. As David Wilt notes, "When the Martians 'transport' themselves to various locations on Earth, their arrival is heralded by flashing lights, a train whistle, and a sort of 'ka-boing!' So much for sneaking up on anybody."[42] Arriving back at the flying saucer, Hercules reports that, while terror has been instilled in the hearts and minds of the Mexican people, the mysterious "Silver Mask" could potentially hinder their mission. Intrigued, Argos personally assumes the task of capturing Santo and Odorica, and teleports directly into Odorica's lab. He explains that he does not wish to destroy them; indeed, between Odorica's "intelligence" and Santo's "strength and integrity," they "will be the seed of a new humanity, more scientifically and morally advanced." As noted, within two short years, in *Santo en el tesoro de Drácula* (1968), Santo himself would be endowed with vast scientific intelligence (the inventor of a time machine) as well as athletic virility and social morality. If this Santo appeared in *Santo vs. la invasión de los marcianos*, one can assume that Professor Odorica would not be needed by the Martians: Santo himself would supply the necessary scientific "intelligence" as well as the "strength and integrity" for a new and better human order. Santo adamantly refuses to collaborate with Argos and the other Martian "murderers of defenseless people and innocent children." Another quasi–lucha libre fight ensues in the lab between Santo and Argos, the highlight being when Argos and Santo trade arm-bars by reversing positions several times the battle verging on Three Stooges–style slapstick comedy rather than tense confrontation. Finally, Argos succeeds in using his Astral Eye to momentarily paralyze Santo, and menaces Professor Odorica, helpless against the physically and mentally superior Argos. However, as luck and a rather strained plot twist would have it, Argos is suddenly overcome by the effects of the Earth's atmosphere (the Martians require pills to counteract the poisonous effects of Earth's air) when his dosage conveniently wears off at this crucial dramatic moment. Argos' temporary incapacitation frees Santo from the effects of the Astral Eye, and he places Argos in a choke-hold while the Martian struggles to swallow another much-needed pill before teleporting to safety.

Greek Aryans: blonde, physically superior Martians with Greek names threaten the Mexican nuclear family (no pun intended) in *Santo vs. la invasión de los marcianos*.

Having succeeded in establishing their menacing presence in Mexico, the Martians begin the second phase of their mission: abducting Earthlings, specifically Mexican citizens, who will become the basis for a new and better breed of humanity the Martians will create. The first captured are Santo's young protégé Luis and his middle-class family. However, given the horror expressed by Luis and his family at the Martian's alien appearance, Argos decides that to better facilitate gathering humans, the Martians must adopt the physical features of Earthlings along with Greek mythological names (leading to the aforementioned "Transformation Chamber" scene). Again, it bears mention that while the Martians attempt to adopt their physical appearance to that of Earthlings, they do not adopt Spanish names that would be appropriate to a Mexican environment, but instead borrow the Greek mythological names that separate them from Mexico and connect them with two common threats in mexploitation films: the past and Europe.

This soon leads to a confrontation at *Club de luchardores*, where Santo is "off to train, for now more than ever I must be prepared for any attack." For several long minutes the viewer watches Santo sharpening his skills with two other wrestlers, and the Martians also closely watch Santo train on their all-seeing, circular screen (panoptic machine) in their spaceship. Again, one is tempted to compare the Martians to a Mexican film audience, watching and marveling at Santo's athletic prowess; moreover, the Martians observe and admire Santo's physical skill in the confines of one of the most important public spaces in the ancient Greek city-state: the gymnasium. While Santo and his fellow wrestlers spar, Artemisa and Diana teleport into the club, still wearing Martian "futuristic" clothing but now looking like decidedly attractive Earth women. After Santo ends his training session, the two Martian women approach Santo's sparring partners, who are obviously intrigued by the mysterious, beautiful women. A series of medium close-ups alternating between the four characters make it clear that the Martian women are hypnotizing the wrestlers. As seen in many mexploitation films, hypnotism is an act not only associated with the spread of evil in modern Mexico, but seductive and sinister *female* sexual power which clouds the moral integrity of the Mexican male. Thus, when Santo attempts to leave *Club de luchadores*, the two wrestlers viciously ambush him, obviously now under the evil hypnotic-seductive control of Martian women. The two bedazzled wrestlers assault Santo as he desperately tries to protect himself (the actual battle only lasts three minutes but seems much longer). Shots of Artemisa and Diana watching with devious, sadistic pleasure the two wrestlers beating on Santo are periodically inserted into the action moments in which evil, attractive, powerful women delight in orchestrating the physical punishment of Santo for voyeuristic, sexual gratification (as seen in *Santo contra las mujeres vampiro* and *Santo contra la hija de Frankenstein*). Nonetheless, Santo valiantly prevails over the two hypnotized wrestlers, causing the Martian women to teleport back to the ship. When Santo asks his wrestling friends what prompted the attack, one answers that the last thing he remembers "is two beautiful women approaching us, and then, *nothing*."

This confrontation marks an important shift in the Martians' strategy and tactics for dominating Earth, relying on the dangerous power of female beauty and seductive hypnosis rather than the masculine force which has so far proven ineffective against Santo. The next scene occurs at a nightclub, where women in evening gowns share their fears and key scientists in tuxedos enjoy cocktails while strategizing how to combat the Martian invasion. In order to avoid widespread panic and disorder, their first tactic will be to convince the public that the Martian invasion is "make believe, and not at all real" (or, "a scary movie"). Hilariously, one scientist comments that the first people they will convince (read: begin lying to) are their *wives*. However, Afrodita and Selena arrive at the nightclub in low-cut gowns, effortlessly hypnotizing and capturing two of the scientists, much to the shock of their spouses, who are helpless in preventing their husbands from being lured away by younger, more attractive women. The next scene shifts to a science-fiction writer and his agent at a restaurant discussing his new novel, which he is postponing because the book's premise, a Martian invasion, has become a dangerous reality. Artemisa appears in the restaurant and easily catches the eye of the novelist; the agent responds to Artemisa's alluring appearance and come-hither gaze by lecherously encouraging the writer to talk to her and congratulating him on his "good luck." As the writer walks out of the frame with a glazed expression, following Artemisa, the viewer is all too aware of his impending fate.

With Martian danger spreading across Mexico, an announcer appears on-screen, delivering a civil defense broadcast over Mexican airwaves; however, he also seems to be addressing the film spectator as he directly faces the camera. He pleads with the Mexican people, and the film audience, to continue with their normal lives until the Martian threat has passed. This cuts to another montage of stock footage of Mexican life, this time focusing on urban nightlife as people gather at an arena. The off-screen narrator provides another explanation: "An intense information campaign was launched using all means of communication to help calm the public. The inhabitants of the city began to enjoy their favorite pastimes again." Specifically, this "favorite pastime" is lucha libre, setting the stage for the obligatory wrestling match featuring Santo. In a plot device taken directly from *Santo vs. las mujeres vampiro*, Hercules attacks Santo's opponent, the Black Eagle, in his dressing room in order to replace him in the ring for the impending "mask vs. mask" match against Santo (a match in which one opponent may remove the mask of the other in order to win, with the loser often forced to adopt a new ring persona afterwords). Hercules' goal is nothing short of publicly defeating, humiliating, and, worst of all, stripping Santo of his iconic mask in the wrestling ring before teleporting the beaten Santo to the Martian spaceship. However, in order to accomplish this task, Hercules must wear his power belt, which Santo notices immediately before the match begins, a clue that something is dangerously amiss.

As in several other Santo films, an important conflict between Santo and a fictional monster takes place in the wrestling ring, mimicking a straight lucha libre match, and acting out traditional técnico verses rudo battles for the benefit of the Mexican public who came to see wrestling matches disguised in the context of a horror film (or, in his case, science fiction). As noted, Hercules signifies an "alien value system"—European antiquity and Nazism. Moreover, Hercules also assumes the role of the masked rudo intent on defeating and unmasking the técnico Santo: a prospect that would certainly end Santo's career as both wrestler and national (super)hero. Thus, this match becomes the centerpiece of the film, and is played out for full dramatic effect. Lasting for ten minutes, the match is filmed almost exclusively through a series of overhead and high-angle shots, often edited together by jump-cuts that propel the match with a frantic, occasionally disorienting momentum. Intercut with the wrestling action are occasional crowd reaction shots, with Morpheo and Kronos, in human form, watching the match in street clothes and with sinister scowls, as well as two Santo fans who are completely baffled by Santo's ring tactics and continually complain about his efforts aimed at removing Hercules' strange belt rather than his all-important mask.

The lengthy battle concludes when Hercules subdues the prone Santo by putting his leg across Santo's back, hooking Santo's elbow with his foot. Effectively locking Santo's arms in place and leaving the back of his head vulnerable, Hercules can undo Santo's mask and wrench it off his head. Holding the mask triumphantly over his head, Hercules parades about the ring; in vulgar Freudian terms, Hercules symbolically castrates Santo and holds Santo's severed penis itself as a trophy. Fortunately, Santo planned ahead by wearing *another mask* under the first! Thanks to his foresight, Santo's identity remains safely hidden, although Santo does undergo the emasculating embarrassment of having his original mask removed by a stronger foe in the public sphere of the wrestling ring. Indeed, losing his mask and the match prompts a livid tantrum from Santo, quite out of keeping with his lectures on good sportsmanship and civil conduct. As Santo storms about the ring and attacks Hercules from behind after losing the match, Hercules responds by further humiliating Santo, tossing the mask (or phallus) he removed from Santo to the ground and contemptuously stomping on it. Even Santo's corner man is stunned by the outburst and attempts to calm Santo: "They will accuse you of fraud. You've already lost." Incensed, Santo responds, "He's not a human being. *He's a Martian!*" Ignoring both his handler and the referee's attempt to establish order in the ring, Santo continues his assault on Hercules and throws him about the ring, easily dominating him before placing him in his signature "Horse Lock." With Hercules immobilized, Santo gains a measure of (phallic) revenge by stripping Hercules of *his* mask. In another borrowing from *Santo vs. the Vampire Women*, Santo's unmasking of Hercules results in the Martian transforming into his true, monstrous appearance: enlarged head, blonde locks, shiny cloak and tights. Morfeo and Kronos transform back into their Martian appearance as well, and as the spectators begin to flee the arena the invaders indiscriminately vaporize those unfortunate enough to be caught within range of their Astral Eyes. Still in the ring, Santo and Hercules continue to battle, with Santo apparently more concerned with personal revenge rather than protecting the Mexican public, until Santo subdues Hercules with a choke-hold. Defeated, Hercules teleports out of Santo's grasp and back to the safety of the ship, with Morfeo and Kronos quickly following. In one of the film's more impressive shots, the sequence closes with a high-angle long shot of Santo standing alone in the ring; he walks to his corner to grab his cape, and, as he surveys the now-abandoned arena, he exits the ring and walks down an aisle to the exit in the background. With Santo unmasked in the ring (but his identity still safe) and the public recreation of lucha libre turned into a chaotic massacre, the shot of the darkened, abandoned arena and Santo's long walk into the background establishes a sense of pessimism which continually grows throughout the remainder of the film.

The scene dissolves to a shot of Santo reading on his bed, still clad in his mask, cape, and wrestling boots and tights. Having again failed to defeat Santo through masculine power (Hercules), the Martians attack Santo with female beauty and guile. The obtrusive sound of Martian teleportation interrupts Santo's reading and ominous music heralds the arrival of Afrodita in Santo's bedroom, appearing human but wearing "Martian" attire. As smoke fills the room, she approaches him, and alternating tight close-ups of Santo and Afrodita convey the act of female seduction via hypnosis. With Santo's back to the camera (or probably a "face-double"), Afrodita removes Santo's mask and slowly, passionately kisses him. Selena appears in the room as well, and also slinks toward Santo and kisses him on the lips. Suddenly, a close-up of Santo, now in his mask, fills the screen. He squints, groans, and shakes his head as the smoke quickly evaporates. "For a moment, I was a victim of your spell," Santo announces, suggesting that his ability to resist the brazen, hypnotic seductions of the Martian women is due to his countermacho status and unwavering sexual morality. Throughout the film, Santo is the *only* male able to successfully avoid being hypnotized (seduced) by Martian women. Their efforts thwarted, the duo then hurriedly teleport back to the spaceship.

With their supply of "atmosphere pills" dwindling, the Martians intensify their efforts to complete their mission by capturing two pillars of Mexican society, Father Fuentes (religion) and Professor Odorica (science). The Martians attempt to capture Father Fuentes first, with Santo demonstrating his uncanny ability to intervene at just the right moment; the scene also affords the opportunity for yet another protracted confrontation between Santo and the Martian musclemen Kronos and Hercules. Finally, after watching Santo battle the two Martians to a draw for several minutes, Father Fuentes reluctantly agrees to accompany the Martians rather than risk Santo's well-being. In contrast, Professor Odorica's abduction is executed through female seduction rather than masculine force. Via their all-seeing "panoptic machine," the Martians learn that a banquet honoring Professor Odorica has been planned. Odorica, explaining that his main priority is quelling the Martian threat, believes the banquet should be cancelled, but his colleagues convince him it must be held in order to show the public that Mexican life is still proceeding in a normal manner. The scene shifts to a nightclub where the banquet is being held; except for the dedicated Professor Odorica, it seems Mexico's scientific community spends more time in nightclubs swilling cocktails than working in their laboratories. The Martians use the occasion as an opportunity to capture Odorica via a rather inventive method: the Martian women infiltrate the nightclub and take the place of the regular showgirls. This affords *Santo vs. la invasión de los marcianos* the chance to briefly veer into the musical genre by featuring a dance routine performed by the attractive Martian women (although it is safe to say that staging Vegas-style revues is not among the many evolutionary advancements the Martians have achieved over Earth). After several minutes of tepid dancing, the Martian women encircle Odorica and teleport him to the spaceship.

Following the successful capture of Father Fuentes and Professor Odorica by the Martians, the dire nature of the Martian invasion is finally revealed to the public. The announcer previously seen directly addressing the Mexican public, asking them to maintain normalcy in the midst of the Martian invasion, is now seen on a TV set in a bar. He dejectedly explains the severity of the situation, and that the Mexican people should not venture out of their homes at night; in a moment of comic relief, the men hastily guzzle their drinks and bolt from the bar. In short, the Martians succeed in paralyzing the Mexican public sphere, its decimation further stressed by a montage made up of stock footage of empty city streets at night, recalling the unpopulated urban landscapes of Antonioni. The off-screen narrator briefly and solemnly comments over the montage: "Since that moment, Mexico's inhabitants did not dare leave their homes at night."

With the crisis in Mexican social order worsening, Santo convinces a promoter to stage a wrestling match, not so much to encourage people to enjoy their favorite urban pastime, but to set a trap for the Martians. Predictably, no one dares attend the match, and Santo and his opponent wrestle in an empty arena. By filming the first minutes of the match entirely in long shots, Crevenna not only renders Santo and the other wrestler as small, insignificant figures, but accentuates the cavernous emptiness of the arena that surrounds the two athletes wrestling for an audience of empty chairs (another moment in which mexploitation meets Antonioni). Nevertheless, Santo's match does have its intended effect by luring the Martians to the arena in order to attempt a final capture. Yet another protracted brawl ensues between Santo and the Martian men, with Santo emerging victorious and, more importantly, acquiring one of the Martian teleportation belts, which he uses to locate the Martian spaceship. Finally able to fulfill his heroic role in Mexican society, Santo rescues the hostages and subdues the Martians, who conveniently die upon succumbing to the effects of the Earth's atmosphere, presumably having exhausted their supply of atmosphere pills.

With the Martians now dead and the hostages freed, it appears that all is well with the Mexican present. However, there is one important consideration left, and Santo decides to return to the Martian spaceship and blow it up. Professor Odorica protests, explaining to Santo that the technology the Martian ship offers could advance science 500 years. Santo corrects him, pointing out that the people of

Earth are obviously not ready for further scientific advancement, with the implication that technology has *already* superseded humanity's capacity to harness it productively ("nuclear energy"). "Professor," Santo firmly tells Odorica, "humanity is not prepared for such progress, and you know it." Unlike the rather corny ending of *Santo contra las mujeres vampiro*, which closes with Santo's public adoringly looking on as he drives away in his sports car, *Santo vs. la invasión de los marcianos* ends with Santo simply walking away from the people he saved as they huddle in the woods. There is a strong sense of resignation rather than jubilation, that while the threat to humanity has been averted, it is only a pyrrhic victory. Ultimately, much of what has been achieved is a greater knowledge of humanity's failings and limitations. The film does not conclude with wrestling fans cheering another Santo victory in the ring or an uplifting civic message, it ends on the off-screen narrator's final ominous warning as Santo, almost oblivious to the Mexican public he rescued, wearily trods past them and into the background of the night forest: "*The human race has been saved, for the moment. Will we learn our lesson? Or will we insist on carrying out crazy nuclear experiments until we disappear from the face of the Earth?*"

Santo y Blue Demon contra Drácula y el Hombre Lobo *(Santo and Blue Demon vs. Dracula and the Wolf Man, 1972)*

Between 1966 and 1970, *fourteen* Santo films were made — an astonishing amount of film production, even if one could argue that by this time Santo's films had become so standardized and predictable that rapid production was hardly difficult. Some of the Santo films of the era were crime-action adventures, such as *Santo, el Enmascarado de Plata contra los villanos del ring* (*Santo, the Silver-Masked Man vs. the Villains of the Ring*, 1966) and *Santo contra la Mafia del vicio* (*Santo vs. the Vice Mafia*, 1970). Other films were patented horror-wrestling sagas, such as *La venganza de las mujeres vampiro* and Santo's initial pairings with Blue Demon: *Santo contra Blue Demon en la Atlántida*, *El mundo de los muertos* (*The World of the Dead*, 1969), *Santo y Blue Demon contra los monstruos* (*Santo and Blue Demon vs. the Monsters*, 1969), and *Las momias de Guanajato* (*The Mummies of Guanajato*, 1970). Several veteran directors oversaw these various Santo projects, including Alfredo B. Crevenna, who directed *Santo, el Enmascarado de Plata contra los villanos del ring*; Gilberto Martínez Solares, who directed *El mundo de los muertos* and *Santo y Blue Demon contra los monstruos,* and the ubiquitous Federico Curiel, who directed *Santo contra la Mafia del vicio, Las momias de Guanajato,* and *La venganza de las mujeres vampiro.*

It was, René Cardona, however, who served as the primary director of the Santo films during this era, and Cardona's Santo films tended towards action-adventure, utilizing a variety of genres besides horror and science fiction, as well as minimizing wrestling sequences (occasionally omitting them entirely). *Operación 67* and *El tesoro de Moctezuma* (*Operation 67* and *The Treasure of Montezuma*; both 1966 and co-directed by Cardona and his son, René Cardona, Jr.) were espionage films modeled on the James Bond formula of foreign intrigue, innovative technology, rugged action, and curvaceous women in revealing outfits (a version of *Operación 67* released internationally even contained topless scenes). In these films, Santo is a secret agent pitted against Asian spies threatening Mexico: in *Operación 67*, their goal is to destroy the economy of Latin America, and specifically Mexico, through a counterfeiting ring; in *El tesoro de Moctezuma*, they are attempting to steal ancient Aztec treasures, strongly echoing the goals of the "Black Dragon" organization in *Las luchadoras contra la momia*. In 1972, Cardona would make *La mafia amarilla* (*The Yellow Mafia*), a similar espionage-crime-action film in which Blue Demon battles the Asian "Yellow Dragon" syndicate. *Santo contra Capulina* (*Santo vs. Capulina*, 1968) was a farce which teamed Santo with popular Mexican comedian Capulina: while not as internationally famous as Cantinflas or Tin Tan, Capulina appeared in more than fifty films from the 1950s to the 1970s.[43] *Santo contra los cazadores de cabezas* (*Santo vs. the Head Hunters*, 1969) was a straight safari-adventure film pitting Santo against savages in the Amazon jungles, although much of the film might be termed "anti-adventure" in that it consists of long scenes of Santo and his entourage endlessly wandering about the rainforests is if they were in an Antonioni film.[44] Perhaps the oddest of all the Cardona-Santo collaborations was *Santo contra los jinetes del terror* (*Santo vs. the Riders of Terror*, 1970), which, like *El pantano de las ánimas* (*The Swamp of the Spirits*, 1956, dir. Rafael Baledón; U.S. title: *Swamp of the Lost Monsters*) and *El quito de la muerte* (*The Cry of Death*, 1958, dir. Fernando Méndez; U.S. title: *The Living Coffin*) combined the horror film and Western genre, with Santo a luchador version of Gastón Santos roaming the Mexican frontier in his silver mask and *charro* duds bringing a gang of desperado lepers to justice while finding time to participate in a makeshift lucha libre match in a nineteenth century Mexican town. To make the film all the more outrageous, a version with female nudity was reportedly released abroad under the title *Los leprosos y el sexo* (*The Lepers and Sex*)![45] If Jodorowsky's *El Topo* was a surrealist Western by design, it could be said that *Santo contra los jinetes del terror* became a surrealist Western by accident. *Santo en el tesoro de Drácula* (1968) and *Santo en la venganza de la momia* (*Santo in the Revenge of the Mummy*, 1970) were the two Cardona films that came closest to the tested Santo formula of alternating between horror and wrestling, with *Santo en el tesoro de Drácula* creating an especially strong sense of familiarity because screenwriter Alfredo Salazar, even by his own standards of recycling, blatantly borrowed numerous pivotal plot points from his pervious work on the *Aztec Mummy* series, as well as *Las luchadoras contra la momia.* Moreover, like *Operación 67* and apparently *Los leprosos y el sexo,* the international version of *Santo en el tesoro de Drácula* included topless women, and was released under the more provocative title *El vampiro y el sexo* (*The Vampire and Sex*).[46]

Following René Cardona's tenure, Miguel M. Delgado directed *Santo contra la hija de Frankenstein, Santo y Blue Demon contra Drácula and el Hombre Lobo,* and *Santo y Blue Demon contra el Dr. Frankenstein* between 1971 and 1973. As noted, Delgado was a well-known and respected director in Mexico who made well over 130 films from 1941 to 1989, including most of Cantinflas' comedies. The Delgado-Santo films are almost throwbacks to the classic Santo films of the early 1960s, differing sharply from emerging trends in mexploitation horror films of the '70s, which were more akin to contemporary American sexploitation films (Cardona's nudie versions of his lucha libre horror films) or Eurotrash sex-horror cinema (the work of Juan López Moctezuma). However, despite the fact that the Delgado-Santo trilogy tends to strongly recall and often liberally borrow from the early 1960s Santo and mexploitation film canon, the glaring Eastmancolor of these later Santo films sacrifices the Gothic moodiness and anachronistic Universal horror film appearance of these early films and clearly dates them as products of the 1960s–1970s. Visually, the Delgado-Santo projects better compare to Hammer rather than Universal horror films, not only by virtue of being in color, but also for their more explicit violence and eventual borrowing from specific Hammer films.

As the self-explanatory title of *Santo y Blue Demon contra Drácula y el Hombre Lobo* indicates, Santo is teamed with another highly popular wrestler, Blue Demon, against two seminal monsters, Count Dracula and the Wolf Man — a sort of mexploitation "all-star cast." The film was one of several Santo film collaborations with Blue Demon (Alejandro Muñoz Moreno), another famous luchador who began starring in his own series of films in 1964, beginning with the eponymous *Blue Demon* and the follow-up *Blue Demon contra el podor satánico* (*Blue Demon vs. the Satanic Power*), both directed by Chano Urueta. In the latter film, Santo himself makes a cameo appearance in order to congratulate Blue Demon on his career choice of fighting for the betterment of Mexican society and offers his assistance in any of Blue Demon's future endeavors, in effect putting the Santo "seal of approval" on the burgeoning Blue Demon film franchise. These early Blue Demon films were produced by Luis Enrique Vergara, who was also producing Santo's films between 1964 and 1965 (*Atacan las brujas, El hacha diabólica, Profanadores de tumbas,* and *El Barón Brákola*). As previously alluded to, Vergara and Santo almost immediately developed an acrimonious business relationship over Santo's fees for his film appearances, and it can be assumed that their rapidly deteriorating partnership served as the impetus for Vergara to create Blue Demon as a box-office rival for Santo, who, perhaps unwittingly, all but officially endorsed Blue Demon's competing film career in *Blue Demon contra el podor satánico.* Vergara himself could also be accused of a certain degree of ruthlessness as a film producer: when Blue Demon suffered a serious head injury in the ring in 1965 and required a long period of convalescence, Vergara promptly hired a popular young wrestler, Mil Máscaras, and began a film series starring *him*. Needless to say, most of Blue Demon's and Mil Máscaras' films were virtual carbon copies of the popular Santo formula, but nonetheless performed well at the box office.

While remembered for their camaraderie battling monsters and other threats to Mexican society on the silver screen, Santo and Blue Demon actually developed a well-known and rather bitter rivalry during their wrestling careers, and for the most part were never close either personally or professionally — a fact which would not be lost on Mexican film audiences. In the early 1950s, Blue Demon and his partner Black Shadow (Alejandro Cruz Ortíz), wrestling as *Los Hermanos Shadow* ("the Shadow Brothers"), were arguably the most popular tag-team of the era.[47] Among their chief rivals was the tag-team *La Pareja Atómica* ("the Atomic Pair"): Santo and Gory Guerrero.[48] A more personal feud developed between Santo and Black Shadow, culminating in a "mask vs. mask" match held on November 7, 1952: Santo emerged victorious and Black Shadow was forced to relinquish his mask. Their hour-long match remains legendary in the annals of lucha libre. Fortunately for Cruz Ortíz, he was popular enough with lucha libre wrestling fans that he simply continued wrestling as Black Shadow minus his mask, rather than being forced to adopt a new ring persona. Blue Demon, vowing to avenge his partner's defeat, wrestled Santo several times in the early 1950s, with Santo playing rudo to Blue Demon's técnico: their most famous bout was a 1953 title match in which Blue Demon defeated Santo. While the rivalry eventually ran its course, it was never officially settled, and the professional acrimony Santo and Blue Demon developed in the ring carried over into their film careers as well. Santo felt that Blue Demon and the growing number of other luchadores starring in highly similar films were riding on the coattails (or sequined cape) of his own successful film career, a perception understandably strengthened by Santo's contentious business dealings with producer Luis Enrique Vergara and the subsequent development of Blue Demon's own film career under Vergara's guidance. Conversely, Blue Demon resented being perceived as a mere Santo imitation and was particularly unhappy about being reduced to the role of Santo's sidekick in their film pairings.

This well-known animosity between Santo and Blue Demon often surfaces as subtext in their films. In several of their collaborations, Santo and Blue Demon are adversaries rather than allies, with substantial screen time devoted to physical altercations between the two wrestlers before they become on-screen partners for the film's finale. In *Santo contra Blue Demon in la Atlántida,* a mad scientist kidnaps and hypnotizes Blue Demon — the brainwashed Blue Demon and Santo battle *each other* throughout much of the film. In *Santo y Blue Demon contra los monstruos,* a similar plot device is used in which a mad scientist kidnaps Blue Demon and creates an evil replica of him; the faux Blue Demon then attempts to murder Santo. One character even remarks to Santo that perhaps their "traditional rivalry" prompted Blue Demon to join the forces of evil. Santo responds, "We were only rivals in the ring." With *El mundo de los muertos*, Santo's aforementioned legendary ancestor, Caballero Enmascarado de Plata (who in this film is not only a legendary fighter of the supernatural but an associate of the Inquisition!), is pitted against Blue Demon's ancestor, Caballero Azul ("the Blue Knight"), suggesting that the legendary Santo–Blue Demon feud "springs eternal" in Mexican culture. Nevertheless, the most overt and hilarious references to the rivalry between Santo and Blue Demon occur in *Las momias de Guanajuato*. While the film focuses on the team of Blue Demon and Mil Máscaras, at one point Mil Máscaras suggests that they should enlist Santo's help as well — an option a deeply-offended Blue Demon immediately rejects. Of course, Blue Demon and Mil Máscaras are eventually captured, and the situation appears hopeless. Fortunately for all parties involved, Santo makes one of his trademark last-minute interventions to save the day; at the end of the film, Mil Máscaras' girlfriend Lina (Elsa Cárdenas) complains to Blue Demon and Mil Máscaras, "We would have avoided a lot of problems if you'd called Santo!"[49]

However, unlike in these previous Santo–Blue Demon films, in which their relationship might charitably be called contentious, *Santo y Blue Demon contra Drácula y el Hombre Lobo* (for the purposes of brevity, the film will henceforth be referred to as *Santo/Blue Demon*) and the subsequent *Santo y Blue Demon contra el Dr. Frankenstein* go to great lengths to establish a close and almost brotherly affinity between Santo and Blue Demon, although their actual personal and professional relationship was far less friendly.

Santo/Blue Demon begins modestly enough with the credits shown in yellow and white letters over a red background. The opening music, provided by Gustavo C. Carrión, is a piano-organ duet that strives to be a sort of ominous funeral dirge, but sounds more like a rudimentary chord exercise between novice keyboard students (a description not at all intended as pejorative).[50] Not to keep lucha libre fans waiting, the film opens with the first of three wrestling matches that appear intermittently throughout the film. Unlike *Santo contra las mujeres vampiros*, *Santo vs. la invasión de los marcianos*, or *Santo en el tesoro de Drácula*, all of which feature critical wrestling matches between Santo and a fictional villain, in *Santo/Blue Demon*, the lucha libre action and the horror film narrative remain distinct and unrelated throughout the course of the film. The three matches periodically alternate with, or simply interrupt, the horror film: they have no actual bearing or effect on the course or content of the narrative. If the three matches were omitted, the horror film itself would not in any way be affected, except that the film would be shorter. In this way, perhaps more than any other Santo film, *Santo/Blue Demon* demands the more "flexible modes of spectatorship" that lucha libre films require from the viewer. By continually alternating between a horror story and unrelated wrestling matches, Santo/Blue Demon constantly frustrates codes of narrative development and continuity seen in Hollywood product. Both incongruous and exasperating, at least for American viewers, the wrestling sequences completely halt the development and flow of the horror film. However, for a Mexican audience, and specifically lucha libre fans, such sequences could, and would, be the highlight of the film.

The match opening the film is between Santo and *Ángel Blanco* ("White Angel"), another popular luchador of the era. However, the match obviously takes place in a wrestling ring constructed in a film studio. In the early horror-wrestling films, the wrestling footage was either stock footage of arena matches, arena matches filmed for subsequent inclusion in a film, or staged matches designed to resemble arena matches as much as possible, including extras playing ringside spectators and the insertion of stock crowd footage. In *Santo/Blue Demon*, all three of the wrestling matches are filmed on this studio sound stage, with static long shots of the wrestling ring intercut with closer shots from another camera. Conspicuously absent from the match scenes are any spectators: there are no reaction shots of excited audience members, and ambient crowd noises are simply dubbed in.[51] In short, the matches throughout *Santo/Blue Demon* are essentially depicted as though they were being shown on television, and are even accompanied by an off-camera announcer who vividly and excitedly describes and comments on the action as if he were broadcasting a televised match — a noticeable departure from early lucha libre films which would show the matches devoid of any "color commentary" (although the wrestling match which serves as a coda to Delgado's previous *Santo contra la hija de Frankenstein* also features an off-camera commentator extolling Santo's wrestling skills, as well as his dedication to public service). In this way, one is struck by the lengths *Santo/Blue Demon* goes to in order to rather blatantly include what amounts to televised lucha libre matches within the film — in effect, defying the government's ban on televised lucha libre by constructing (thinly) disguised "television broadcasts" of lucha libre matches within a horror film.

The growing excitement generated by Santo and Ángel Blanco's match is suddenly interrupted after each wrestler has won one fall, and the third, deciding fall of the match is about to begin. The wrestling action abruptly cuts to shots of large, metal bat-head ornaments that spit jets of flames in an eerie grotto, signalling the beginning of *Santo/Blue Demon's* horror film components. Eric (Wally Baron) — a slovenly, bearded hunchback — lurks near two coffins lying on the floor of the subterranean lair. He portentously announces that the moment has arrived to resurrect the monsters in his charge, Count Dracula (Aldo Monti, reprising his role from *Santo in el tesoro de Drácula*) and Rufus Rex, the Wolf Man (Augustin Martínez Solares, Jr.). Since no other characters are in the scene with him, Eric's plot exposition-as-monologue is directed at the film audience, reminiscent of Tundra's lengthy opening speech in *Santo vs. the Vampire Women*, which similarly exists to summarize the film's plot for the viewer. Eric is a highly parodic horror film caricature, a sort of synthesis of Dracula's psychotic, obedient lackey Renfield (*Dracula*) and Dr. Frankenstein's misanthropic, deformed assistant Fritz (*Frankenstein*). While one can trace Eric's lineage to a long tradition of classic horror film servants, his presence serves a specific purpose for contemporary Mexican film audiences. David Wilt notes that Barron was a well-known character actor who "excelled in playing oily entrepreneurs [and] crooked politicians."[52] Along with Barron himself being known for characters associated with the odious aspects of Mexican capitalism and its insular political system, Barron's character Eric, with his ill-fitting suit, bushy beard, and long, unkempt hair, suggests a sort of left-wing intellectual. Given that one of the rudos featured in the lucha libre sequences is a long-haired wrestler known as "Renato the Hippie," it is possible to infer a certain level of vilification of Mexican radicalism and counter-culture in *Santo/Blue Demon*. At one point in the film, Eric even contemptuously dismisses Santo as "a retrograde man who still believes in truth and justice," defining Santo as a sort of political anachronism in the wake of the world-wide political unrest of the late 1960s, a period in Mexican history that would forever be summarized with one word: *Tlatelolco*.

On October 2, 1968, after several weeks of sporadic confrontations, 5,000 to 10,000 students staged a protest in Tlatelolco Square (the Plaza of the Three Cultures) in Mexico City. At 6:00 pm, orders were given to open fire on the protesters (no government official ever accepted responsibility for issuing the order). A slaughter of unarmed students and civilians by police, army, and paramilitary forces ensued. Not only were students bayoneted and gunned down, some in execution fashion, but government forces raided nearby apartments in search of fleeing students and killed numerous residents.[53] The Mexican government originally claimed less than a dozen people were killed, but eventually raised the "official" death figure to 32. However, the final body count was over *ten times* that total, with at least 325 fatalities being attributed to the evening-long massacre. In the wake of the horror at Tlatelolco and its devastating effect on Mexican political order, Santo represents a dated symbol of political idealism from which Eric, who epitomizes the current crisis in Mexican politics (corruption, radical dissent), explicitly wants to distance himself. Ultimately, the most important aspect of *Santo/Blue Demon* is how the film itself ambivalently negotiates the status of Santo as "a retrograde man who still believes in truth and justice."

The film cleverly cuts from two more shots of the bat-head ornaments spitting flames to a shot of an elderly man lighting his pipe. The viewer is introduced to the Cristaldi family: Professor Luis Cristaldi (Jorge Mondragón), his daughter Laura (María Eugenia San Martín), her daughter Rosita (Lissy Fields), and the young maid Josefina (Lourdes Batista). The elderly Professor Cristaldi is most impatient and worried, expressing an urgent need to meet with Santo. Laura implores him to patient, reminding him, "We don't live in the city anymore," suggesting that the Cristaldi family is already endangered by the fact they are not in an urban setting but live in the countryside: the traditional location of evil monsters and supernatural danger. As in other mexploitation films, Professor Cristaldi combines the roles of the head of the family (patriarchy) and respected scientist (modernity), although Professor Cristaldi's relationship to science is quickly problematized by the film. Laura Cristaldi serves as the film's *traditional woman*, completely defined by her family relationships: she is an obedient daughter and devoted mother who is not a faithful wife only because she was tragically widowed at a young age. It is Laura's longing for marital fulfillment, both sexually and domestically, which leads to her eventual seduction and murder by the charming but thoroughly evil Wolf Man, Rufus Rex.

Having briefly introduced Eric and the Cristaldi family to the viewer, the film abruptly shifts back to lucha libre action and the deciding round between Santo and Ángel Blanco, which Santo naturally wins. He returns to his dressing room, somewhat narcissistically decorated with a large photo of Santo's head and a velvet painting of Santo. Patiently waiting is Lina (Nubia Marti), Santo's girlfriend. Lina's important presence throughout *Santo/Blue Demon* typifies a key development in Santo's film persona: romantic interest. As David Wilt notes, in his early films Santo has absolutely no private life: he seems to exist solely to battle rudos, crime, and monsters. In later films Santo frequently has a girlfriend, but not at the expense of allowing this private life to interfere with his responsibilities in the public sphere of Mexican life.[54] Not surprisingly, Santo's sexual life is quite consistent with the political image of the countermacho: "celibate or monogamous." In his early films, Santo is *celibate* simply by virtue of having no personal life; in his later films, Santo is *monogamous*, and one can also assume that pre-marital sex is something neither his virtuous *chica moderna* girlfriends would allow, nor would the countermacho Santo himself condone. (One unintended irony of establishing Santo's romantic life in these later films is that different actresses portray Santo's girlfriends in each film, resulting in Santo accumulating a fair number of attractive girlfriends over the course of his cinematic career — suggesting he may have a bit of the swaggering, womanizing *macho* in him after all.) In *Santo en el tesoro de Drácula*, Santo and Luisa are engaged to be married, yet their relationship is passionless to the point of being platonic: when Santo mentions their plans for the future it sounds as if he is discussing a potential business merger rather than an impending marriage. In *Santo contra la hija de Frankenstein*, Norma exhibits a personal closeness and strong physical attraction to Santo, confiding to her sister Elsa, "When we are alone, he takes the mask off. If you saw him without it, you would also be crazy for him." The fact that Santo can unmask when they are alone suggests a high degree of intimacy and a component of eroticism in their relationship: Santo can "expose himself" to Norma, who can view his most private, personal body part — his *face*, rather than his genitals (although 1965's *El hacha diabólica* contains a scene in which Santo actually removes his mask for his girlfriend; but he is not directly facing the camera, and a stand-in was used). In this sense, a fundamental difference arises in the status of Santo's iconic mask between the early 1960s and the early 1970s. In *Santo contra las mujeres vampiro*, it is not simply the villainous vampire women who seek to remove Santo's mask and strip him of his iconic power, even the heroine Diana betrays the feminine "weakness" of longing to know the true identity of the man behind the mask and must be corrected by her father who reminds her that Santo's true identity is none of her personal business. By the early 1970s, Santo not only has a private life and personal, romantic relationships in his films, he can even "unmask" or "reveal himself" to women in moments of domestic privacy. In short, the separation between the "public Santo" and the "private Santo" becomes much more pronounced in these later films. Santo is not simply "a figure of perfect justice" whose role in the public sphere subsumes any private life (*Santo contra las mujeres vampiro*, *Santo vs. la invasión de los marcianos*), but is much more of the conventional superhero balancing his civic responsibilities with elements of a private life. One of the more subtle but important ways the later Santo films construct a distinction between the public Santo and the private Santo is that by the late 1960s Santo is no longer constrained to wearing his wrestling outfit in every scene, as in *Santo contra las mujeres vampiro* or *Santo vs. las invasión de los marcianos*. While Santo obviously never voluntarily removes his mask in his films (excepting *La hacha diabólica*), he is allowed to wear clothing appropriate to his surroundings when not in the ring: business suits, leisure wear, turtleneck sweaters and slacks, sweatshirts, and, in one hilarious scene from *Santo en el tesoro de Drácula* in which Santo responds to a late-night emergency knock on his door, a bathrobe!

When Santo greets Lina in the dressing room, he immediately plants a warm kiss on her lips. This immediate physical contact is in stark contrast to Santo's relationship to Norma in the previous *Santo contra la hija de Frankenstein*, which is quite literally a "look-but-don't-touch" voyeuristic relationship. Norma watches Santo wrestle twice during the film, once on television and once in an arena (of course, the scene of Norma watching lucha libre on television is especially striking because lucha libre was still banned from television at the time). Shots of Norma shouting encouragement, blowing kisses, and making suggestive facial expressions are periodically inserted into both match sequences, strongly implying that watching Santo wrestle is a source of intense sexual pleasure for Norma. During the film's concluding match, Santo immobilizes his opponent in a head scissors and waves to the crowd; Norma responds by lasciviously winking at him. Yet while Norma demonstrates obvious sexual arousal watching Santo in the ring, and can even see him without his mask when they are alone, there is no physical contact between the two in the film (explaining Freda Frankenstein's sexual-sadistic obsession not with killing Santo and Norma, but with threatening or attempting to *blind* the two throughout the film, in that the "sex" in their relationship is manifest through *sight* and not physical contact). In contrast, Lina, who can display actual physical affection for Santo, does not even bother to watch him in the ring but casually reads a magazine in his locker room until the match finishes.

With Santo's wrestling obligations completed, Lina informs him that her uncle, Professor Cristaldi, urgently needs to discuss "something important and strange" with him. The film quickly cuts to the Cristaldi mansion where the next several minutes are spent in Professor Cristaldi's study while he provides another long plot exposition, reiterating many of the points Eric previously cited by reading Santo a menacing, anonymous letter (sent by Eric) informing the Cristaldi family of their impending doom. In order to prove the letter is not simply "a bad joke" as Santo suggests, Professor Cristaldi reads a long passage from a book written 400 years ago. Learning of a pact formed by Count Dracula and the Wolf Man to conquer the world, the alchemist Elco Cristaldi created a magic dagger and killed Dracula and the Wolf Man. With his dying breath, Dracula swore that he would return one day to destroy the Cristaldi family line and turn them into "abominable zombies." Of course, the main conflict in *Santo/Blue Demon* revolves around resurrected monsters seeking revenge on those in the present: a standard narrative — and ideological — trope. Not surprisingly, Alfredo Salazar is credited with the screenplay for *Santo/Blue Demon*, which should serve as a red flag for the viewer that there will be an abundance of familiar plot points and themes derived from his own (and other) previous mexploitation films. However, it is notable that the heroic monster slayer of the past is not a fabled ancestor of Santo, specifically "Caballero Enmascarado de Plata" from *El barón Brákola, El mundo de los muertos* and, implicitly, *Santo contra las mujeres vampiro*. Rather, Elco Cristaldi is a nondescript magician-scientist known only to his immediate family. In this way, Santo is not connected with Mexican history and the heroic legends of the past, but rather entirely associated with modern Mexico: the countermacho — a political stereotype that not only came under fire in the aftermath of Tlatelolco but is also ultimately critiqued throughout the course of *Santo/Blue Demon*. Laura is perplexed that her scholar-father, a "man of science," could believe such an improbable, irrational story, and she expresses strong doubts about any supernatural threat. Professor Cristaldi admonishes her for her naiveté: "The limits of science go beyond those of mystery. The powers of the occult reach many planes. *Some are devices for good*" (emphasis added). In this regard, *Santo/Blue Demon* takes a far different position on the conflict between the supernatural and modernity than in many mexploitation films, as it grants a place for "the mysteries of the occult" in Mexican society. Both the alchemist Elco Cristaldi and Professor Cristaldi embody a *synthesis* of "science" and "the occult" which is now necessary to defeat the monsters of Mexico's past returned to destroy the present. This concession of a possible, let alone *useful*, role of "the occult" in modern Mexico is quite startling, considering occultism, with its roots in irrationality, superstition, and the supernatural, is vilified in many previous mexploitation films (*Muñecos infenales*, *El barón del terror*, *Santo contra las mujeres vampiro*, *Atacan las brujas*, etc.).

Fearing for the safety of his family, Professor Cristaldi asks Santo for his help. Santo vows to protect them — a vow that Santo is, at best, only partially successful in keeping throughout the course of the film (yet another way the film will ultimately question Santo's mythic ability to protect Mexican society). Indeed, Eric soon abducts Professor Cristaldi from his mansion, and the scene quickly returns to the grotto that houses the coffins of Dracula and Rufus Rex. In the film's most violent moment, Eric suspends the bound Professor Cristaldi upside down over Dracula's skeletal remains and cuts his throat, allowing the blood to drip onto Dracula's corpse and return him to life. Of course, horror film aficionados will recall a virtually identical, if much bloodier, scene in Hammer's *Dracula, Prince of Darkness* (1966), and one can easily assume the scene was "borrowed" from the well-known Hammer film. Revived by the spilled blood of a Cristaldi, Count Dracula transforms from a skeleton into a robust, handsome man in the familiar black apparel of a vampire (although the discerning viewer will notice, perhaps as a nod to 1970s fashions, that the lining of Dracula's cloak is actually plaid!). Cristaldi's bloody corpse is then hung over the coffin of Rufus Rex, who is similarly revived.

Dracula now provides further plot exposition, explaining the necessity of capturing human slaves and converting them into an army of vampires and wolf men — the first stage of his vengeance. After two brief shots of the metal bat-head ornaments spitting flames, the film cuts to a dungeon now suddenly filled with numerous humans captives chained to the wall, all of whom will soon be transformed into vampires (the women) and wolf men (the men). Later, when Laura Cristaldi is killed by Rufus Rex, she subsequently reappears as one of Dracula's red-clad *vampire* slaves, suggesting a strict gender division of the monsters' minions: the status of "wolf man" seems to be gender specific (a wolf *man*) and exclusively reserved for men in *Santo/Blue Demon*. There are no "wolf women" in the film; although, also in 1972, Santo would indeed confront female werewolves in *Santo vs. las lobas* (*Santo vs. the She-Wolves*, dir. Jamie Jiménez Pons). David Wilt perceptively notes the highly condensed nature of this sequence, which omits crucial and potentially exciting footage depicting *how* so many humans were captured in such a short span of time, and instead simply has a character state or explain this key plot development to advance the narrative, reflecting the frustrating tendency in *Santo/Blue Demon* to *describe* rather than show action sequences."[55] Throughout *Santo/Blue Demon*, much of the action is expressed through character dialogue or monologue rather than the actual on-screen depiction of such events. While this provides for many monotonous moments in the film by sacrificing narrative action in favor of exposition, the emphasis on "action" shifts almost entirely to the three wrestling matches interspersed and showcased throughout the, again suggesting that the horror film narrative may simply be designed to kill time between the lucha libre action.

Understandably concerned about Professor Cristaldi's sudden disappearance, Santo, Lina, and Laura attempt to enlist the police. However, when Santo mentions the supernatural (vampirism and lycanthropy), the police are, needless to say, skeptical, even if the theory comes from someone as respected as Santo. Realizing that the law will be of little help, Santo says, "I'll ask a loyal and brave friend of mine for his help — a formidable ally who could be of great help." Lina innocently asks, "Who is he?" In order to provide the obvious answer to Lina's query, the camera, right on cue, cuts to a shot of Blue Demon standing in the corner of the wrestling ring as the off-camera wrestling announcer excitedly bellows: "BLUE DEMON!" For the next several minutes the viewer is treated to a straight wrestling match between Blue Demon and the aforementioned rudo "Renato the Hippie," which comes as a welcome respite from the slow, dialogue-driven nature of the film thus far. Blue Demon easily wins in two successive falls, and after the match Santo explains the dire situation to Blue Demon in the locker room. Blue Demon responds by donning the "radio-watch" Santo once gave him. The two shake hands, with Blue Demon proudly telling Santo that they "will fight together again for truth and justice"–the very political ideals previously dismissed by Eric as "retrograde."

From this point on, *Santo/Blue Demon* sustains the horror narrative uninterrupted to its resolution, with the

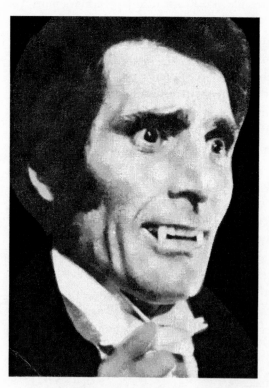

A suave vampire: Aldo Monti as Count Dracula in *Santo y Blue Demon contra Drácula y el Hombre Lobo.* Monti also played Count Dracula in René Cardona's *Santo en el tesoro de Drácula* (*Santo in the Treasure of Dracula,* 1968).

film becoming a series of episodic events that strain credibility even by mexploitation's loose standards of narrative logic. But, despite this flurry of events, *Santo/Blue Demon* still manages to offer more than its share of plodding moments, largely due to its continual emphasis on expository dialogue over on-screen action. Rufus Rex, now in his human form as a handsome, well-dressed man-about-town, has relocated to an apartment with the express intent of seducing and sacrificing Laura Cristaldi. Hilariously, when Eric tells him how "good" he looks, Rufus Rex conceitedly replies, "Yes — *very good*," expressing complete confidence in his masculine, seductive, "cocksure" powers and depicting him as the classic womanizing *macho*. A fake kidnap attempt is staged in the streets, courtesy of the gangsters in Eric's employ, with Rufus Rex intervening to save Laura from the mock-attack. The lonely Laura is easily smitten by Rufus Rex, and when Laura and Lina excitedly engage in gushy girl-talk about this potential new love interest in Laura's life, Santo and Blue Demon react with obvious he-man discomfort. Rufus Rex also becomes the target of Blue Demon's suspicions, which Wilt argues stems from Blue Demon's own implied romantic interest in Laura Cristaldi.[56] Following Rufus Rex to a meeting with Eric, Blue Demon watches the two through the window from a perch in a tree. Aware that they are being observed by Blue Demon, Eric devises a ruse: they stage a conversation that makes it appear that Eric has kidnapped Professor Cristaldi and Rufus Rex is working to secure the (dead) Professor's release. Blue Demon falls for the scheme and alerts Santo via the radio-watch about this new development. Soon in Santo's convertible, the two luchadores follow Eric through the streets to a warehouse, accompanied by some odd surf-rock-meets-cocktail-jazz music (courtesy of Carrión). Inside the building, Santo and Blue Demon, believing they are about to apprehend Eric, instead are ambushed by the gangsters in Eric's employ and held at gunpoint (here Eric serves as a bridge between the threat of supernatural evil and the problem of urban crime). After taunting the two wrestlers, the gangsters decide to kill Santo and Blue Demon by incinerating them in the warehouse stove, but will first perform the ultimate injustice and unmask them. Inexplicably, Santo and Blue Demon offer absolutely no resistance to this awful fate, and simply submissively turn their backs to the criminals so they can remove their masks.

Fortunately for the two helpless luchadores, Lina disobeyed Santo's orders to "stay home and stay safe" and stowed away in the back seat of Santo's convertible. Following them into the warehouse, Lina intervenes and prevents their humiliating unmasking by driving a forklift into a stack of boxes which tumble onto the gangsters, throwing the scene into disarray. Taking advantage of Lina's literally "face-saving" initiative, Santo and Blue Demon pummel the gangsters with masculine fury while Lina phones the police, who conveniently arrive just as the gangsters have been beaten into submission. Lina's actions are a refreshing change from those of previous Santo film heroines, specifically Norma in *Santo contra la hija de Frankenstein*, in which Santo must constantly rescue Norma and Elsa, the classic "damsels-in-distress," with his romantic relationship becoming a complication in fulfilling his duties to the Mexican public due to the constant need to save his powerless girlfriend from dangerous situations. Lina is the exemplary *chica moderna*: young, urban, modern, sexy, independent, and impertinent (but nonetheless virtuous). In this scene, Lina strongly recalls mexploitation's foremost *chicas modernas*, Gloria/Loreta Venus and Golden Rubi in René Cardona's early *Luchadoras* films. Much like the repeated and often hilarious need for the wrestling women to rescue their ineffectual boyfriend detectives from danger in *Las luchadoras vs. el médico asesino*, genre and gender conventions are briefly turned on their heads in *Santo/Blue Demon*—it is Lina, a *woman*, who must intervene in order to prevent the defeated and vulnerable luchadores from suffering the worst of all possible fates: losing their masks.

In order to implement his plan of seducing and sacrificing Laura, Rufus Rex meets with Santo and Blue Demon, employing his diabolical charm to further the charade that he is an ally in their quest to locate Professor Cristaldi. After Rufus Rex provides Santo and Blue Demon with a map that will supposedly lead them to the Professor's location, the luchadores investigate and locate Professor Cristaldi, now an "abominable zombie." The undead Professor mindlessly attacks Santo while Eric ambushes him from behind, knocking Santo unconscious. Producing a large knife, Eric is about to plunge it into Santo's heart; fortunately, Blue Demon decides to investigate the scene as well, forcing Eric and the undead Professor to flee before Santo can be murdered: a rare moment in the Santo–Blue Demon film canon in which it is *Blue Demon* who rescues *Santo*. When Santo regains consciousness, Blue Demon asks him if he located Professor Cristaldi. Santo answers that he did see the Professor, "or better yet, some kind of corpse behaving like a robot!"

Unfortunately, Santo and Blue Demon entrusted Rufus Rex with the responsibility of safe-guarding Lina and Laura. Immediately following the luchadores departure, Lina loudly sighs and says she is going to her room to read — an obvious excuse to leave the new romantic couple alone. Laura asks Lina to watch the house instead so she and Rufus Rex can take a walk in the garden. The scene cuts to a shot of the full moon in the night sky: a wolf howl, male animal grunts, and a woman's scream all accompany the image. Obviously, Rufus Rex has transformed into a wolf man and fulfilled his plan of "sacrificing Laura with the next full moon"; however, the sacrifice's unsettling sounds denote nothing short of a brutal sexual assault. This strikingly defines the difference between the two primary female characters, Lina and Laura, in *Santo/Blue Demon*. Lina, the *chica moderna*, is not only "impertinent and impatient," but intervenes at a crucial moment to rescue the luchadores from being unmasked and symbolically losing their iconic power in Mexican society. In contrast,

Laura, the "traditional woman," is utterly incapable of defending herself from the supernatural seduction and violence of Rufus Rex.

The following morning, Laura's disappearance has been discovered, and the police inspector reports, "Blood was found in the woods ... *human blood*." While he mentions that the police have Rex's apartment under surveillance, the inspector snidely suggests to the visibly distraught Lina that a lovelorn and infatuated Laura may have simply "run off" with Rufus Rex, implying that her carnal desires may have overtaken her social responsibilities to her family.

The scene shifts to the caves, where Dracula congratulates Rufus Rex on his successful attack on Laura, who now resides "in the caves of the walking dead." Dracula then proclaims it is now his turn to fulfill his part in their pact of revenge, and his next victim will be Lina, who he will turn into "one of his own species ... and [who will] be my slave for eternity." The implication is that the confrontation between the evil seducer of innocent *chicas modernas* (Dracula) and the sexually moral countermacho (Santo) is becoming personal, with Dracula's goal not simply to eliminate a Cristaldi, but to seduce, enslave, and steal Santo's girlfriend.

The film returns to the Cristaldi manor, where Santo and Blue Demon intently play chess while Lina reads a book in a chair in the background. The camera slowly zooms in to a medium close-up of Lina and pauses while Dracula steps into the right side of the film frame, appearing outside of the window behind Lina; the camera then slowly zooms in to a close-up of Dracula. He hypnotizes Lina, the act portrayed via the usual visual conventions of mexploitation cinema — alternating tight close-ups between Dracula and Lina. Succumbing to Dracula's evil power, Lina silently rises, and the scene cuts back to Santo and Blue Demon concentrating on their chess match. Lina walks into the far background of the shot and out the front door, the wrestlers too absorbed in their chess game to notice her departure (perhaps a vestige of "their traditional rivalry" does still exist). The camera cuts to a medium close-up of Dracula in the fog-shrouded garden of the Cristaldi manor, then tracks with him as he walks to the right, where Lina, standing motionless, enters the film frame, completely under Dracula's hypnotic-seductive spell. He slowly moves Lina's hair away from her neck and is about to bite her on the throat when suddenly a voice calls out "Lina!" (resulting in a sort of vampire *coitus interruptus*). The next scene shows Santo in the garden, desperately searching for his missing girlfriend. Thwarted by the timely intervention of Lina's true love, Dracula flees, and she is saved for the moment. However. as these events unfold, perhaps the film's most (unintentionally?) humorous moment also occurs. As the maid Josefina sleeps, a bald, diminutive, elderly vampire with oversized fangs enters her room. More laughable clown than sinister vampire, he's a comical parody of the gaunt, grim Count Orlock in Murnau's *Nosferatu*. He bites Josefina on the neck before transforming into a rubber bat and stealing away into the night.

Back in the safety of his lair, Dracula resumes his attack on the remaining Cristaldis, especially Lina. In a highly theatrical moment, the camera focuses on a darkened doorway as a shadow-shrouded figure enters the film frame. Stage lights from below slowly flood the frame, revealing Count Dracula staring directly at the camera, which gradually zooms-in to a close-up of Dracula's face. Once more Dracula begins to hypnotize his female victims, this time by "long-distance." Through the standard pattern of alternating close-ups, Dracula first beckons Lina to his chambers and then contacts the previously-bitten Josefina, ordering her to bring Rosita to his lair as well. While Santo retires to Professor Cristaldi's study to research the occult, Lina, again in a hypnotic trance, wanders out of the Cristaldi mansion. Noticing her departure, and alarmed by her unresponsiveness, Blue Demon follows her into the woods, where he is soon ambushed by three wolf men and captured in a net. Josefina, similarly hypnotized, wakes Rosita and orders her to get dressed, informing her she is bringing Rosita to her mother; they also wander off into the woods. Santo's research uncovers crucial information regarding the importance of the magic dagger (apparently Santo was not paying attention during the Professor's long exposition early in the film in which the Professor explained the critical role of the dagger in detail). Noticing that important artifact is no longer with the Professor's collection of other occult objects, Santo begins to search the mansion, discovering the dagger in Rosita's bedroom as well as realizing that everyone has suddenly and mysteriously disappeared from the Cristaldi home. Santo contacts Blue Demon via the radio-watch, and, despite being chained to a wall in Dracula's dungeon, Blue Demon relays the location of the monsters: a cave underneath an old house in the woods. Santo hurries to investigate.

The entranced Lina arrives first at Dracula's mansion, and for the second time, Dracula attempts to make her his vampirical (and sexual) slave, only again to be interrupted at the last second, this time by Eric. Eric anxiously informs Dracula — and the film audience — that Santo is on the way to the haunted mansion with the magic dagger; Eric helpfully adds that he learned of this vital development from one of three wolf men who encountered Santo in the woods — he was the only one not killed by Santo, and escaped back to the mansion. The viewer certainly wishes this violent confrontation between Santo and the wolf men had been depicted on-screen — rather than the several interminable minutes of the principal characters meandering about the woods in hypnotic trances, especially when one recalls earlier Santo films such as *Atacan las brujas* or *Santo vs. las invasión de los marcianos*, which featured not only the requisite wrestling sequences but extended brawls between Santo and various monsters.[57] Josefina and Rosita arrive at Dracula's mansion as well; Josefina promptly and cruelly shoves Rosita to the floor upon their arrival and then callously walks away, presumably to join her fellow vampire women in the "caves of the walking dead." Understandably frightened, Rosita roams about

Dracula's mansion alone, first briefly encountering her undead and unresponsive grandfather, and then her mother, clad in the blood-red gown all of Dracula's vampire slave-women wear. Taking her daughter by the hand ("Mama, your hand is very cold!"), Laura leads Rosita to the underground catacombs. Fortunately, Rosita drops her doll and turns back to retrieve it, but Laura, completely oblivious to her daughter's absence, continues onward and enters the red-lit "caves of the walking dead," the heavy stone closing behind her. Like Josefina, Laura is never seen again. One might argue that Laura, the traditional woman who succumbs to the corrupting, seductive evil power of a monster from the past (Rufus Rex), can no longer fulfill her proper societal role in the present: that of devoted mother.

Instructing Eric to confront Santo, Dracula flees to the sanctuary of the caves. When Santo arrives at the mansion, he is promptly ambushed by Eric, who throws a gas grenade at Santo. It explodes at Santo's feet, the fumes quickly rendering him unconscious. Searching Santo, Eric finds the magic dagger and raises it, about to stab Santo. However, Eric suddenly realizes that possessing the magic dagger gives him a great advantage over Dracula; he can use it to force Dracula to produce the vast treasure Eric feels is owed him for his dedicated service (according to the film's own mythology, it would have been impossible for Eric to kill Santo with the magic dagger in the first place — it is only effective against evil monsters). Eric returns to Lina, still locked in Dracula's bedroom, and offers to help her escape if she can explain how to use the dagger. However, suddenly and quite hilariously, the dagger magically spins around in Eric's palm and plunges itself deep into his expansive stomach. Dying, he utters his classic final words: "*I committed so many crimes that I stopped being human!*" It serves as a fitting end to the bearded villain who so derisively dismissed Mexican ideals of "truth and justice," as if Eric's rejection of such noble concepts made him a "monster" as much as any specific evil deeds.

Able to escape the dangerous confines of Dracula's bedroom, Lina finds Santo helplessly sprawled on the floor of the mansion and revives him. Once again rescued by Lina, and perhaps more than a little embarrassed by it, Santo firmly orders her to return to the Cristaldi mansion. Of course, she only pretends to follow Santo's orders and instead trails him to the underground cave where the monsters have gathered and are preparing to torture one of their own: the cowardly wolf man who fled from Santo during the (unseen) confrontation in the woods. Setting a plank across a pit full of spikes, Rufus Rex orders the lackey to cross it while Rufus twists it back and forth: if the wolf man can successfully cross the pit he will escape further punishment. Predictably, he falls to his doom. Count Dracula and Rufus Rex announce that Blue Demon will be next, with the added disadvantage of having his hands tied behind his back while he "walks the plank." Despite the overwhelming odds against him, Blue Demon manfully stays on the plank until Santo can rescue him. A melee between the two luchadores and several wolf men (finally!) ensues,

Blue Demon socks Rufus Rex in the jaw during the finale of *Santo y Blue Demon contra Drácula y el Hombre Lobo.*

allowing Santo and Blue Demon to demonstrate some impressive wrestling moves in the context of the horror film battle between good and evil. The implicit tension between Rufus Rex and Blue Demon explodes when the two finally square off, man to (wolf) man. Unable to defeat Blue Demon as a man, halfway through their fistfight the overmatched Rufus Rex transforms into a wolf man before cowardly fleeing from Blue Demon. While Santo stands at the edge of the pit of spikes, Count Dracula and Rufus Rex surround him. Blue Demon throws a rope pulley to Santo (the same device used to hoist Professor Cristaldi over the coffins). In a moment of swashbuckling verve, Santo swings from the rope and kicks both Dracula and Rufus Rex into the pit of spikes (an ending is borrowed from *El mundo de los vampiros*, in which Count Subotai meets a nearly-identical fate). Horribly impaled by these spikes, the two monsters meet their demise (so much for needing the magic dagger).

Having defeated the monsters, Santo and Blue Demon return to the Cristaldi mansion, where Lina is reading the fairy tale "Little Red Riding Hood" to a sleeping Rosita. The incorporation of "Little Red Riding Hood" is highly ironic. The fairy tale genre is inscribed into the horror film, and, as noted, Little Red Riding Hood appeared several times in Mexican children's films, including her quite unnerving treatment in *Caperucita y Pulgarcito contra los monstruos* (*Little Red Riding Hood and Tom Thumb vs. the Monsters*, 1960, dir. Roberto Rodriquez; U.S. title: *Little Red Ridding Hood and the Monsters*). Moreover, the Little Red Riding Hood fairy tale is about a female menaced by a monstrous male wolf. In *Santo/Blue Demon*, Little Red Riding Hood is not necessarily represented by Rosita and her brief encounter with the monsters. Rather, Little Red Riding Hood is represented by Laura Cristaldi, who is seduced, murdered, and implicitly raped by the Wolf Man, Rufus Rex. While little Rosita sleeps, Lina wonders how to explain these horrible events and the loss of her dearest family members (her grandfather, her mother, and her nanny). Lina asks Santo, "What will we tell her when she wakes up?" Santo responds with a very inadequate solution: "That it was a dream." Blue Demon nods and adds, "A nightmare." Then, almost as an afterthought, Blue Demon suddenly reminds Santo that they have a match tomorrow and they better get some rest. The film closes with a lucha libre coda: a tag-team match featuring Santo and Blue Demon against Ángel Blanco and Renato the Hippie (the reappearance of the *same* two opponents time and again leads one to assume that the three matches were filmed simultaneously). As if to expunge the tragic ending from the film, the match celebrates the exploits of Santo and Blue Demon, who easily defeat their opponents, as if the routing of the rudo by the técnico in the melodramatic spectacle of the wrestling ring is all that is necessary to demonstrate that all is well with Mexican society (although the obvious irony is that Santo and Blue Demon were actually bitter tag-team *rivals* during their long wrestling careers).

However, despite the final images of the two técnicos triumphing in the ring, *Santo/Blue Demon* is not a "happy ending." In *Santo/Blue Demon*, Santo is far from being "a figure of perfect justice." At best, Santo is fallible, and at worst simply inept. Even Santo's girlfriend must come to his rescue twice in the film: the *chica moderna* saving the manly, iconic luchador. Santo and Blue Demon, despite their best efforts, cannot prevent the violent deaths of Professor and Laura Cristaldi, and the resurrection and subsequent defeat of the monsters has exacted a high price: an awareness of the limits of modernity over unexplainable evils, the virtual destruction of the traditional family, and the demystification of Santo's heroic image. The tragic demise of the family patriarch-scholar (Professor Cristaldi) and loving mother (Laura Cristaldi) will be pitifully explained away as "a dream ... a nightmare." In this sense, *Santo/Blue Demon* inherently reflects the fact that the simple moral lessons and political solutions expressed in the early Santo films are no longer adequate in a Mexico that has endured its own share of turmoil in the wake of the world-wide student uprisings, political upheaval, and brutal violence of the late 1960s (manifest most dramatically and traumatically with the Tlatelolco massacre). When Santo decides they will tell the child Rosita, the future of Mexico, that it was all "a dream," perhaps it is an admission by Santo, the film's "retrograde man who still believes in truth and justice," that "the fairy tale" has been the lucha libre genre, "the dream" the political and cultural myths celebrated by the lucha libre genre, and "the nightmare" the harsh political realities of Mexico.

5

Las Luchadoras

From Chicas Modernas to Wrestling Women

René Cardona was one of Mexican cinema's most prolific filmmakers, directing over 140 films from virtually every genre over a career spanning almost *five* decades (1937–1985): melodramas, comedies, adventures, Westerns, horror, lucha libre films, exploitation, and even the surreal kiddie-film classic *Santa Claus* (1959), aptly described by Rob Craig as "a singular cross between Luis Buñuel and a cheesy Saturday morning kid's TV show."[1] From 1962 to 1968, Cardona also contributed six *Luchadoras* ("Wrestling Women") films to the mexploitation canon, all produced by Guillermo Calderón Stell: *Las luchadoras vs. el médico asesino*; *Las luchadoras vs. la momia*; *Las lobas del ring* (*She-Wolves of the Ring*, 1964); *Las mujeres pantera* (*The Panther Women*, 1966); *Las luchadoras vs. el robot asesino* (*Wrestling Women vs. the Killer Robot*, 1968); and *El horripilante bestia humana*. The first two "Wrestling Women" films, *Las luchadoras vs. el médico asesino* and *Las luchadoras contra la momia,* were among the wave of Mexican horror films imported and dubbed into English by K. Gordon Murray in the 1960s, and released under the respective titles *Doctor of Doom* and *Wrestling Women vs. the Aztec Mummy.* Like several other Murray imports, they became fixtures on late-night American television and eventually acquired an almost mythic cult-film status.[2]

While not an official part of the *Luchadoras* film canon, Cardona's bewildering classic *La Mujer Murciélago* (*Bat Woman*, 1967) could certainly be considered part of this cycle and merits its own brief discussion. *La Mujer Murciélago* starred Maura Monti as Bat Woman: Monti was featured as Afrodita in *Santo vs. las invasión de los marcianos* and Eritrea in *El planeta de las mujeres invasoras* (*Planet of the Women Invaders*, 1965), a "straight" science fiction film directed by Alfredo B. Crevenna which concentrated on well-proportioned women aliens instead of Santo battling burly Martians. Clearly inspired by the Batman-Batgirl DC comics, or, more likely, the *Batman* television series of the mid–1960s, Bat Woman thwarts the efforts of a mad scientist (Roberto Cañedo) attempting to create a race of superhuman fish-men using the pituitary glands of women wrestlers he has kidnapped and murdered for his fiendish experiments (it probably goes without saying that

The North Pole of Dr. Caligari: Santa Claus (José Elias Moreno) in his hallucinatory Expressionist–Art Deco palace in *Santo Claus* (1959). (Courtesy Rob Craig.)

Alfredo Salazar wrote the film). Featuring a black bikini to complement her cape, cowl, and arm stockings, Bat Woman's costume does not so much resemble the tight black body suit worn on *Batman* by Batgirl (Yvonne Craig), but instead prefigures the quasi–S&M gear donned by whip-wielding Halle Berry in *Catwoman* (2004). Coincidentally, around the same time Cardona made *La Mujer Murciélago*, Jerry Warren made *The Wild World of Batwoman* (1966), a parody of *Batman* about a secret society of crime-fighting "Batgirls" that emphasized extended go-go dancing sequences as much as any efforts at battling evil. While Warren did not plagiarize *La Mujer Murciélago* for *The Wild World of Batwoman*, he did manage to include footage of Dr. Krupp recycled from *La momia azteca* and, for reasons known only to Warren, footage culled from the trailer for the science fiction film *The Mole People*.[3]

The first three "Wrestling Women" films starred mexploitation legend Lorena Velázquez as "Gloria Venus," although in *Las luchadoras vs. la momia* and *Las lobas del ring*, her character is renamed "Loreta Venus." Given that Greek and Roman mythology is frequently used to codify characters as villains in mexploitation films by referencing them to European culture and values, one is struck by the fact that Velázquez's character receives the name of the Roman goddess of love. Something of an icon of mexploitation cinema, Velázquez appeared in such films as *El planeta de las mujeres invasoras*, *Santo contra los zombies*, and *El hacha diabólica*. Besides her *Luchadoras* films, Velázquez is also remembered for her starring roles as Zorina, queen of the vampire women, in *Santo contra las mujeres vampiro,* and Mayra, queen of the witches, in *Atacan las brujas*. Alongside Velázquez was American actress Elizabeth Campbell as her tag-team partner "Golden Rubi"—Campbell's other mexploitation credits include *El planeta de las mujeres invasoras* as well as the Santo spy film *Operación 67*. With *Las mujeres pantera*, Campbell remained in the role of Golden Rubi, but Velázquez was replaced as "Gloria Venus" by another mexploitation veteran, Ariadna Welter (*El vampiro*, *El barón del terror*).

Like the other lucha libre films of the era, Cardona's *Luchadoras* cycle blended horror film conventions and clichés, comic book action, episodic narratives, comedy, and, of course, astringent wrestling sequences. One exception was *Las lobas del ring,* a straight wrestling melodrama with a crime subplot added for good measure; the film featured a virtual all-star cast of popular actresses who frequently appeared in mexploitation films: Velázquez, Campbell, María Eugenia San Martín, Sonia Infante, and Rosa María Gallardo. The other exception is arguably *El horripilante bestia humana*, in that the film only features three brief wrestling scenes in its early stages; by the halfway point it becomes a horror film emphasizing the murders of unsuspecting Mexican citizens by the titular ape man. Nevertheless, both *El horripilante bestia humana* and *Las luchadoras vs. el robot asesino* borrow greatly from *Las luchadoras vs. el médico asesino;* and like several other Cardona wrestling-horror films of the era, alternate versions with female nudity were released internationally: *Las luchadoras vs. el robot asesino* as *El médico loco y el sexo* (*The Mad Doctor and Sex*) and *El horripilante bestia humana* as *Horror y sexo* (*Horror and Sex*).[4]

Certainly the most obvious aspect of the *Luchadoras* films is that they feature beautiful, shapely women instead of muscular, masked luchadores. Whereas the films of Santo or Blue Demon obviously emphasized their wrestling abilities over their dramatic skills (many times the voices of the luchadores were dubbed in postproduction by professional actors), the *Luchadoras* films starred well-known actresses (Velázquez, Campbell) and stressed their obvious on-screen sex appeal rather than their athleticism. In the action and wrestling sequences, the actresses were frequently doubled by professional women wrestlers, and the alternation between Velázquez and Campbell and their obvious stunt doubles not only provokes a great deal of unintentional humor, but creates a quite disruptive and disorientating effect for the film audience, rendering the matches surreal theater rather than exciting lucha libre action.[5] Such moments in Cardona's films demonstrate his relative indifference to basic rules of continuity editing, the most blatant example being the end of *Santo en el tesoro de Drácula*, in which the final battle between Santo and Black Hood's forces takes place in a parking lot at night, but was clearly filmed during daylight hours!

As Rubenstein argues, the dominant discourses of modernity and tradition in Mexican popular culture were often framed by the *representation of women*. It is this representation of women in the early *Luchadoras* centuries that becomes the sub-genre's most fascinating and problematic aspect. The *Luchadoras* films represent a rather remarkable departure for a society defined by what Carlos Monsiváis termed "brutal sexism" by having *women* assume the male luchador's crucial role of battling for the betterment of Mexican society, in and out of the wrestling ring. Dispelling stereotypes of feminine passivity, the luchadoras not only confront threats to Mexican society but "man-handle" the villains themselves, particularly in *Doctor of Doom*, in which the wrestling women assume the heroic, "masculine" role due to the ineffectual efforts of their boyfriend-detectives. Both *Doctor of Doom* and *Wrestling Women* not only depict the main female characters as *chicas modernas*, but as dynamic, powerful women actively engaged in fighting threats to mexicanidad and modernity, quite unlike "damsel-in-distress" or "passive victim" stereotypes (Diana in *Santo contra las mujeres vampiro*, Norma in *Santo contra la hija de Frankenstein*, Laura in *Santo y Blue Demon contra Count Drácula and el Hombre Lobo*). Heather Levi argues that lucha libre was one of the few practices in Mexican popular culture that actively *encouraged* the participation of women rather than discouraging it or even denying it altogether: "The participation of women as lucha libre spectators was significant, considering that some kinds of public space, notably the cantina, were formally closed to women until the 1970s, and the gendering of other public spaces, such as the cinema and the rock concert, was sometimes subject to violent contestation."[6] While certainly Levi's focus is on the opportunity afforded to the female *spectator* in the public sphere of lucha libre (in contrast to the other closed, exclusively male, even homeosocial public spaces in Mexican popular culture), it is possible to argue that Cardona's *Luchadoras* films further open the public space of lucha libre for women, who are not simply allowed into the world of lucha libre as enthusiastic, admiring, even voyeuristic *spectators* of masculine wrestling action (Norma in *Santo contra la hija de Frankenstein*), but become active *participants* in the ring and, by extension, the public sphere.

However, the status of women in these films is also typical of the conservative gender politics of mexploitation. One is struck by how the *Luchadoras* films perpetuate sexism in the ways feminist film scholar Laura Mulvey argues cinema depicts women: a two-fold process which "over-values" women by fetishizing the female body as sex-object, while simultaneously "under-valuing" women by routinely subjecting female characters to "narrative punishment" over the course of the film.[7] In *over-valuing* the luchadoras, these films certainly fetishize their very attractive stars Velázquez and Campbell; and one obvious strategy in casting two stunning, statuesque actresses as evil-fighting luchadoras in place of beefy luchadores is to simply provide a degree of mildly risqué sexual excitement for male spectators and substitute one male fantasy for another: the buxom Amazon verses the sexy, submissive female. The camera closely follows the wrestling women's exploits as they parade around in form-fitting wrestling tights in the ring and gym, and clinging sweaters and tight pants out of the ring: all of which continually emphasize their bosoms and buttocks. The *Luchadoras* films also indulge in the titillating thrill of watching women "cat-fight," although these battles take place in the civil, respectable world of the wrestling ring. One can ultimately suggest that the space made for the luchadoras in these films does not empower them in Mexican society, but rather exploits them as objects of voyeuristic-fetishistic pleasure for men.[8] Conversely, women are often "under-valued" in the *Luchadoras* films by making them victims of sexually-charged violence and unwilling individuals whose bodies are the site of grotesque experiments. While the *Luchadoras* films engage in common mexploitation debates — modernity and mexicanidad—the most important aspect of these films is their framing of these issues through the *representation of women*, resulting in highly problematic critiques of gender politics.

Las luchadoras vs. el médico asesino (Doctor of Doom, *1962)*

Doctor of Doom begins with a brief but important pre-credit, two-shot sequence. The first shot depicts an attractive woman walking down a dark city street alone. As she nears the camera, she becomes aware she is being followed and quickens her pace, glancing behind her several times at the mysterious men shadowing her. This shot jump-cuts to a medium shot of the woman, still glancing backwards and hurrying forward, when two large, hairy arms emerge from behind the corner of a building and grab her from behind. A hideous, subhuman man-monster is revealed — a ghastly brute with patches of thick hair covering its body. While this attack is a prologue to the horror film narrative, given the opening's *film noir* tone and urban violence theme, there is a certain sense that the spectator is watching a brutal street crime unfold as much as a monster film. The assault lacks the Gothic eroticism of horror film vampirism and instead contains an urban seediness and grim realism more comparable to the low-budget American sexploitation "roughies" of the mid–1960s than to traditional mexploitation or Universal and Hammer horror films. The dark urban surroundings become very familiar over the course of the film, as *Doctor of Doom* is set exclusively in *the city*, the modern milieu of Mexican life, with any depictions of, or even references to, traditional rural life nonexistent in the film. Equally important, the monsters in the film (Gomar, Vendetta) are the awful and dangerous products of unrestrained and irresponsible science roaming the city streets rather than being resurrected, supernatural beings ominously dwelling in the countryside. In short, the focus of *Doctor of Doom* is exclusively on *modernity*: urban life, scientific progress, and *chicas modernas*.

The scene of the woman being attacked in the street suddenly cuts to a shot of a statuesque woman standing in the middle of the wrestling ring: Gloria Venus. As a tag-team luchadora match unfolds, the opening credits are shown over the action. The lucha libre sequence itself is a barrage of wrestling action propelled by jarring jump-cuts, with luchadoras appearing in and out of the ring almost at random: mexpolitation as done by Godard. Most of the wrestling shots in this sequence are actually taken from the wrestling match shown halfway through the film. Certain moments are recognizable in both matches, as is the stock footage of cheering crowds. Moreover, in other crowd reaction shot under the opening credits viewer clearly sees the characters of Professor Wright (Roberto Cañedo — name changed from "Professor Ruiz" in *Las Luchadoras vs. el médico asesino*) and the two detectives, Armando Campos (Armando Silvestre) and Chema (Chucho Salinas), who are given the all–American names "Mike Henderson" (Silvestre) and "Tommy Johnson" (Salinas) in both *Doctor of Doom* and *Wrestling Women vs. the Aztec Mummy.* Given that these three characters are not introduced into the narrative until later in the film, their presence at this "first" match of the film is incongruous, to say the least. (Also, probably unintentionally, the title *Doctor of Doom* appears over a shot of Professor Wright, immediately informing the audience of his secret identity as the evil "Mad Doctor.") In an attempt to disguise the recycled footage, Cardona not only uses jump-cutting to fragment the sequence, but *flips* the footage of the entire lucha libre sequence: The right side of the frame in the second match is the left side of the frame in the opening credits, and characters reverse their positions accordingly. While presumably this flipping was simply a cost-saving measure to avoid shooting an additional wrestling sequence, midway through the film the viewer experiences a disorienting sense of *déjà vu* when he sees the same footage again in an unabridged, more coherent, and reverse-oriented form supposedly depicting a *different* match.

After the credits conclude, a long shot depicts Gloria defeating one of her opponents by putting her foot on her back and stretching the opponent's arms behind her, forcing her to submit; the opponent's partner charges in the ring, and Gloria quickly and easily defeats this second woman as well. The viewer easily discerns that Gloria's partner for most of this match — Elizabeth Campbell — is now a different woman: she is much shorter and wears a different outfit. The shot cuts to the referee raising Gloria hand's in triumph, with the victor hardly the worse for wear, her make-up and hairdo still intact. This shot dissolves to the interior of the woman's locker room, and Gloria enters, followed by her sister Alice (changed from "Alicia" in *Las luchadoras vs. el médico asesino,* played by Sonia Infane). When Alice proclaims that she thought Gloria might lose, Gloria hilariously replies: "I hate to be called a braggart, sis, but up to now no woman has pinned me!" Beyond the obvious sexual-voyeuristic thrill the film offers, specifically the well-built Gloria in her wrestling tights "cat-fighting" in the ring, the issue of male voyeurism is addressed in a far more subtle, but equally important way. It is through *the camera* that the male spectator can access and enter "forbidden" places and spaces exclusively reserved for women: namely, their *locker-room.* This voyeuristic promise seems on the verge of fulfillment when Gloria tells her sister she wants to "take a quick shower" before they go out. However, the exciting possibility for the male spectator that he might see Gloria naked is quickly dashed when she hangs her towel over the shower wall and walks out of the shot — and out of the field of vision of the camera and male spectator. Obviously the lack of nudity is dictated by Mexican film industry censorship guidelines at the time, but it is worth noting that by 1968's *El horripilante bestia humana* (or, more correctly, *Horror y sexo*), depicting the naked luchadora within the space of the locker room becomes far more important than depicting the fighting luchadora in the space of the wrestling ring itself.

Alice mentions that she would be afraid of getting a "broken arm" in the ring, and the scene cuts to a close-up of an IV inserted into the crook of a woman's elbow. A long sequence ensues wherein two surgeons perform an operation on the woman's brain. Lasting several minutes, it is filmed in an almost documentary manner, as if the viewer were watching an actual operation unfold. A close-up of an arc of electrical current is repeatedly inserted to signify the status of the patient's life. Suddenly the arc stops, and the shot cuts to a close-up of the woman turning her head to one side: she is dead. As the two doctors discuss the operation's failure and their other medical experiments, Cardona deliberately keeps their identities concealed. During and after the operation, their faces are covered by surgical masks; after they remove their masks, Cardona continues to make a concerted effort to film the pair without revealing their faces. While feeding the brutish ape-man Gomar, the same monster seen attacking the woman in the opening sequence, their heads are obscured by hanging slabs of raw meat. In other shots they are shown with their backs to the camera or from the waist down, such as in the long takes focusing on their feet as they pace back and forth. Obviously Cardona's intention is to keep the viewer in suspense by not revealing the identity of "the Mad Doctor," although more than enough heavy-handed clues appear throughout the film so that the identity of the Mad Doctor should come as no surprise.

The hidden faces of the doctors would seem to ease the dubbing process quite considerably in that voices would not have to approximate the movement of their unseen mouths. Nonetheless, this stretch of dialogue offers some of the strangest verbalizations ever to appear in a Murray mexploitation film. Much like with the convoluted syntax of *The Brainiac* (in particular, its opening tribunal sequence), it is possible the strange and strained nature of the dialogue lies in the original Spanish script — or translating the original Spanish script *too* literally — rather than mistranslating the script for dubbing purposes.

Having killed the woman during the operation, the doctor hangs his head: "Another failure — and that makes the *fourth* one." His assistant expresses his own theory to the doctor — and the film audience — about *why* their experiments have failed:

> All of the brains that we've tried to transplant up to now have come from *totally uneducated women*. They had no preparation whatsoever, and their IQs were *extremely low*. Don't you believe we'd achieve better results from a superior brain with a high IQ from a young, intelligent woman?

The doctor concurs: "I couldn't be absolutely certain about it — but there is a strong possibility you might be right." Noting that, "the female of the species reacts more positively to these experiments, for many biological reasons" (*why?*), he decides the next brain transplant effort will use "an *intellectual* woman ... one that has selected a *professional* career" (emphasis added). As the bizarre dialogue continues, the viewer soon realizes that these men are not "surgeons," but "mad scientists," and what appears to have been brain surgery has actually been a fiendish scientific experiment. In Portillo's *Aztec Mummy* films or Cardona's *Santo en el tesoro de Drácula*, science is a means to promote social and cultural progress though it inadvertently produces potentially disastrous consequences: specifically, resurrecting monsters from the past. In contrast, in *Doctor of Doom*, as with *Santo contra la hija de Frankenstein* or *Santo y Blue Demon contra el Dr. Frankenstein*, science serves no useful social function whatsoever, and is only arrogantly committed to producing freakish nightmares of nature. In fact, *Santo y Blue Demon contra el Dr. Frankenstein* is virtually a remake (or even parody) of *Las luchadoras vs. el médico asesino*. Santo and Blue Demon assume the Gloria Venus and Golden Rubi roles, and two *female* detectives, Marta (Ivonne Govea) and Carmen (Sonia Aguilar), fill in for "Mike Henderson" and "Tommy Johnson." (This gender turnabout prompts a hilarious observation by Dr. Frankenstein: "Cops wearing pants don't bother me. It's the ones in skirts that make me uncomfortable.") Additionally, the central premise for both films is identical (a mad scientist kidnaps young women to experiment with brain transplants); key plot points (the entire ending) and specific scenes (the opening brain surgery sequence) are recycled; and even character names are reused ("Alicia," "Dr. Ruiz"). Of course, Alfredo Salazar wrote the story and co-wrote the screenplay for *Santo y Blue Demon contra el Dr. Frankenstein.*

While *Doctor of Doom* serves as a warning about the dangerous potential excesses of science in modern society, the *representation of women* in this critique of scientific progress is also pivotal, and *Doctor of Doom* features a disturbing convergence of science, sadism, and sexism. One of the more unsettling aspects of Cardona's work is the tendency to reduce women and their bodies to scientific "guinea pigs" (and in the case of *El horripilante bestia humana*—or, rather, *Horror y sexo*— "sexy guinea pigs"). In *Santo en el tesoro de Drácula*, the ideal subject for Santo's time machine is a woman; Santo explains that women are "four times less susceptible" to the effects of time travel (presumably for "many biological reasons"), and the burden of testing the time machine inevitably falls upon Santo's fiancée, Luisa. In *Doctor of Doom,* not only do women's bodies fall under the domain of science, but the *status* of women in Mexican society is also defined by science. "Uneducated," and presumably lower-class, women are the initial subjects for these diabolical experiments, in that lower-class women had (and have) the fewest rights in Mexican society and the least amount of say over their bodies. However, the more intelligent, career-orientated, and middle-class a woman is does not signify increased social respectability; rather, it means she is an even *better* candidate for brutal experimentation on her body.

The setting shifts to the *chica moderna* Alice diligently working as a laboratory assistant for the milquetoast scientist Professor Wright. When he discusses Alice's activities from the previous evening with her, the Professor also offers a firm lecture on the dangerous position Alice is placing herself in by cavorting about the city at night without a male escort, especially considering the awful murders of young women that are currently making headlines. Alice dismisses his concerns about her safety, and displays flighty indifference towards such ghastly current events: she insists that she'll be fine because she carries her "lucky rabbit's foot" with her at all times. In this sense, Alice's inevitable death is not only the result of her disregard for social mores, but her belief in an irrational superstition. The sequence in the lab abruptly cuts to a shot of a television set and a news announcer delivering a report about the series of murders of young women in the city. In that no character is shown watching a television (nor does it appear in any other scene), the television report essentially functions as a moment of on-screen narration (inventively disguised as a news broadcast) inserted into the film as a means to provide plot exposition for the viewer. Nonetheless, the announcer delivers his report with all the convoluted oratory one would expect from a Murray import:

Reports show these nocturnal acts are continuing and the police are still accusing that criminal who has caused so much public discussion. Due to his actions, he has been named "the Mad Doctor." The woman he killed last night is in the morgue. She was found early this morning and as always happened, police found marks showing the brain had been removed from the unfortunate girl's body.

Following the TV news report, the scene shifts to the police station, where the viewer is introduced to the two police detectives working the Mad Doctor case: the handsome "leading-man" Mike Henderson and his "comic-relief" sidekick, Tommy Johnson. They have made no progress toward solving the murders, much to the irritation of their portly, chain-smoking, boss ball-busting (Armando Acosta): "I only say that this particular criminal is disconcerting!" From the police conversation about "this disconcerting criminal" the film cuts to the headquarters of the hooded Mad Doctor, who, along with his similarly hooded assistant, appears before a group of hired thugs. This figure of a "mad scientist" *and* "criminal mastermind" certainly borrows from low-budget serials and is common in mexploitation film, specifically the *Aztec Mummy* series (Dr. Krupp/"The Bat") and the later *Santo en el tesoro de Drácula* ("Black Hood," eventually revealed to be a noted scientist, Dr. Kur). The Mad Doctor and his assistant are accompanied by the hulking ape-man Gomar, the hideous product of the Mad Doctor transplanting a gorilla's brain into a man (Gomar is portrayed by Gerardo Zepeda, who seemed to have a monopoly on mexploitation ape-man roles and played virtually identical monsters in *El horripilante bestia humana* and *Santo contra la hija de Frankenstein*). Explaining that Gomar will accompany them to capture their next victim — one he has personally selected — the Mad Doctor hands his henchmen a photo of Alice.

The close-up of the photo dissolves to a shot of Alice working late in the lab, as ominous shadows appear behind her and discordant music bursts forth from the soundtrack. The viewer suspects it is Gomar and the criminals breaking into the lab. However, it turns out to be Professor Wright (another obvious clue to the identity of the Mad Doctor). Again he expresses his concerns for Alice's safety and demands that she go home, even offering to escort her. Alice declines his gentlemanly offer, which predictably leads to her putting herself in the potentially dangerous situation she has already been warned about: being a woman out alone at night in the city. Of course, Alice's reckless disregard for social convention results in her abduction by the Mad Doctor's gang. Unlike the barfly and prostitute who become the early victims of the monster in *The Brainiac*, peripheral females "punished" for their obvious "immorality" and sexual availability to men, Alice is *not* punished for violating sexual codes of conduct, but simply because she has the audacity to be an unmarried, career-minded *chica moderna* who walks the streets of Mexico at night without benefit of proper male escort. Like the film's opening violent abduction, Alice's kidnapping also takes place on dark city streets, again

112

recalling the gritty violence directed against women in American sexploitation roughies rather than the comic book exaggerations and horror film clichés of most mexploitation films. However, seemingly to diffuse the *noir* depiction of the abduction, played out in all its sinister realism, the film immediately and abruptly veers back into the parodic, comic excesses of mexploitation horror. The very next shot shows the taxi the criminals are using almost running into a police roadblock. Gomar is ordered to handle the cops; having foreseen this very possibility, the Mad Doctor devised a hilarious bulletproof suit for the ape-man: a mask and bulky suit apparently made of sheet metal and flannel underwear. As bullets ricochet off him, Gomar murders a few police officers with his bare hands and some lucha libre body slams, allowing the criminals to escape with Alice.

The experiment, however, is a complete disaster, and Alice quickly dies on the operating table. The Mad Doctor concludes that the failure of his brain transplants was the result of focusing on the "intellectual capacity" of his victims. Realizing it made no difference whether he used a lower-class "uneducated" woman or a middle-class "professional woman with a high IQ," the Mad Doctor concludes that they must next try the experiment on a woman of great *physical* prowess who might withstand the shock of the brain transplant. At its most sexist, the film demonstrates a ruthless Cartesian separation of the mind and body, suggesting not only that "the mind" is distinct and separable from "the body," but that the brain, or "the mind," of a woman is simply an interchangeable, irrelevant element easily exchanged between bodies, given the proper subjects. Regardless of whether a woman is "uneducated" or "intelligent," the success of transplanting the brain (*mind*) from one woman to the next is entirely dependent on the resiliency of her *body*. In short, the status of the woman in Mexican society is that she is *a body* first and foremost, and *a mind* second. The Mad Doctor informs his henchmen that they "must find women of incredible physical stamina, but at the moment I don't know where to start to look for them."

In obvious answer to the Mad Doctor's question, the film cuts to a scene of various luchadoras working out in the gym. Naturally, the physically impressive body of a luchadora is best suited for the next phase of the Mad Doctor's cruel experimentation on the female body. As well as introducing Golden Rubi into the narrative, the film's focus on wrestling training sessions is important for two contradictory reasons. One, it allows a degree of sexual fetishization of the female body itself by the camera, and often times the scenes in the gym simply serve as a means to display Gloria and Golden Rubi in wrestling tights that accentuate their well-endowed figures. However, the luchadora gym also becomes a female homeosocial space where *women* can exercise power in a male-dominated culture. In a scene probably included simply as comic relief, a muscular man walks into the gym and helps himself to the ladies' weightlifting equipment. When a luchadora objects, he puts his palm in her face and rudely shoves her to the ground. Rather than "lie down and take it," the rest of the luchadoras react with a furious barrage of throws and kicks before piling on the now-humbled and helpless man. Gloria and Rubi react by heartily laughing at the embarrassing predicament the man has brought upon himself with his macho conceit, and it is at this point that *Doctor of Doom* begins to problemize, parody, and even subvert gender politics; and the critique grows more pronounced as the film progresses.

After Gloria and Golden Rubi meet, the camera once again enters the most intimate area of luchadora life, the women's locker room. Gloria and Golden Rubi sit close to each other on the massage table and begin to untie their wrestling boots, briefly encouraging the male spectator's hopes that not only will he see them undress, but that the luchadoras may actually make out. Their intimacy and the implied possibility of a lesbian relationship between the two is exaggerated by the next sequence: a lengthy close-up head shot of Golden Rubi expressing her admiration for and concern about Gloria; while Gloria, in turn, invites Golden Rubi to move in with her to ease her loneliness after the recent death of her sister Alice. To solidify their new relationship, an obligatory wrestling match follows, featuring the newly-formed tag-team of Gloria Venus and Golden Rubi, who are pitted against two squat, rotund luchadoras, "Bertha Galindo" and the rather ironically-named *La Gacela* ("the Gazelle"). This information is provided by a poster outside the arena advertising the match, which the film viewer is able to read as the camera focuses on it and slowly pans downward (since the poster is in Spanish, in *Doctor of Doom* a voice-over narrator explains the necessary information in English). The inclusion of the poster suggests an attempt to give a certain air of "authenticity" to the match. Additionally, not only do numerous extras play the parts of match spectators, but Cardona liberally intercuts stock footage of actual excited lucha libre fans into the action to further make the matches appear real. At one point in the match, Tommy even encourages Mike to "join in" and boo La Gacela as she egotistically prances about the ring, perhaps cueing the film audience to join in and boo as well — to treat the film as an actual wrestling match rather than a narrative film (Mexican film audiences would often join in and vocally express their support or disdain for the onscreen wrestlers). In this way, the insertion of stock footage of crowds cheering the action not only attempts to give the wrestling match a sense of realism, it also provides a reminder for the film audience to "join in" and directly participate in the onscreen matches.

At the level of developing the narrative, the match is important because Professor Wright, who previously expressed a strong distaste for the violence of lucha libre to Alice, can be seen in the front row of the arena. Mike and Tommy also show up for the match, under the pretext of their detective work but obviously for the voyeuristic enjoyment of watching women wrestle. Aware that Mike has both a professional and romantic interest in Gloria, Tommy cautions him, "You better watch out and not get fresh with her because she'll put her foot in your mouth, sonny — and so long teeth!" The film at once admits that the spectacle of the luchadora is a sexual thrill for the male spectator, yet also cautions the male spectator that he may only "look, but don't touch." Much like how Norma's relationship with her wrestling boyfriend (Santo) is limited to voyeuristic sexual pleasure without physical contact in *Santo vs. la hija de Frankenstein*, Mike's romantic interest in Gloria is similarly defined by voyeuristic desire. Indeed, if the male spectator (Mike) risks "getting fresh" and intruding on the space of the female fetish object of his voyeuristic interest (Gloria), he may end up facing dire physical consequences. In short, the sex object in the form of the *luchadora* is not necessarily a "passive" object existing solely for male visual pleasure, but one that can literally fight back if her space is invaded.

While the bodies of Velázquez and Campbell are fetishized by their wrestling tights, the wrestling action is ultimately more strange and surreal than exciting, let alone erotic. Velázquez and Campbell are doubled by actual wrestlers, and the substitutions are painfully obvious to the film viewer, particularly in Velázquez's case (her stunt-double is noticeably shorter and heavier). This is not to say that any sexual excitement is negated by the appearance of a "less attractive" body, but rather that the male spectator must continually orientate himself between the *two* distinct bodies representing Gloria, resulting in continual breaks in verisimilitude, and denying the scenes any chance to create an idealized, fetishized female body. The match produces further estrangement between the film and audience as it becomes clear that much of the match has previously been seen in the opening credits. Besides the sense of *déjà vu,* this produces a certain degree of confusion as to how the match fits in with the narrative proper. Whereas Santo films insert straight lucha libre matches between luchadores, which demand the audience temporarily "unsuture" themselves from the horror film narrative in favor of watching lucha libre spectacle on its own merits, this wrestling sequence in *Doctor of Doom* not only *detaches* the viewer from the narrative, but completely *bewilders* the viewer.

The match concludes with Gloria and Golden Rubi victorious, and they hug triumphantly in the ring. This dissolves to a shot of Professor Wright tentatively knocking on the door of the locker room, and the women inviting him inside. In one of the more intriguing shots from the film, the camera tracks Professor Wright walking from outside the locker room door, through the door itself, and into the locker room, all in a single shot (the hallway and locker room are obviously a set rather than an actual location). Once again, the shot establishes the unlimited power of the camera to "penetrate female spaces" (so to speak). While Professor Wright must be "invited" into the private, gender exclusive space of the women wrestlers, the camera can, and *does*, enter and intrude on their space at will, literally "moving through walls." Within moments, Mike pokes his head through the open door, surveys the scene inside the locker room, and *then* asks, "Mind if I come in?" His polite request to be admitted into the locker room is merely a formality in that he has *already* physically entered their space. Tommy follows, and the detectives are introduced to Golden Rubi, who promptly sets Tommy cringing from the power of her handshake: a comic parody of the masculine ethic of having a firm handshake. When expressing their surprise at seeing Professor Wright at the match, he again stresses that he is not a wrestling fan, but only came to deliver some information about on Alice's fiancé that the police might find useful. He departs, and the detectives quickly invite the luchadoras out for "supper and dancing," dispelling any potential lesbian relationship between Gloria and Golden Rubi by establishing an important heterosexual counterpoint of two romantic couples — Gloria and Mike, Golden Rubi and Tommy — in relation to the male couple (leading man/comic relief) and especially the female couple (the luchadora tag-team).

After their exhausting match and romantic evening of "supper and dancing" with Mike and Tommy, Gloria and Golden Rubi sleep in Gloria's bedroom: Gloria in pajamas and Golden Rubi in a frilly nightgown. Shadowy figures can be seen at the window, and their presence awakens Golden Rubi, who alerts Gloria. Gloria convinces her to pretend she is still asleep, and both lie in bed awaiting the intruders. However, when the Mad Doctor's henchmen enter their bedroom through the window and attempt to abduct them, the two luchadoras bolt out of bed and effortlessly pummel the intruders to the strains of overwrought, *film noir*–style jazz. The sequence creates a hilarious dichotomy between the fetishized, idealized image of the Mexican woman and their unlikely "masculine" power and behavior. The men are sent scurrying out the bedroom window in defeat, and the ironic social commentary and comedy is certainly not lost on Cardona. In an ingenious bit of filmmaking, a profile shot of Gloria and Golden Ruby looking left, out the bedroom window in profile, slowly dissolves to a profile shot of one of the Mad Doctor's beaten henchmen, also looking to his left. He occupies the exact same position in the film frame as Golden Rubi in the previous shot, and through this dissolve one witnesses nothing short of the transformation of a woman into a man and a man into a woman: their faces and bodies temporarily blur into one genderless form. By virtue of defending herself in a "masculine" manner, Golden Rubi becomes a "man"; conversely, by taking the brunt of a "masculine" beating, the henchman becomes a "woman." The camera pans left, revealing two more beaten henchmen: faces bruised, eyes blackened, their suits in disarray. Accompanied by comic, mocking music (of the type usually reserved for cartoon animation), the pan allows the viewer to dwell on the henchmen's hilarious, humiliating, and emasculating embarrassment at the hands of Gloria and Golden Rubi. To add insult to injury, the pan stops at the Mad Doctor standing in his hood and gown, while Harry ("Marcado" in *Las luchadoras vs. el médico asesino*) pathetically complains: "But look, chief, why didn't you tell us those two girls were *wrestlers*? You should've seen the way they threw me around!" Further irony comes from the fact that Harry is played by Jesús "Murciélago" Velázquez, a legendary rudo in the lucha libre world known for his ruthlessness and toughness in the wrestling ring, and quite possibly the last person the Mexican public would believe could be beaten up by two women in their night clothes. Unmoved, the Mad Doctor berates the men for their pathetic display of masculinity. Despite the overt elements of sexism and misogyny that underscore the film, *Doctor of Doom* also demonstrates a satirical questioning and even potential subversion of traditional gender roles established by the horror genre, as well as Mexican society.

This segues into perhaps the most perverse moment of the film. A high-angle shot shows Gloria, seated in profile on the right side of the frame, gazing upward at an unseen male's face; directly across from her face on the left is a man's *crotch*. The shot implies the act of fellatio: Gloria is about to administer, or has just finished administering, oral sex on the man. The shot zooms out to reveal Mike standing next to her: it is *his* crotch adjacent to her face. Far from complimenting her on her (masculine) reaction to the abduction, Mike admonishes her: "If they do return, it is best if you react in *another* manner — that is, if you intend in helping *the law*" (emphasis added). Gloria's wonderful, indignant reply: "I think you could talk *plainer!*" Assuming there will be another abduction attempt directed at the luchadoras, Mike suggests they *allow* themselves to be kidnapped and taken to the Mad Doctor's hideout; Mike and Tommy will follow and triumphantly arrest the Mad Doctor and his gang. The very idea that Gloria and Golden Rubi should allow themselves to be abducted is important for two reasons. One, it corrects the evident cracks developing in the horror genre by suggesting that women assume their "proper" role in the horror film as passive victims while men retain the status of heroes and rescuers (in *Santo y Blue Demon contra el Dr. Frankenstein* this issue becomes a moot point by having *luchadores* Santo and Blue Demon replace the luchadoras, and *women* replace the men as detectives). Two, it suggests that the status of a woman's body is not simply as an object for *science* to explore at will, but an object for *the law* to exploit and manipulate for its own ends as well.[9] This becomes manifest in the aforementioned first shot of the sequence, in which Gloria assumes a submissive posture in relation to Mike and his crotch. Between this emphasis on his penis and his role as a police officer, he embodies the phallocentric order of the Law itself. In short, what Mike expects, even demands, is that Gloria and Golden Rubi conform to the needs of a patriarchal order if they "intend on helping the law [the Law]." In this way, male domination over the domain of the female body is not only presented in the evil and brutal excesses of *science* exhibited by the Mad Doctor, but by the police, *the law* itself (embodied by Mike and his crotch), which essentially demands that the women conform to and "donate" their bodies to the law to serve its own purposes.

Further complicating and hilariously satirizing the relationship between *the law* and *the woman* is the burgeoning romantic relationship between the statuesque Golden Rubi and the diminutive Tommy. After Mike explains his plan, a profile shot shows Golden Rubi on the right and Tommy on the left. He is at least six inches shorter than her, his head at the level of her breasts. "Don't worry, baby doll, I intend to watch out for you," Tommy proudly proclaims, his gaze directed entirely at her bosom. Golden Rubi responds by lifting him off his feet by his collar and kissing him. "I feel safe and protected!" she purrs, and then drops him in a heap into a chair. Her actions clearly parody and utterly mock her adoring words: Golden Rubi is the strong and protective partner in the relationship, Tommy's superior in every way.

Following the plan of the law, Gloria and Golden Rubi wander the dark city streets in their clinging white sweaters and tight black pants, acting as seductive female "bait" for the Mad Doctor. Of course, the Mad Doctor's henchmen attempt another abduction, utilizing the ape-man Gomar (once again clad in his iron mask and bullet-proof clothing). Rendering the two women unconscious with blows to the head, Gomar carries them to a waiting car, one under each arm. Mike and Tommy follow and locate the Mad Doctor's hideout, but are easily overcome by his assistant and his gang. With the men (the law) failing to execute their part of the plan, it is left to the wrestling women to save the day. Gloria fortunately regains consciousness and revives Golden Rubi, and it is through the efforts of the luchadoras that the Mad Doctor's gang and his loyal assistant are apprehended. His hood removed, the Mad Doctor's assistant is revealed to be Boris, Dr. Wright's assistant (at this point the film practically screams out the true identity of the Mad Doctor, but no one seems to be listening). Boris is taken to police headquarters, but suddenly and mysteriously dies at the moment he is about to reveal the Mad Doctor's identity. The police discover that Boris was killed by a poison needle fired by a mechanism hidden in someone's mouth, presumably the Mad Doctor's. Though explicitly stated that the only people in the room were the police, the luchadoras, the arrested henchman, and Professor Wright, and so the Mad Doctor has to be one of them, no one deduces the identity of the prime suspect. In fact, the scene ends with Mike facetiously noting that the Mad Doctor may be Professor Wright, who nods, "That's right...." Connecting Professor Wright's "admission" to the next shot, the scene dissolves to the hooded Mad Doctor himself, laughing proudly and maniacally: "Once again, I've made the police look like fools!" He orders his remaining henchman, Harry, to round up some more thugs in order to put his next plan into effect: the murder of "that detective and his stupid sidekick ... I'm going to set a *good* trap!"

Dressed for action: detectives in business suits, wrestling women in form-fitting tights in *Doctor of Doom.* **From left to right: Lorena Velázquez, Armando Silvestre, Elizabeth Campbell, and Chucho Salinas. (Courtesy Rob Craig.)**

The scene shifts to the luchador gymnasium. Mike and Tommy nonchalantly walk in, and Mike casually leans against the parallel bars and lewdly nudges Tommy, pointing out that they can watch the luchadoras train. "The law" is not only free to enter exclusively female spaces of its own volition (the locker room, the gym), but can even engage in some quick voyeurism. After marveling at a wrestling demonstration by a new luchadora, Gloria and Golden Rubi happily greet their new boyfriends the detectives in their officious business suits contrasting hilariously with the luchadoras in their figure-enhancing wrestling tights. Mike explains that he will give Gloria and Golden Rubi radio-watches that will allow them to stay in contact at all times, thus allowing the law to constantly monitor the women. The scene also has Tommy and Golden Rubi engaging in some additional absurdist romantic banter. Golden Rubi remarks that the radio-watches are "marvelous, really," to which Tommy responds, "Not as marvelous as you, you lovely redhead." Rubi caresses his cheek with her hand and says, "I'd say the same thing about you, you five-foot lightning bolt [?!]." Tommy swoons, "This woman loves me *dearly!*"

In a deliberate attempt to throw the audience off course, Professor Wright is seen being held at gunpoint by two of the Mad Doctor's hooded henchmen. Forced to call Mike and Tommy and lure them to his home, Professor Wright apologizes profusely when the criminals abduct the detectives. At the Mad Doctor's laboratory hideout, Cardona offers a wonderfully exaggerated, clichéd shot of Mike and Tommy surrounded by the Mad Doctor's gang. The Mad Doctor's ominous, oversized shadow looms in profile on the wall, diabolically pointing as he portentously orders the detectives taken downstairs and thrown into the "Death Chamber" located next to Gomar's cell. A wonderfully excessive and devious device culled from comic books or serials, the Death Chamber is a small room bordered by Gomar's cage on one side and a wall of spikes (that slowly move towards Gomar's cage) on the other. The victims will be crushed into bloody pulps which Gomar can then devour like his rations of raw meat. With a painful death imminent, Mike anxiously contacts Gloria via the watch-radio, and sends a homing signal to lead for the luchadores to them. The radio-watches are thus used to affect the exact *opposite* of their intended purpose: rather than allowing the masculine order of the law to monitor the women, they must now be used so the women can locate and rescue the men. While Mike and Gloria frantically coordinate a rescue, Tommy and Golden Rubi find time to engage in another hilarious exchange. "You better hurry, honey," Tommy pleads, "or we are not going to walk down the altar together!" Golden Rubi's reply: "Don't say such things, small hero — I'll be there like white lightning!" Desperately awaiting their rescue by the luchadoras, our heroes (to use the term loosely) struggle to survive in the Death Chamber, their frantic efforts producing broad, even surreal, slapstick comedy instead of dramatic tension (whether the comedy is intentional is open to interpretation). Mike hoists Tommy over his head, and the small man sets himself perpendicular to Gomar's cage and the spiked wall, temporarily stopping its crushing movement toward them. With Gomar flailing his arms through the cage, it's as if Luis Buñuel directed a Republic Studios serial starring Dean Martin and Jerry Lewis.

Thus, at the film's most critical dramatic point, it is yet again the women who must now rescue the male heroes and preserve the masculine law. Again clad in matching tight white sweaters and black slacks, Gloria and Golden Rubi follow the signal, somehow astonished that it leads to the very same building where Boris and the first batch of henchmen were captured. Proceeding to the basement, the luchadoras are ambushed by the Mad Doctor's henchmen in black hoods. Gloria and Golden Rubi quickly and easily dispatch them with a furious display of wrestling moves and fisticuffs, and the criminals beat a hasty retreat while the luchadoras rescue their detective boyfriends (again). Once more, by adopting the masculine role of rescuers of their inadequate boyfriends, they hilariously place genre and gender stereotypes in question. The Mad Doctor himself is finally cornered in his lab, and it is *Gloria* rather than Mike who physically confronts the villain, first punching him in the jaw and then throwing a vial of acid in his face. As he throws himself about the lab in agony, the Mad Doctor knocks over volatile chemicals and a fire erupts around him. The viewer fully expects the film to end at this point, especially when Gloria states, "I guess this is the end of the Mad Doctor," and Mike adds, "You know, it's a shame we couldn't find out his *real* identity, but he's paid for all his crimes now!" However, after everyone flees the burning lab, Gomar escapes from his cell and rescues the Mad Doctor, carrying him to safety. The highly episodic construction of the film's plot, and in particular this false ending, certainly reflects the influence of serials, although the more cynical viewer might argue that the film needed an additional final battle between the luchadoras and the Mad Doctor simply because it would not have been long enough otherwise.

In any event, the scene returns to the gym where the luchadoras are back at work, training for their upcoming matches, the threat of the Mad Doctor apparently ended. However, when the promoter asks Gloria if she has seen the new wrestler, who has been missing for two days, Gloria gasps, "*Is it possible?*" The shot of the pensive Gloria cuts to a shot of the Mad Doctor, his back to the camera, his henchman Harry facing him. Explaining that it is time Harry learned his "true identity," the Mad Doctor lifts the hood and reveals his face, the camera zooming in to a close-up reaction shot of Harry. "It's not *possible!*" gasps Harry, echoing Gloria's amazemen; but once again, it *is* possible. The scene abruptly switches back to the gym, where the promoter announces that he is going to "phone the police." Immediately afterward, an off-camera woman's voice informs Gloria that she is "wanted on the phone." The dialogue and twin references to the phone link the promoter's phone call to the police to Gloria being "wanted on the phone" (as if he were actually calling *her*), ironically implying that Gloria has indeed become "the police," the embodiment of the phallocentric law in the form of a masculine woman. Indeed, in many ways Gloria and Golden Rubi *have* become "the law," all but officially displacing their feeble detective boyfriends in bringing justice and order to Mexico.

However, it is actually Professor Wright phoning Gloria, inquiring into her wrestling schedule for what the viewer soon learns is far from polite curiosity about her career. Wright is shown only in profile from the left side, and when he hangs up the phone his voice becomes quite sinister. He turns to face the camera, exposing the now-hideously scarred right side of his face — the result of the acid thrown by Gloria. Coming as absolutely no surprise, Professor Wright is (finally) revealed to be the Mad Doctor. Vowing revenge against Gloria, Professor Wright devises a fiendish plan: transplant Gomar's gorilla brain into the body of the missing woman wrestler he abducted and use the monster to murder Gloria in the wrestling ring. The scheme becomes particularly important because the Mad Doctor does not simply combine an animal (ape) with a human (man), creating a *social* aberration of "man" and "beast"; by combining Gomar's ape brain with a *woman* (the luchadora), he creates a *sexual* aberration as well: an *ape-man-woman,* with Gomar's tremendous, primitive, and *masculine* power placed in the body of a woman. The Mad Doctor names his new creation "Vendetta" in obvious reference to his plan to kill Gloria, and adorns her in a wrestling outfit and black mask with a white lightning bolt on the forehead (at the risk of over-interpreting, this makes Vendetta a "five-foot lightning bolt" like Tommy). Via some plot exposition (allowing Roberto Cañedo to indulge in some wonderful overacting), Professor Wright explains that Vendetta is under his complete "hypnotic" control and will unquestioningly serve his evil designs. Early in the film, when Gomar's brain was in the body of a *man*, the Mad Doctor mentioned the great difficulty he had in hypnotically controlling his creation; with Gomar's brain now housed in a *woman*'s body, the Mad Doctor can easily and completely control the creature via hypnosis, even at "great distances" (recalling Count Dracula's seemingly limitless long-distance hypnotic power over women in *Santo y Blue Demon contra Drácula y el Hombre Lobo*). "Tremble, Gloria Venus! *Trrr-emmm-ble!!*" the Mad Doctor insanely proclaims in close-up, bursting into devious laughter.

Now acting as Vendetta's manager, Professor Wright abandons the surgical mask and hood that previously hid his true identity and signified him as both "mad scientist" (surgical mask) and "criminal mastermind" (hood). He now wears a lucha libre mask decorated with the visage of a demonic monster, thus giving Professor Wright a *new* evil role in the film: *rudo.* He issues a public challenge to Gloria to wrestle Vendetta for the championship title, which Gloria accepts. With the stage set for a find battle between Gloria and Vendetta in the ring, the horror film narrative becomes integrated with the spectacle of lucha libre action for the climactic confrontation of the film. As with the previous match, a poster advertising the bout between Gloria and Vendetta is shown, the camera slowly panning downward so the audience can read the advertising material (again an English voice-over in *Doctor of Doom* summarizes the Spanish poster). However, the match itself is proceeded by another brief intrusion by the camera into the gender exclusive space of the women's locker room. While Golden Rubi expresses her concerns over the impending match, Gloria confidently lounges on a massage table in her wrestling tights, striking a somewhat contorted and stylized pose as she ties her boots. The tableaux is reminiscent of a pin-up photograph, and the camera certainly takes advantage of the moment to fetishize Gloria's body. This fetishization continues when Gloria enters the ring, with the camera focusing on her as she holds the ring

Luchadora Gloria Venus (Lorena Velázquez*)* meets masked *rudos* the Mad Doctor and ape-man-woman Vendetta in *Doctor of Doom.*

ropes, and stretches and poses her body into several more pin-up style positions. Introduced to her adoring fans by the ring announcer as "the champion of our people," Gloria Venus becomes a national allegory representing both the idealized, sexy, Mexican *chica moderna* and the "masculine" power fighting against the scientific/sexual/social monster Vendetta (who is said to be from Paris, thus coding her as a European threat as well).

Indicative of how Cardona filmed many of the wrestling matches for his *Luchadoras* and *Santo* films, a static, high-angle long shot assumes a spectator's position over one of the corners of the ring, allowing the whole ring to be shown in a sort of diamond shape within the confines of the film frame. This shot allows the viewer to see the entire ring and assume the position of a wrestling fan in the arena itself, thus promoting a sense of recreating an actual lucha libre match experience for the film audience. Intercut with this long, high-angle shot of the match are inserts of medium shots from outside the ring and close-ups of the luchadoras battling inside the ring, and it is through alternating the long and medium shots of stunt doubles with the close-ups of Velázquez (and Campbell) that Cardona records the matches (as noted, the success of blending the actresses and their stunt doubles onscreen is inconsistent, to say the least). As the match progresses it is quickly evident that Vendetta combines the role of horror film monster and the classic rudo—she employs a variety of illegal tactics, the most obvious being an attempt to strangle Gloria with her bare hands while the Mad Doctor encourages Vendetta to kill Gloria through his hypnotic power. Fortunately, while Gloria is being mercilessly assaulted in the ring, Golden Rubi intervenes. Recognizing Harry in the crowd, she chases him under the bleachers and applies a painful wrestling hold on his arm. Essentially torturing him physically, she extracts a full confession: Harry informs her that Vendetta's manager is actually the Mad Doctor who is actually Professor Wright, and Vendetta is going to kill Gloria in the ring. Summoning the police to arrest Harry, Golden Rubi then enters the ring to stop Vendetta's assault on Gloria. Her efforts serve as stark contrast to those of Mike and Tommy, sitting ringside, who are apparently too wrapped up in the voyeuristic spectacle of the "cat-fight" to notice (or care about) the potential danger Vendetta poses. In one hilarious shot, Vendetta strangles Golden Rubi in the corner of the ring, just above Mike and Tommy's ringside seats: the two detectives turn and stare at each other, dumbfounded, seemingly unable — or unwilling — to interfere. Despite being able to enter *private* female spaces at will (the gym, the locker room), the men, or "the law," cannot or will not enter the *public* female space of luchadora spectacle in the ring, and must remain only passive, albeit agitated, spectators (perhaps because if they do violate the space of the luchadora spectacle in the ring, it's "so long, teeth!"). Indeed, their involvement is literally reduced to the rules of participation allowed by lucha libre: cheering and booing as spectators rather than physically intervening in the melee as agents of the law.

As the match disintegrates, Vendetta, urged on by the Mad Doctor, alternates her vicious assaults between Gloria, Golden Rubi, and even the referee, who vainly tries to preserve order in the wrestling ring. Finally, Golden Rubi relays the vital information regarding the true identity of Vendetta's manager to Mike and Tommy, who promptly set off in pursuit of Professor Wright (unable or unwilling to take any action against Vendetta in the ring, they immediately pursue the male Mad Doctor). Summoning Vendetta via his hypnotic powers, the two flee, and the Mad Doctor strangely decides that the best place to escape from the police is atop a water tower. With the film now about to officially end, traditional gender roles in the horror genre almost miraculously return to normal. Mike and Tommy suddenly assume the masculine roles of heroes, while Gloria and Golden Rubi literally become reduced to helpless bystanders, their involvement in the conclusion of the film reduced to close-up reaction shots as they pensively watch the scene unfold with their mouths agape. While the horrid Vendetta must be expunged from the film for being a sexual and social aberration — an ape-man-woman — it can also be said that Gloria and Golden Rubi are *also* sexual and social aberrations–masculine women in a society of "brutal sexism" — and must be returned to their proper gender roles before the film can end: perhaps the greatest moment of "narrative punishment" in the film.

Mike climbs up the water tower to confront the Mad Doctor and Vendetta "man to man," and "man to ape-man-woman," respectively. Tommy, demonstrating surprising and considerable marksmanship, shoots both the villains from his vantage point on the ground, sending them plummeting to their deaths. Professor Wright is finally unmasked by Mike, who carries the mask like a trophy, again recalling the symbolics of lucha libre rather than the horror film. By unmasking the villain, Mike achieves masculine mastery over him, and he holds the mask as if it were an emasculated opponent's severed penis. Proudly, he consoles Gloria: "Don't worry — it's all over now. Your sister has been avenged." Mike takes full credit for bringing Professor Wright to justice, signified by the symbolic castration of the villain by the phallic Law. The heroic deeds of the luchadoras throughout the film are conveniently ignored and even forgotten in the end. With the return of normal gender roles in the horror film, normalcy is also restored to Mexican society, a normalcy that must include the inequality of women. Ultimately, however, *Doctor of Doom* can neither escape sexism nor successfully perpetuate it. As the film attempts to finally establish the phallocentric order of the law (the Law), it has left too many obvious contradictions in its wake through the critical role the luchadora plays in the film, continually upstaging and besting the men. The foundation the film lays for a patriarchal order is revealed to have numerous all-too-visible flaws.

Las luchadoras contra la momia
(Wrestling Women vs. the Aztec Mummy, *1964)*

Las luchadoras contra la momia is sometimes considered part of the *Aztec Mummy* film series, which actually only encompassed the three *Aztec Mummy* films made by Rafael Portillo in 1957. Understandably, this perception is fueled by *Wrestling Women*'s abrupt shift from a serial-style action film pitting the luchadoras against the evil Asian "Black Dragon" secret society to a horror-film finale featuring a resurrected Aztec mummy. Moreover, *Wrestling Women* does not simply allude to Portillo's films but includes footage from *La momia azteca* to explain the origins of the Aztec treasure and curse. However, as the original Spanish title suggests, the Wrestling Women are simply battling "the mummy," with the specific reference to the fabled "Aztec Mummy" of previous films an advertising addition to the title on K. Gordon Murray's part. While *Wrestling Women* certainly references and even parodies Portillo's *Aztec Mummy* saga, it does not follow the *Aztec Mummy* films as such, and neither features nor chronicles the further adventures of any of the characters or situations originally seen in Portillo's films.

Rather, *Las luchadoras contra la momia* is a direct sequel to *Las luchadoras vs. el médico asesino*, and all the principal actors reprise their roles, albeit with minor name changes: Lorena Velázquez is now "Loreta Venus" instead of "Gloria Venus," Armando Silvestre is now "Armando Ríos" rather than "Armando Campos," and Chucho Salinas becomes "Chucho Gómez," rather than "Chema" (Elizabeth Campbell remains "Golden Rubi"). Moreover, these name changes match the first name of the character with the first name of the actor playing that character: Armando Silvestre is still appropriately "Armando," Chucho Salinas is now "Chucho," and Lorena Velázquez becomes "Loreta" (the "t" in her character's name simply substituted for the "n" in her real first name). A "self-reflexivity" is established, a conscious effort made to blur the separation between "character" and "actor" and dismantle the illusion between reality and fiction by giving the main characters identical or nearly-identical names as the actors.' One assumes these changes would not go unnoticed by the Mexican audiences for whom the film was intended. In Hollywood it would be unthinkable to change a character's name for a sequel (for instance, changing Bruce Willis' "John McClane" in *Die Hard* to "Bruce McClane" without explanation in the subsequent *Die Hard* sequels). Tellingly, Murray's English-language versions provide more continuity between the two films, with Silvestre again called "Mike Henderson" and Salinas "Tommy (Johnson)" in *Wrestling Women vs. the Aztec Mummy*.

The title's emphasis on the mummy is highly misleading in that the mummy does not even appear until the final stages of the film. One is reminded of the "false advertising" in *The Robot vs. the Aztec Mummy*, where the much-anticipated battle promised by the title is an extremely brief confrontation crammed into the final few minutes of the film (the robot itself does not even appear until the last quarter-hour). A more accurate title for *Las luchadoras contra la momia* might be *Las luchadoras contra el Dragón Negro* (*Wrestling Women vs. the Black Dragon*), in that much of the film is devoted to the struggle of the film's heroes against the Black Dragon and its attempts to steal the ancient Aztec treasures.[10] In this way, the Black Dragon serves as a metaphor for a foreign power and "alien value system" threatening mexicanidad by attempting to plunder Mexico of its cultural heritage, with the role the Black Dragon plays in the film and its obvious threat to mexicanidad setting a rather reactionary tone for the film. Beyond the degree of racism the film generates by the stereotypical depiction of Asians (all played by Mexican actors), *Wrestling*

Women conflates Japanese and Chinese cultures into one blanket category of "Yellow Peril." The Black Dragon is lead by Prince Fujiyata (Ramón Bugarini), with his judo-expert sisters providing the muscle in the organization: the name "Fujiyata" is Japanese, and judo is a Japanese form of martial arts. However, with his ornate robes and hat, not to mention his droopy mustache, Prince Fujiyata is obviously modeled on the legendary Chinese criminal mastermind Fu Manchu from Sax Rohmer's novels, and most famously brought to life on the screen by Boris Karloff in *The Mask of Fu Manchu* (1932, dir. Charles Brabin).[11] To explicitly add the contemporary specter of revolutionary Communism into the Black Dragon's overall Oriental menace, one of Prince Fujiyata's henchmen is named "Mao" (played by the decidedly non–Asian Jesús "Murciélago" Velázquez). This obvious reference to Chairman Mao Tse-Tung, then leader of Communist China, would be lost on American audiences because the character's name is continually mispronounced as "Mayo" in Murray's dubbed version.[12] As noted, such an Asiatic threat to Mexico as that seen in *Las luchadoras contra la momia* would appear in subsequent Cardona films where Santo or Blue Demon battle Asian criminals and spies (*Operación 67, El tesoro de Moctezuma, La mafia amarilla*). Moreover, an anti–Communist message would also be in keeping with contemporary Mexican politics of the early 1960s, an era of Communist activity in Latin America. Fidel Castro came to power in Cuba in 1959 and joined the Soviet Bloc in 1961, becoming the first Marxist-Leninist country in the Western Hemisphere.[13] Marxist insurgency movements were also active in a number of Latin American countries in the early 1960s: Guatemala, Venezuela, Columbia, and Peru. And, while Mexican foreign policy was fairly ambivalent about Communism abroad, there was a profound concern over the spread of communism within its *own* borders, with Mexican presidential administrations of the Cold War–era adopting staunch, even repressive anti–Communist political measures.[14] *Las luchadoras contra la momia* was made in the twilight of the López Mateos administration; and while claiming to pursue policies not merely of the "left" but the "extreme left," the López Mateos administration stressed mexicanidad, capitalist development, and democratic ideals rather than socialist revolution (during Mateos' presidency, Communist activists were fired from their positions in schools and labor unions, and sometimes jailed outright).[15] In this political context, the primary focus of *Wrestling Women* becomes a cultural battle — or "national allegory" — fought between the luchadoras (Mexico, democracy) and the Black Dragon (Asia, communism), culminating in a highly public battle for cultural superiority in the wrestling ring between the luchadoras and the Fujiyata sisters.

Wrestling Women begins with the credits shown over quasi-documentary footage of Aztec ruins. While obviously inferring the critical role played by the Aztec Mummy, which the film only belatedly provides, the images do suggest the importance and centrality of Aztec *history* and the film's central theme of whether Mexico or an obtrusive "foreign" culture will control Mexico's ancient past. Following the credits, the film suddenly shifts to a tone more fitting of *film noir,* strongly recalling the beginning of *Doctor of Doom.* In the first shot, a car careens down a dark city street into the foreground, and a body is roughly thrown out of the car. This cuts to a newspaper headline reporting the murder of a prominent archeologist by the criminal Black Dragon organization. A long shot of a car on a desolate stretch of road follows, and a body is again tossed from the car into a ditch. A second newspaper headline detail's the disappearance of a second scientist, Dr. Van Dine. The scene then switches to a close-up of a bloodied man laying on a table, with the camera panning upward to reveal an evil, menacing Oriental: Prince Fujiyata in his full Asian regalia. Not only resembling Fu Manchu, Fujiyata shares Fu Manchu's delight in torturing Westerners, and he smiles sadistically as smoke billows from the bottom of the frame: the shot cuts back to the man on the table, with a smoldering cattle brand now pressed against his chest.

The scene dissolves to another *noir* shot of the city at night. The viewer sees a visibly upset man, later revealed to be archeologist Dr. Mike Sorva (Julián de Meriche, his character name changed from "Miguel Sorva" in *Las luchadoras contra la momia*). Aware he is being followed by Mao, Dr. Sorva seeks refuge at the National Arena, where luchadora matches are being held. His arrival also allows the film to shift to a lucha libre sequence, which has no bearing on the plot, forcing the (American) spectator to delay any narrative gratification. In a shameless bit of film recycling, this first lucha libre sequence in *Wrestling Women* is actually the same match footage shown (twice) in the previous *Doctor of Doom.* However, while the wrestling footage is recycled, the sequence offers three new reaction shots of Lorena Velázquez standing in the corner of the ring watching Golden Rubi wrestle. Unfortunately, Velázquez now sports a much different, shorter hairstyle than she wore in *Doctor of Doom.* The intercutting between two-year-old wrestling footage of Velázquez in the ring, an obviously different stunt double, and the new reaction shots (with alternate hairstyle) make for quite obvious lapses in continuity and produce a jarring, estranging effect on the viewer. Needless to say, Loreta Venus and Golden Rubi emerge victorious (how could they not?— they've won the same match *three* times over the course of two films!), and they return to the privacy of the women's locker room. As in *Doctor of Doom,* the locker room only affords somewhat limited privacy. While the male *characters* may not freely enter the women's sanctuary, the *camera* (and the male film spectator) has unlimited access. The camera itself is positioned *inside* the locker room, and the luchadoras enter and sit down on a bench to relax. "Those two wrestled like *bobcats!*" Loreta sighs, perhaps unintentionally classifying the confrontation as a "cat-fight." However, as they are about to undress, Golden Rubi notices a man hiding behind a pillar in the locker room. Fearing the presence of a Peeping Tom, they indignantly ask who he is and why he is there, shocked that a man has entered their locker room without permission. And so, due to Dr. Sorva's intrusion into the girls' private space, the male spectator is (also) denied any possibility of seeing the luchadoras about to undress

Dr. Sorva offers a nervous and embarrassed apology, explaining that he is an archeologist and colleague of Mike Henderson's uncle, Dr. Lewis Tracy (changed from "Luis Trelles" in *Las luchadoras contra la momia*). Dr. Sorva desperately needs to contact Mike, now Loreta's fiancé. Obviously, the relationship between Mike and Loreta blossomed considerably since *Doctor of Doom*, and a key aspect of *Wrestling Women* is the film's focus on the *heterosexual* pairings established between the principal characters in the previous *Doctor of Doom* (Loreta and Mike, Golden Rubi and Tommy). In doing so, *Wrestling Women* minimizes the important "same-sex" relationships between the two women (the powerful luchadoras) and the two men (the bumbling detectives) — relationships that were integral to *Doctor of Doom*'s subversion of gender stereotypes in the horror film and even Mexican society. As if on cue, Mike and Tommy conveniently arrive at the locker room to congratulate their respective girlfriends on their victory. With the principal characters, and *couples*, now assembled, Dr. Sorva engages in some lengthy and highly melodramatic plot exposition, the unintentional humor enhanced by the excited, high-pitched voice assigned to the character in Murray's dubbing. Explaining the back story for the benefit of the characters, as well as the film viewer, Dr. Sorva reveals that he, Dr. Tracy, and three other archeologists discovered a codex which will potentially lead to an ancient Aztec treasure. However, the Black Dragon learned of the codex and is now attempting to steal it. Three of the archeologists have already been murdered, leaving only Sorva and Tracy remaining. Understandably in fear for his life, Dr. Sorva adamantly insists that he has no part of the codex, a strident admission which proves to be Sorva's undoing: Mao has been eavesdropping on the conversation through a window and promptly kills Sorva with a poison dart upon learning that he can be of no use to the Black Dragon in locating the codex.

Following a scene at the Black Dragon's hideout, which allows Prince Fujiyata to provide further plot exposition and elaborate on his ruthless goals regarding the codex and Aztec treasure, the scene shifts to the home of Mike's uncle, Dr. Tracy, where the luchadoras and detectives are gathered. Dr. Tracy introduces them to Charlotte Van Dine ("Chela Van Dine" in *Las luchadoras contra la momia,* played by Maria Eugenia San Martín). Charlotte's father was one of the three archeologists killed during the film's opening montage, and she is now under the (paternal) protection of Dr. Tracy. As seen in a number of mexploitation films, Dr. Tracy is a character who is both a dedicated man of science (modernity) and a strong father figure (patriarchy). This latter role is especially pronounced by casting Victor Velázquez in the role of Dr. Tracy. A seasoned Mexican actor, he was also Lorena Velázquez's father, providing a genuine "father-daughter" relationship within the film which would be known to Mexican audiences. Dr. Tracy engages in yet *another* lengthy plot exposition detailing the archeological expedition's find, and modifies (or corrects) the narrative to explain that the Black Dragon has *already* stolen part of the codex. Tracy plans to further divide the remaining codex he possesses into three separate segments, with each section assigned to three different people who will retrieve and protect the pieces when he contacts them at the appropriate time.

Unfortunately, while Dr. Tracy is hiding the three parts of the divided codex in various parts of the city, Mao abducts Charlotte. The scene shifts to Charlotte tied to Fujiyata's torture table, and Fujiyata explains his plans for Charlotte with all the verbosity one would expect from a Murray-Mexican import:

> Now, watch while I dominate this girl's will — and use her as an instrument to help us find those who are struggling against us. I can even make her *kill*. Just a few injections, and my hypnotic power will start to make her hate the ones she now considers to be good friends.

Fujiyata's nefarious designs for Charlotte suggest a number of connotations. One, of course, is the common motif in mexploitation films of aligning hypnotism with villainy. Two, the scene is borrowed from a much longer, similar scene in *The Mask of Fu Manchu* where the title villain not only tortures a young Anglo man, but injects him with a strange serum, apparently made through equal parts "science" and "sorcery," which will make the Anglo a servant under Fu Manchu's complete control. Three, and perhaps most importantly, in the context of the anti–Communist subtext of the film, Fujiyata's act is tantamount to Communist "brainwashing," designed to turn Charlotte against her friends and allies as a "Manchurian Candidate" (or "Fu Manchu[rian] candidate") under the control of Fujiyata and the Black Dragon organization.

The luchadoras and the detectives are gathered at the Tracy home when a large package arrives for Tommy. Inside is a sombrero with a hotel key hidden in the hat lining and a message from Dr. Tracy, who now has apparently gone into hiding. Unknown to the heroes, the Black Dragon has wire-tapped the phone and planted a hidden camera in the Tracy home, allowing Fujiyata to monitor their plans and conversations. As David Wilt notes, the camera is not "hidden" at all (it is shown numerous times and is plainly visible on a bookshelf in the living room), but for all intents and purposes it functions as a *movie* camera, "capable of tracking, panning, zooming, and even looking in other rooms."[16] In this regard, the viewer is struck by how many scenes from the film set in the Tracy home actually unfold onscreen while shown on Fujiyata's small television set; thus the viewer watches a sizable amount of the film unfold within the confines of a TV set. This creates further "self-reflexivity" in the film, in that the audience is not only watching a low-budget, serial-style B-horror film, but watching a low-budget film being shown *on a television set*. One might recall *Santo vs. la invasión de los marcianos* and the Martians who appear on television to broadcast their sinister warnings to Earth — they must remind Mexican television viewers that they "are not actors in a scary movie" (which, of course, they are). In his later *Santo en el tesoro de Drácula*, Cardona employs a similar strategy to create a sense of ironic estrangement and self-referential commentary on the film's status. Having sent his girlfriend Luisa back in time to a previous life via his time machine, Santo can conveniently watch her encounter with Dracula in late nineteenth century Mexico on a television monitor. Luisa's past life plays out as a fairly straight horror film, owing an obvious and considerable debt to the original *Dracula*, as well as the mexploitation classics *El vampiro* and *El mundo de los vampiros*. While watching her former life transpire on the television monitor, Santo is essentially watching a mexploitation vampire film on television.

Realizing that the sombrero is a signal to find part of the codex, Mike orders Tommy to retrieve it. Golden Rubi, putting her arm around her diminutive boyfriend, announces she will accompany Tommy "so I can give him protection." Tommy adoringly and *literally* "looks up to her" (Chucho Salinas being several inches shorter than Elizabeth Campbell) and blurts, "You're my guardian angel — as an Amazon, you're the greatest!" Much like in the previous *Doctor of Doom*, the romantic relationship between Golden Rubi and Tommy is played primarily for comic relief, but it also satirizes the traditional romantic couple, emphasizing the obvious physical superiority of the powerful "Amazon" over the puny man.

The two go to the hotel to recover the codex, but are ambushed by the Black Dragon's men. They are captured and subdued: Tommy tied to a chair; Golden Rubi, a bit more provocatively, bound to the bedpost (recalling a tamer version of Bettie Page's legendary bondage photos with Irving Klaw, or John Willie's *Bizarre* magazine bondage photography). Mao repeatedly slaps Tommy's face, demanding he reveal the (unknown) location of the codex, but a knock on the door interrupts Mao's interrogation. Loreta and Mike burst into the room, rescuing Golden Rubi and Tommy while capturing two Black Dragon henchmen. As previously suggested, *Doctor of Doom* emphasized the relationships between the two men (the detectives) and especially the two women (the luchadoras) as much as the heterosexual pairings. Specifically, one can recall the scene in which the luchadoras defend themselves from the Mad Doctor's thugs in their bedroom without benefit of male protection, and, of course, the memorable scene when the *two women* must rescue the *two men* from the confines of the Mad Doctor's insidious Death Chamber. However, with heterosexual relationships predominant in *Wrestling Women*, one heterosexual couple (Loreta and Mike) rescues the other heterosexual couple (Golden Rubi and Tommy). Except for their tag-team matches and the all-important forthcoming battle with the Fujiyata sisters, there is virtually no interaction between Loreta and Golden Rubi outside the ring that does not include or revolve around the men in their lives.

In one of many obvious continuity lapses in the film, Mao and the others report to Prince Fujiyata that they have acquired the first part of the codex, although they were clearly still seeking the location of the codex when Loreta and Mike forced them to flee the hotel. Seemingly disinterested in the codex but fascinated by his henchmen's violent encounter with the wrestling women, Fujiyata already envisions the (sexually) exciting possibility of watching his sisters battle the luchadoras, a premise that will allow the film to construct an eventual *all-female* confrontation, with males only minimally involved as passive spectators. "How would you like to face those girls and match your strength against them?" he asks. The camera zooms out to reveal the Fujiyata sisters in profile, one on each side of the frame. They nod approvingly. Fujiyata laughs deviously and envisions "*a delightful show*: [emphasis added] the best trained girls in judo in Asia against two girls who are great wrestlers. How much time do you need to tear them to pieces?" "Three minutes!" the sisters reply in hilarious unison.

Still under Fujiyata's hypnotic control, or "brainwashing," Charlotte returns to the Tracy home to await further orders. Again, much of this sequence featuring Charlotte alternately unfolds, onscreen and within the confines of Fujiyata's TV monitor, continually reminding viewers of the film's status as a low-budget mexploitation film they might themselves be watching on television. Seeing Tommy arrive via his hidden camera, Fujiyata orders Charlotte to reach under the pillow of her bed, where a hypodermic syringe has been placed (this sequence demonstrates the amazing, even "panoptic," ability of Fujiyata's stationary surveillance camera to actually see into two different rooms). Charlotte jabs the syringe into Tommy's arm while he lounges on the couch, and Fujiyata attempts to hypnotize Tommy in his drugged state via a radio transmission, but to no avail: not that Tommy resists through indomitable will, but natural silliness. Tommy responds to Fujiyata's increasingly aggravated hypnotic interrogation with a series of weak jokes and *non-sequiturs* intended as comic relief ("Well, what a deep voice you have, Grandma dear!").[17] Strained comedy aside, the scene does suggest the great gender disparity regarding the status of hypnosis in mexploitation films. While women are highly susceptible to hypnosis by men, men are much more resistant to the hypnotic power of their fellow men. In *Doctor of Doom,* the Mad Doctor talked of the great difficulty he had controlling the male Gomar through hypnosis, but how he could easily command the female Vendetta (of course, evil *women* who practice hypnotism in mexploitation films can bend the will of men and women with great ease and social consequence — Tundra, Freda Frankenstein). When Rubi and Loreta enter the scene, they are both subdued by Charlotte's hypodermic needle: under Fujiyata's hypnotic machinations and "brainwashing" program, Charlotte indeed becomes a pawn of the Asiatic threat against her fellow Mexican citizens. As luck would have it for Fujiyata, a messenger arrives with a package addressed to Charlotte from Dr. Tracy. Informing Charlotte the that codex section assigned to her is hidden in her post-office box, the Black Dragon can now easily acquire the second part of the codex.

With only one remaining part of the codex free of the Black Dragon's clutches, Mike realizes the urgency of the situation. Using directions provided by Dr. Tracy, Mike is able to deduce the location of the final piece of the codex: the National Arena. Of course, Fujiyata still monitors them via the hidden camera, and learns of its location as well. Both factions immediately converge on to the arena, and another brawl ensues between the heroes and villains in the women's locker room, with Mike taking possession of the remaining piece of the codex and threatening to set it on fire. Realizing that the two parties have reached an impasse regarding the codex, Prince Fujiyata proposes a unique solution: rather than continuing the cloak and dagger intrigue, he suggests the dispute over the codex could be settled by a public match pitting the Fujiyata sisters and their judo skills against the wrestling prowess of the luchadoras, the winner receiving the loser's parts of the codex. (Cardona and Alfredo Salazar would reuse this key plot point in *Santo en el tesoro de Dràcula* when Santo and Black Hood's son "Atlas" — another villain's name derived from Greek mythology–wrestle publicly for the ownership of the coded artifacts that lead to Dracula's treasure.) However, Fujiyata's idea of a winner-take-all sporting duel is not so much motivated by a desire for a civil resolution to the dispute but by Fujiyata's perverse fascination with seeing his sisters battle Loreta Venus and Golden Rubi in "a delightful show." Mike is adamantly opposed to the idea, but Loreta overrules her boyfriend and accepts the challenge: "Let's get this thing over with once and for all!" Loreta's impatient statement also speaks for the film viewer as well; considering how chaotic, confusing, and episodic the film's plot has become, her desire to settle the narrative mess parallels the audience's own wish for narrative unity and resolution. They agree on a match in two weeks, and, as a gesture of good faith, Fujiyata releases Charlotte from his hypnotic spell.

While Fujiyata's idea may not make any narrative sense, it does allow for a long lucha libre sequence to be inserted into the film. More importantly, the match constructs a thinly-veiled cultural conflict between Mexico (the luchadoras) and Asia (the Fujiyata sisters); however, there is the irony that one of Mexico's defenders, the Golden Rubi, is actually an American. The luchadoras can be seen as "national allegories" whose "private destinies" mirror Mexico's "embattled situation" — the encroachment of an "alien value system" which threatens to appropriate their history and culture. However, unlike most mexploitation films which code this foreign threat as some type of European influence (Greek and Roman antiquity, Nazi Germany), in this case the threat to mexicanidad is specifically Asiatic and Communist. Moreover, while *women* assume the role of "national allegories" for their respective countries rather than men, and the match opens a space for the luchadoras to actively participate in the Mexican public sphere, the luchadoras are also defenders of a Mexican national culture that is permeated with sexism and works towards women's inequality. Certainly one can argue that the role of the luchadora is not so much defending national honor and culture, but rather to promenade in wrestling tights and provide "a delightful show" to satisfy male voyeuristic pleasure.

As a preface to the match, the viewer sees a long shot of a lucha libre poster advertising the confrontation, with the camera panning slowly down its length. As in *Doctor of Doom*, a voice-over narrator provides a loose translation of the Spanish poster:

> Sensational fight between members of *the weaker sex*—Judo experts against wrestlers: Loreta Venus! And the Golden Rubi! Against the Oriental Judo Champions Lien and Tzu! (emphasis added).

While the "weaker sex" disclaimer does not appear on the poster and seems to be an addition in the English dubbing, this mention of a "sensational fight between members of the weaker sex" is quite ironic in that the match is a an important battle for cultural and national identity and sovereignty in which *women*—"the weaker sex"–are assigned the crucial roles of defending their respective nations and cultures. The first names of the Fujiyata sisters, which *are* plainly visible on the Spanish poster advertising the match, become significant as well. Not only are their names Chinese rather than Japanese, but the name "Tzu" serves as an important reference point to Sun Tzu, the ancient Chinese philosopher and author of *The Art of War*, the first philosophical work on the strategies and tactics of war (among those influenced by *The Art of War* was Mao Tse-Tung). Not only is the specter of Communism associated with the Black Dragon Society ("henchman Mao"), but via the Fujiyata sister "(Sun) Tzu," so is the philosophy of war, the battle between nations: the Mexican luchadoras versus the Asian judo champions.

The shot of the poster cuts to Loreta and Golden Rubi preparing for the match in the locker room, while Mike and Tommy anxiously wait with them. Mike continues to express reservations about the match, and is especially concerned that the Fujiyata sisters will be employing an unfamiliar fighting style that could result in not only losing the match and the codex, but serious injury. Loreta responds with her own hilarious, condensed version of *The Art of War*: "Their advantage is the Japanese method, but don't rule out the many tricks we use—applying pressure holds—and we can punch them if they get too rough on us!"

Much like the climactic match between Gloria Venus and Vendetta in *Doctor of Doom*, the match between the luchadoras and the Fujiyata sisters is shown primarily via a high-angle long shot from a camera positioned in the seats over one of the ring posts, which takes in the entire ring. With this long shot situating the film viewer in a position to watch the action from the perspective of a wrestling spectator in the arena, medium shots and close-ups of the combatants in the ring are inserted to propel the match, alternating between the obvious stunt doubles (in the long shots) and actresses Velázquez and Campbell (in the medium and close-up shots). Reaction shots of Mike and Tommy in the crowd appear throughout the match, and they are joined by Charlotte and Dr. Tracy, who has apparently come out of hiding to see the pivotal bout (Tommy, of course, also provides running comic commentary over the course of the match). Similarly, reaction shots of Prince Fujiyata and Mao are also inserted, with Fujiyata eschewing his Oriental attire in favor of a respectable business suit for the event. Stock footage of actual lucha libre crowds complete the scene, but it is the *same* familiar stock footage the viewer has seen in *all* the previous matches from *Doctor of Doom* and *Wrestling Women*.

As the two teams enter the ring, the statuesque luchadoras, clad in their wrestling tights and sequined capes, stand in stark contrast to the diminutive Fujiyata sisters wearing traditional judo robes. This not only provides a contrast between the Amazonian luchadoras and the squat Fujiyata sisters, but their costumes clearly code them as representing their respective cultures: the glamorous Mexican luchadoras verses the practitioners of a "foreign" fighting style (judo) and embodiments of an "alien value system" (Asia). The match begins, with the Fujiyata sisters easily dominating the luchadoras and winning the first fall, leaving Golden Rubi and Loreta lying stunned and beaten in the ring. However, the luchadoras make a remarkable recovery, and quickly and easily win the second fall. In particular, Loreta humiliates her opponent by holding her upside down in a painful submission hold as she smiles at the crowd, and Golden Rubi soon forces the other Fujiyata sister to submit as well. With the third and deciding round beginning, Mike and Tommy express grave concerns about Loreta and Golden Rubi's ability to win the match, but it is apparent the luchadoras have gathered momentum. Indeed, the Fujiyata sisters' tactics deteriorate into mostly utilizing desperate chops and kicks, apparently unable to effectively use their judo holds and throws on the physically superior luchadoras or their culturally superior grappling style of lucha libre. In a repeat of the second round, Loreta forces one of the sisters to submit, and Golden Rubi follows by forcing the other to submit as well. Successful in their defense of mexicanidad, the luchadoras proudly stand in the center of the ring, the referee holding their arms high in triumph, the crowd jubilantly celebrating their heroic effort.

With the luchadoras victorious, Prince Fujiyata, accompanied by Mao, arrives at the locker room to fulfill his end of the agreement by surrendering the codex to

"As an Amazon, you're the greatest!" Golden Rubi (Elizabeth Campbell) achieves physical and cultural supremacy over a Fujiyata sister in *Wrestling Women vs. the Aztec Mummy.*

Mike, who passes it to Dr. Tracy to ensure its authenticity. Satisfied that the codex is complete, Mike springs his own trap on Fujiyata. Pulling out his gun, Mike informs the Asians that their gentlemen's agreement said nothing about arresting them for the murder of the three archeologists. Mike and Tommy place Fujiyata and Mao in police custody, but the detectives' triumph is brief. Overhearing the arrest, the Fujiyata sisters ambush Mike and Tommy, bombarding the detectives with a barrage of savage karate chops and judo throws. Their attack not only allows their brother and Mao to escape, but provides Mike and Tommy with an emasculating, embarrassing beating at the hands of two petite women. "Those cute little Orientals attacked us!" Mike reports incredulously. In this sense, one can see a certain resonance with the subversion of gender stereotypes that makes *Doctor of Doom* such a richly problematic text. The authoritative male figures of "the law" (Mike and Tommy) prove to be utterly ineffectual in maintaining social order as compared to the mighty efforts of the so-called "weaker sex"—the luchadoras who become defenders of mexicanidad over the Fujiyata sisters, who in turn effortlessly defeat the (masculine) law.

The film returns to Prince Fujiyata's hideout where Mao suggests stealing back the codex. Fujiyata, now back in his Oriental attire, endorses a far different plan, a sage bit of philosophy which could easily be derived from Sun Tzu's *The Art of War* or Mao Tse-Tung's *Little Red Book*: "At times it is convenient to let your enemies work out their own ideas. Perhaps they'll work for *us*. You must remember that patience is the greatest of virtue ... sooner or later, *they* are going to show *us* the way, and at that moment I'll plan my actions." The scene shifts to the Tracy apartment, where the heroes are attempting "to work out their own ideas." Dr. Tracy strongly considers abandoning his work of translating the codex, disturbed by the harm it has caused. Charlotte urges him to continue so the efforts of her father and the other dead archeologists will not have been in vain. Loreta adds that the recovery of a vast Aztec treasure could serve to improve Mexican society, and "the government can use it for public works." As noted, *Wrestling Women* was produced near the end of the López Mateos presidency; part of that administration's political program were efforts aimed at the betterment of the lower class, although the motivation of the López Mateos presidency to provide such reform may have been to quell Communist sentiment rather than improve social and economic conditions.[18] Persuaded of the potential benefit the treasure could have on the present, Dr. Tracy decides to translate the codex. Still under Black Dragon surveillance, Dr. Tracy announces, "I've finished at last, and this story that the codex tells us is something that only can be described as extraordinary!" Dr. Tracy sits behind his desk, which the film viewer sees within the confines of Fujiyata's television monitor, and begins another lengthy plot exposition that he peppers with quotes from (fictional) academic sources in order to lend scientific credibility to his remarkable story.

The scene dissolves from Dr. Tracy to a painted backdrop of an ancient Aztec city. Alongside Dr. Tracy's authoritative voice-over narration, footage culled from Portillo's *La momia azteca* is shown, once again detailing the mildly sordid story of two young Aztecs, the maiden Xóchitl and a sorcerer named Temozoc (in Portillo's *Aztec Mummy* films, Xóchitl's forbidden lover was the Aztec warrior Popoca, who in *Wrestling Women* is now mentioned as the author of the codex). Dr. Tracy takes an almost perverse pleasure in stressing Xóchitl's sexual virtue, repeating several times over the course of his narration that Xóchitl was a "radiant virgin," a "maiden," and "pure" prior to meeting Temozoc. However, the couple succumbed to forbidden carnal desires, causing them to be cursed eternally for their sexual transgression against the gods and Aztec society. The deflowered Xóchitl was sacrificed to appease the gods, and her body adorned with a necklace-style breastplate inscribed with the location of a vast Aztec treasure. Buried alive next to her, Temozoc is doomed to spend eternity guarding his dead lover and the breastplate's secrets.

Watching Dr. Tracy explain the saga of Xóchitl and Temozoc, Fujiyata exclaims, "I have never heard anyone talk such utter nonsense!" Mike expresses an eagerness to find the treasure, but Dr. Tracy explains that there is "a curse" attached to the breastplate, and those who disturb it will risk death. While Mike, like Fujiyata, is skeptical of any curse, Dr. Tracy warns him, "Don't scoff at the supernatural, because there are certain mysteries that either science or man's intelligence have been able to unravel." While Dr. Tracy, like Professor Cristaldi in *Santo y Blue Demon contra Drácula y el Hombre Lobo*, admits that the power of the supernatural is vast, and that science may not have the ability to understand it, he does not share Cristaldi's belief that the supernatural may possess the potential for good. *Wrestling Women* has thus far focused primarily on the cultural and ideological struggle between mexicanidad and the "alien value system" which threatens it, the national allegorical struggle between Mexico (democracy) and Asia (Communism). However, consistent with numerous other mexploitation films, the dichotomy and conflict between *the present* (rationalism, science) and *the past* (superstition, the supernatural) is introduced into *Wrestling Women* as well, and the disastrous consequences of disturbing the past ultimately far outweighs any possible benefits (the *Aztec Mummy* trilogy, *Santo en el tesoro de Drácula*).

Against his better judgment, Dr. Tracy is convinced to lead an expedition to the Aztec pyramid that houses Xóchitl and Temozoc. The scene begins with the same establishing shot seen in the opening credits, a long shot of an Aztec pyramid accompanied by an ominous burst of brass-dominated music (beyond creating a suitably foreboding mood, this music is noteworthy in that it was later recycled as the main theme for *El horripilante bestia humana*). Several minutes are spent watching the luchadoras and their entourage roaming about Aztec ruins, all the while being observed by Prince Fujiyata and his gang. The sequence is made up of twelve long takes, virtually all of which are either long shots or extreme long shots of the various parties wandering about as small, barely discernable figures amid the desolate desert and Aztec monuments — one is tempted to say that for a few minutes *Wrestling Women* is Cardona's version (or unintentional parody) of an Antonioni film. After watching and following the luchadoras and the others, Fujiyata simply orders everyone back to the hideout, prompting frustrated criticism from one of the henchmen whose objection to Fujiyata's inaction mirrors the viewer's own impatience with the film's inactivity and anti-climactic resolution at this point. Eventually locating the pyramid containing the tomb of Xóchitl and Temozoc, the luchadoras and the others explore dim passageways for at least two minutes of screen time, at times becoming all but invisible in the darkness, save for their flashlights, which leaves the viewer essentially watching a black screen.[19] Finally, they locate the crypt, finding Xóchitl's skeleton on a slab, rats gnawing on her bones. Tommy's reaction: "Looks *dead* to me, Professor!" "Don't be stupid!" impatiently responds

Dr. Tracy. Upon removing Xóchitl's breastplate, Temozoc stiffly rises from his grave, now an emaciated mummy with a skeletal head: at last, the monster advertised and promised in the film's title makes his long-overdue appearance.

Escaping to the home of Dr. Tracy, and understandably upset from their frightful encounter with Temozoc, the luchadoras and the others ponder the situation, with Dr. Tracy providing the obvious (and humorous) explanation: "The monster is supernatural." In a classic Murray *non-sequitur*, Charlotte adds, "Frankly, I'm scared that something in this situation is terrifying!" The film once more halts in order for Dr. Tracy to offer yet more plot exposition. Again quoting from an academic textbook, he details the magical powers of the Aztec "witch-doctors" such as Temozoc, powers which include being able to shape shift into other animal forms. This source pointedly notes that the magic of such Aztecs "is almost the same in many cases as the sorcery used in the Middle Ages in Europe." Thus, Temozoc's supernatural power is tied to European necromancers as much as Aztec magic, and the threat of the "supernatural" is not simply tied to an undead monster of *the past*, but is also distinctly referenced as being similar to the forces of supernatural evil of (pre-modern) *Europe*, another common threat to mexicanidad in mexploitation cinema.

Aware that Dr. Tracy now possesses the breastplate, Fujiyata and his henchmen attempt to seize it under the cover of darkness. However, night also brings the mummy Temozoc, searching for the breastplate and the violators of the crypt, with Temozoc arriving in the city by assuming the form of a bat. In this respect, Temozoc is indeed much closer to (a European) vampire than (an Aztec) mummy. A brief and quite clumsy battle ensues on the streets outside the Tracy home between the Aztec Mummy and the Black Dragon gang, who are quickly disposed of by Temozoc (where are the Fujiyata sisters when they need them?). Following his thrashing of the Black Dragon hoods, Temozoc again transforms into a bat and flies into the bedroom window, past the sleeping and unsuspecting luchadoras. The scene cuts to Dr. Tracy and Charlotte, both of whom have fallen asleep at his desk while translating the breastplate. Mimicking (or parodying) the gait of the monster in *Frankenstein*—wobbling unsteadily with his arms outstretched—the Aztec Mummy enters the film frame and slowly walks towards the desk. Just as he is about to strangle Charlotte, a rooster crows and the monster recoils in horror at the first rays of sunlight (like a vampire, Temozoc cannot function in daylight). The mummy backs away, moving steadily backwards toward the camera, until his shoulder blades fill the entire screen (with viewers half expecting the mummy to fall into their laps). This odd close-up jump-cuts to a shot in the bedroom of the bat literally flying out the window backwards — Cardona simply reused the original footage of the rubber bat flying *into* the bedroom and reversed it![20]

The next day's newspaper headline reports that the Black Dragon gang members were savagely killed by "a strange monster" that left behind their "badly-mangled bodies." Certainly a violent, bloody assault is not the impression one gets from the brief, choppy, and stagey fight between Temozoc and the Black Dragon members (although "badly-mangled bodies" would become the *raison d'être* of the subsequent *El horripilante bestia humana*'s American version, *Night of the Bloody Apes*). However, the mass murder of the Black Dragon organization does mark their abrupt departure from the film, allowing the new conflict of the past (Aztec mummy) versus the present (luchadoras) to become the story's focus. One might even suggest that the foreign invaders that threatened mexicanidad, the Black Dragon, are finally obliterated by the very forces of the (supernatural) Aztec past they so arrogantly underestimated and ruthlessly tried to appropriate.

Alarmed by this newspaper report, Charlotte has a dramatic change of heart, deciding that the breastplate must be returned rather than risk the vengeance of Temozoc. She enlists Tommy to take her to the crypt, despite his comic protests. Their bizarre discussion veers more towards the absurdist theater of Alfred Jarry's *Ubu* plays than horror film dialogue, their stiff and convoluted syntax magnified by the odd emphasis and awkward pauses that characterize a K. Gordon Murray import:

> CHARLOTTE: The breastplate must be returned, or undoubtedly the mummy will be coming for us.
> TOMMY: *That's* all I need.
> CHARLOTTE: What's the matter? Are you afraid?
> TOMMY: Who? No — well, I think ... we better be careful. Maybe that stupid mummy has fits and undresses. Who knows what he has beneath his clothes?
> CHARLOTTE: Look, he's sleeping now. During the day he won't harm you — when the sun goes down, that is when you must be careful. That's why I think we better go now.
> TOMMY: You're very sure he's sound asleep now, aren't you? Maybe he'll feel a draft suddenly and go out and get a blanket —
> CHARLOTTE: Well, don't talk *nonsense*!
> TOMMY: We better wait for the rest to get here and go shoulder to shoulder — *firmly*!
> CHARLOTTE: I assure you they couldn't be convinced easily that the mummy is a threat to our safety. What about it?
> TOMMY: You're dragging me. I don't like it!

Tommy and Charlotte return to the pyramid to replace the breastplate, a trek that the viewer becomes quite familiar with by the time the film reaches its conclusion. Virtually every time a given character or group of characters reach or leaves the pyramid crypt, Cardona repeatedly shows the character(s) in a long shot traversing a long dirt road into the background or foreground, and then includes a high-angle extreme long shot of the characters arriving at or exiting the pyramid itself. Once inside the pyramid, Tommy and Charlotte wander its dark passageways before becoming separated, at which time Tommy demonstrates his usual flair for comic ineptitude and cowardice by abandoning Charlotte in the pyramid. As Tommy returns to the city to get the others, the film retraces his journey by first showing the high-angle extreme long shot as he exits the pyramid, and then the long shot of the dirt road as he sprints down it toward the foreground of the frame.

With Charlotte now alone in the pyramids and sunset quickly approaching, Tommy returns to Dr. Tracy's home to inform everyone of Charlotte's predicament, which unfortunately he does with more heavy-handed attempts at comic relief through broad physical comedy and pantomime. Finally realizing the severity of the situation, they hurriedly rush to Charlotte's rescue. For the next few minutes Cardona constructs a montage devoid of dialogue, perhaps recalling the cross-cut chases and rescues filmed by silent cinema pioneer D.W. Griffith: the car containing the luchadoras and the others careening through the streets; Charlotte wandering the dark passageways; Temozoc slowly reviving from his daily slumber; stock footage inserts of the setting sun on the horizon (in fact, this is the same shot used to signify the sun*rise* when Temozoc is forced to flee the Tracy home). Temozoc begins to pursue Charlotte through the passageways, finally cornering her as the camera alternates between close-ups of the mummy walking directly toward the camera and Charlotte cowering in fear in the dimly-lit pyramid corridors. A medium close-up of Charlotte collapsing in the darkness cuts to the long shot of the dirt road as Dr. Tracy, the luchadoras, and the detectives rush toward the pyramid (the *third* time this shot is used to depict various characters nearing or leaving the pyramid within a span of a few minutes).

This all-too-familiar scene dissolves to a medium long shot of the crypt, showing Charlotte tied to a slab next to Xóchitl's skeleton. Recalling the earlier scene where she is tied to the table in Fujiyata's lair, it could be said that Charlotte is placed in this same dangerous situation *twice* by the film's respective villains, each acting in their own dastardly and culturally-specific ways. The first time Charlotte undergoes the process of "brainwashing" by Asians; the second time, she is about to be subjected to the ancient Aztec punishment of human sacrifice. [21] Fortunately, the luchadoras, the detectives, and Dr. Tracy arrive in time to prevent Charlotte's death, and they square off in a final confrontation with the mummy, which plays out as a surreal, slapstick anti-climax rather than a tense, dramatic finale. When the protagonists attempt to ward off Temozoc with torches (apparently he is afraid of fire), Temozoc opts to transform into a bat and aimlessly flies about the room. "Look, Loreta, he's a vampire now!" Golden Rubi exclaims. The bat flies out of the left side of the film frame, and Temozoc immediately reenters the shot, now back in his original form as a mummy. "He's a mummy again!" Dr. Tracy observes, explaining the obvious to the film spectator. As Temozoc walks out of the right side of the frame, Loreta adds a wonderful *non-sequitur*: "He's disappeared: *Look*!" Loreta not only points out that the mummy has literally disappeared from the shot, but makes the absurd comment that one can "look" to see that the mummy is now "invisible." In actuality, Temozoc has not disappeared but transformed himself into a small tarantula crawling on Charlotte's stomach. As Charlotte squirms in fear, the Aztec necklace falls on the floor. However, in the very next shot, when Dr. Tracy swipes the tarantula off her body, the breastplate is again draped over her bosom. In a subsequent shot of her on the table, the breastplate is again *off*, and in the next shot of Charlotte, pleading for Dr. Tracy to untie her, the breastplate is again *on*. The obvious continuity gaffes could be dismissed as filmmaking incompetence; however, they also disorientate the viewer and subvert any possibility of filmic realism (as mentioned, basic rules of continuity editing never seemed to be a pressing concern for Cardona). With Temozoc having courteously become a tiny insect, Mike, Tommy, and the luchadoras can easily subdue Temozoc with a blanket. Now a mummy again, but with his head covered by the blanket, which deprives him of his supernatural powers (his eyes are the source of his powers), Temozoc is securely chained to a support pillar while Dr. Tracy rescues Charlotte. When Dr. Tracy picks up the elusive breastplate and hands it to her, she instead places it on Xóchitl's skeleton: "No, Professor — this belongs to Xóchitl!" Charlotte states the ideological message of the film: what is from the past must *stay* in the past in order for the modern world to safely progress. As everyone flees the crypt, Temozoc struggles to free himself from the chains and inadvertently loosens the pillar, causing the roof to crash down upon the tomb, burying him and the secret of the Aztec treasure. The camera cuts to the luchadoras and the others standing in awe outside the pyramid; the shot pans to the right and upward to show the exterior of the pyramid in long shot. Dr. Tracy speaks, his disembodied voice and authoritative tone essentially becoming off-camera narration supplying a brief epilogue: "Well, I guess this is the end of our search. Who can tell how many centuries more the Aztec treasure will remain hidden?" At the moment the word "Aztec" is said, the scene cuts to Temozoc buried in the rubble of the crypt, eyes wide open, staring directly at the film audience. The word "Aztec" is literally connected to the supernatural evil of the past, buried but nonetheless still quite vigilant over its secrets, reminding the viewer than any attempt to disturb the past will also disturb the evil associated with the past.

Perhaps more so than any other mexploitation film, *Wrestling Women* engages in an ambitious ideological campaign overtly promoting mexicanidad and modernity. Initially, the luchadoras and their allies must confront a contemporary, external political threat to Mexican society and culture in the form of the Black Dragon secret society, with its none too subtle allusions to Asian Communism. Yet as this *external* threat is extinguished, an equally insidious *internal* threat to Mexican social order and progress must be defeated: the specters of Mexico's past in the form of supernatural evil. It is only through defeating *both* its external and internal enemies that mexicanidad and modernity are preserved.

6

El horripilante bestia humana (Night of the Bloody Apes, 1968)

The only other "Wrestling Women" film dubbed into English and released in America was the final film of the series, *El horripilante bestia humana* (*The Horrible Human Beast*, or, more literally, *The Blood-Curdling Human Beast*), a loose remake of *Las luchadoras vs. el médico asesino*. An alternate version of *El horripilante bestia humana* with additional violence and female nudity was released internationally under the more sensational and self-explanatory title *Horror y sexo* (*Horror and Sex*). Also in 1968, Cardona made *El vampiro y el sexo*, the version of *Santo en el tesoro de Drácula* with topless vampire women, as well as *El médico loco y el sexo* (*The Mad Doctor and Sex*), a version of *Las luchadoras contra el robot asesino* that also included female nudity (obviously, one can spot a trend in the titles of the nude versions of Cardona's lucha libre films). However, *El horripilante bestia humana*, like *Santo en el tesoro de Drácula*, was only released in Mexico under the "A" (all-ages) authorization, which would have precluded the possibility of Mexican audiences seeing the violence and nudity presented in the various *Sexo* films. In that ratings of Mexican films range from "AA" (children's films) to the rarely used "D" certification, had *Horror y sexo* itself been released in Mexico it would have probably earned a "C" authorization (the rating given to most films with nudity and violence); the fact that *El horripilante bestia humana* did not even garner a "B" authorization indicates that Mexican audiences saw a very mild version of Cardona's film.[1] In 1972 the film appeared in America under the title *Night of the Bloody Apes* in an edited form — with even *more* sex and especially violence. American sexploitation director Jerald Intrator is credited for "additional scenes"; Intrator is best remembered for his burlesque revue film *Striporama* (1953) and the sexpolitation film *Satan in High Heels* (1962). *Bloody Apes* also later gained some notoriety through its inclusion on the famous "Video Nasties" list of objectionable

144

films banned in Great Britain in the 1980s (not due to its violence and nudity, but primarily due to the inclusion of stock footage of actual open-heart surgery).

Admittedly, this discussion of *El horripilante bestia humana* is based on the English-dubbed version *Night of the Bloody Apes* (for the remainder of this chapter the film will be referred to as *Bloody Apes*), a version that went through a considerable degree of cinematic translation for American audiences, not only in its sometimes peculiar dubbed dialogue, but in the additional sex and violence added to Cardona's film by Intrator. Nonetheless, Cardona himself made a fairly explicit version of *El horripilante bestia humana*, or what would have been *Horror y sexo*. All the featured actresses clearly do their own nude scenes: Norma Lazareno as luchadora "Lucy Ossorio" has two locker room sequences that feature her in the nude; Noelia Noel (Luisa in *Santo en el tesoro de Drácula*) briefly appears as a woman savagely stripped and assaulted in a park by the ape-man (played, of course, by Gerardo Zepeda); and the character Elena is shown naked from the waist up on the operating table prior to having her heart surgically removed. In the prelude to the notorious "girl in the shower" rape and murder sequence, the ape-man carries the female victim to her bed, completely naked except for the towel that strategically (and barely) covers her pubic region, and then begins to awkwardly and disturbingly stroke her body (to state the obvious, all these scenes were excised from the "A" version released in Mexico). However, while much of the nudity was supplied by Cardona, most of the violence was only *implied* by Cardona: the viewer sees the moments just prior to the attacks (the ape-man stalking and roughly grabbing its victims) and the immediate aftermath (the ape-man unceremoniously throwing its limp victims to the ground). Ultimately, it appears that most, if not *all*, of *Bloody Apes*' legendary graphic gore should not be credited to Cardona but instead to Jerald Intrator, who filmed and inserted the grisly extreme close-ups during the various murders: showing ripping flesh, blood-soaked clothes and faces, the infamous "eye-gouging" sequence, and other gory sights. If nothing else, Intrator deserves credit for making an effort to integrate the additional scenes, as opposed to Jerry Warren, who infamously cannibalized *La momia azteca* and added endless footage of American actors explaining the plot to create *Attack of the Mayan Mummy*, (1964). However, a close viewing of the many violent and visceral moments in *Bloody Apes* does reveal continuity flaws, ranging from very subtle to rather evident, especially differences in clothing, *mise en scène*, and the sometimes noticeable replacement of one actor for another.

In these respects, it is difficult to even consider *Bloody Apes* as part of Cardona's "Wrestling Women" series. As *El horripilante bestia humana*'s original title suggests, it is not the luchadora Lucy Ossorio who is the star of the film, but rather the monstrous and murderous "blood-curdling human-beast" of the title. Granted, the female lead is a luchadora; three brief lucha libre matches occur early in the film that bear little (or no) relation to the plot; and the story itself is derived from

Las luchadoras vs. el médico asesino. However, despite *Bloody Apes* being based on *Las luchadoras vs. el médico asesino*, Alfredo Salazar, while credited with "general production," does not receive a story or screenplay credit for *Bloody Apes*, which is instead credited to René Cardona and René Cardona, Jr.[2] Rather than imitating the first two *Luchadoras* films, and mexploitation as a whole, *Bloody Apes*' graphic if unconvincing violence and occasional "tits and ass" moments situates the film alongside American low-budget horror or even sexploitation films of the era, particularly the seminal early 1960s "ghoulies" of Herschell Gordon Lewis (*Bloodfeast, 2000 Maniacs, Color Me Blood Red*). When comparing the grainy black and white footage, mild sexual innuendo, and comic book action of the first two *Luchadoras* entries with the garish Eastmancolor, gratuitous nudity, and (inserted) grisly violence of *Bloody Apes*, the films seem decades apart, rather than a scant few years. In this way, one might suggest that the rather sudden shift from lucha libre adventure to the random violence in *Bloody Apes* mirrored the conditions of Mexican political life in the late 1960s (*El horripilante bestia humana* was made the same year as the Tlatelolco massacre, and theatrically released in Mexico in February of 1969, only four months *after* Tlatelolco). While *Bloody Apes* varies considerably from *Las luchadoras vs. el médico asesino* in its narrative, and obviously in its content, it does share its predecessor's obsession with issues of Mexican modernity: urban life, the perils of science and progress, and *chica modernas*. The crisis of 1968 epitomized by Tlatelolco shattered the unconditional belief in the vision of a modern Mexico, and rather than simply being a *remake* of *Las luchadoras vs. el médico asesino*, *Bloody Apes* is a *revision* of *Las luchadoras vs. el médico asesino* told through the blood-stained perspective of Tlatelolco.

As a sort of advertisement for the amount of blood seen in the film, the opening credits of *Bloody Apes* features a montage of red liquid (blood) dripping down the screen, forming pools, creating abstract patterns, coalescing and even "curdling" onscreen over a black background while the credits appear in yellow lettering. The clashing red, yellow, and black hues are heightened by the garish quality of Eastmancolor. (Much less expensive than Technicolor, Eastmancolor was the choice of many American low-budget exploitation filmmakers, including Herschell Gordon Lewis). These credits are accompanied by the main theme, a menacing musical motif that reoccurs throughout the film, usually during the "man-to-monster" transformations or the many murders. Composed by Antonio Díaz Conde, the theme is recycled from his score for *Las luchadoras contra la momia*; however, Díaz Conde embellishes and updates the original, ominous, brass-dominated melody with some modernist, avant-garde flourishes and atonal, dissonant blasts of organ and woodwinds — as if Karlheinz Stockhausen rearranged the original score.

The credit sequence fades out to reveal the first shot of the film: a lucha libre mask hanging on top of a coat rack. One is immediately stuck by the red color of the mask, recalling the color that dominate the opening credits. The camera slowly pulls back to reveal Lucy, a young, blonde woman in a matching red wrestling outfit, as she takes the mask from the coat rack. Interrupted by a knock on the door, Lucy walks across the locker room, the camera tracking with her as she answers. It is her boyfriend, Arthur Martinez (Armando Silvestre, the lone holdover from the first two *Luchadoras* films, reprising his role as police detective and luchadora boyfriend). After is a brief, extraneous insert of an excited lucha libre audience, the scene cuts back to Lucy facing the camera, putting the mask on while Arthur assists, standing behind her. The camera slowly zooms in to a close-up of Lucy as she adjusts the mask while Arthur secures it around her head. The slow zoom-in fetishizes and eroticizes the act of placing the mask over Lucy's head, as if the two were indulging in some bondage foreplay. However, the masking (and unmasking) of Lucy is not only infused with an element of eroticism and sexual power, it also establishes a pattern throughout the film where Arthur, the luchadora's boyfriend, is effecting and even controlling the transition between the private Lucy and her public luchadora persona in the ring. One of the key subplots of the film is that Arthur would like to remove Lucy's mask *permanently*: he wants her to quit her wrestling career in favor of marriage and the tranquility of domestic servitude. Thus, the status of the mask itself becomes important in *Bloody Apes*. With Santo and other luchadores, private identity is subsumed by an iconic, public persona; only in the most private or intimate moments of his life might the luchador voluntarily remove his mask. Conversely, in the early *Luchadoras* films, Gloria Venus and Golden Rubi do not wear masks, presumably to avoid obscuring their movie-star good looks. However, this absence of a mask allliviates the need to protect their private identities, allowing them to function as wrestling women both *in* the ring and *out* of the ring: Amazonian bombshells who fight for mexicanidad in the public sphere of the wrestling ring against the Fujiyata sisters, or pummel criminals who have the audacity to invade the private space of their bedroom. (Unlike the statuesque Lorena Velázquez or Elizabeth Campbell, actress Norma Lazareno is of fairly average height and build.) At the opening of *Bloody Apes*, Lucy is shown in the first shot of the film *without* her mask, immediately pointing out to the audience that the luchadora is very much a "mere mortal" behind the mask. A strong distinction is established between "the public Lucy," the fighting luchadora, and "the private Lucy," a pretty but quite ordinary young woman much more concerned with her romantic and career problems than with defending Mexican society from potential threats to its stability.

The close-up of Lucy in the mask jump-cuts to a close-up of Lucy poised for action in the wrestling ring. The mask's pointed features suggest both cat ears and devil horns, especially when one considers the blazing red color of Lucy's luchadora costume. To reference American comic book characters, one might describe the outfit as a cross between Catwoman, Batgirl, and Daredevil. In this way, the costume casts Lucy's luchadora image as a sort of feline/devil hybrid, equal parts "cat-woman" (or "panther-woman," recalling the evil title characters in Cardona's earlier *Las mujeres pantera*) and female Satan (all that is missing is a pointed tail). Moreover, it is never specified whether Lucy's ring persona is that of técnico or rudo (unlike Gloria Venus and Golden Rubi, who are clearly técnicos loved by their many fans). While Lucy is initially established as the film's heroine, Lucy's luchadora persona is also immediately and textually problematized by being associated with the same images of social danger that dominate the film: bloodshed (the color red) and animal violence (Lucy as a "cat-woman" in comparison to the "ape-man" monster of the film). The implication is that Lucy-as-luchadora is a *dangerous* rather than *heroic* force in the film, even aligned with the film's monster rather than opposed to it.

The first of three lucha libre sequences begins, pitting Lucy against a green-clad, masked luchadora named Elena. As in virtually all of Cardona's other wrestling-horror films, the matches are filmed primarily via a stationary, high-angle long shot that encompasses much of the ring and adopts a spectator's point of view from the stands. Intercut with this recurring long shot of the action are ring-level medium shots and close-ups of the wrestlers, as well as inserts of spectators reacting to the action. Even more so than with Lorena Velázquez and Elizabeth Campbell in the first two *Luchadoras* films, and probably due to the fact that Lucy is a masked luchadora, Cardona almost exclusively substitutes a stunt double for Norma Lazareno in the wrestling sequences. Except for a few close-ups of Lucy, especially her horrified reactions after she tosses her opponents from the ring, the stunt double is used entirely throughout the matches. Moreover, it is obvious to the viewer that the double is clearly *not* Lazareno; she is much larger and heavier, providing the usual discontinuity which is typical of Cardona's wrestling sequences in his *Luchadora* films.

After several minutes of wrestling action, the match ends in tragedy: Lucy throws Elena out of the ring and she lands on her head, fracturing her skull. The scene cuts to a nurse at the hospital switchboard; she receives an emergency phone call from the arena and dispatches an ambulance. This scene, however is not intended to provide narrative continuity with the last scene, but instead introduces Dr. Krellman (José Elias Moreno), the chief surgeon of the hospital. The film abruptly shifts to following Dr. Krellman (quite literally — the camera focuses on his back) as he walks to his car, where his scarred, limping assistant Goyo (Carlos López Moctezuma) awaits him. Goyo is a parodic throwback to the horror film tradition of misshapen, obedient servants of mad scientists, and he constantly and comically refers to Dr. Krellman as "master" (it is later explained that Dr. Krellman saved Goyo's life through experimental surgical procedures after medical science

6. El horripilante bestia humana (Night of the Bloody Apes, *1968*)

Lucy demonstrates her unfortunate tendency to throw her opponents out of the ring in *El horripilante bestia humana* (*Night of the Bloody Apes*).

had given up hope). The role of Goyo is also a sort of reprise for Carlos López Moctezuma, who appeared as the hunchbacked lackey Juan to the witch Selma (Rita Macedo) in *La maldición de la Llorona* (like Wally Barron, López Moctezuma was a popular and respected character actor in Mexican cinema). The two depart in Dr. Krellman's station wagon, exiting the hospital parking lot while the ambulance heads toward the wrestling arena in the other direction, indicating that the film is indeed moving in "two different directions."

The film now shifts its focus to Dr. Krellman, demonstrating how *Bloody Apes* shares an often frustrating narrative tendency of mexploitation films as a whole by alternating between relatively unrelated plot lines and characters, and even abruptly interrupting scenes as they build dramatic tension or excitement by briefly intercutting to other characters, as if to purposely diffuse any narrative momentum. The viewer must adapt to *Bloody Apes* on its own narrative terms, rather than apply rules of spectatorship learned from watching Hollywood films (where there is a strong, central, coherent, and linear narrative drive that all the characters circulate around). The film continues to concentrate on Dr. Krellman, who breaks into the city zoo to steal a gorilla. His bizarre criminal activity is soon explained when the viewer learns that Dr. Krellman's son, Julio (Augustín Martínez Solares, Jr.), is suffering from leukemia, with known medical science unable to prevent Julio's imminent death. A long, protracted zoom slowly brings the camera from a medium shot of a group of doctors gathered around Dr. Krellman, all explaining the hopeless situation regarding Julio's failing health, to a tight close-up of Dr. Krellman's face as he determinedly ponders the situation, lending a heavy-handed, melodramatic, even soap-operatic staginess to the scene. Throughout *Bloody Apes,* one is struck by the frequent zooms that Cardona incorporates; his repeated and exaggerated use and *overuse* of the zoom lens inevitably recalls the film techniques of 1960s and '70s Eurotrash horror films, specifically those of Spanish horror-exploitation film master Jess Franco (notorious for his infatuation with the zoom lens), and even perhaps some of the Italian *giallo* horror films masters (Mario Bava, Dario Argento) who frequently used the zoom lens, albeit with a bit more discretion and subtlety than Franco or Cardona.

Given his son's dire situation, Dr. Krellman decides to undertake a radical and completely preposterous surgical procedure. Explaining to Goyo — and the film audience — that gorilla blood is more "powerful" than human blood, Dr. Krellman postulates that it may have the capacity to fight Julio's leukemia. However, because Julio's system is too weak to support a massive transfusion of gorilla blood, the gorilla's heart must be transplanted into Julio as well. As Dr. Krellman finishes his absurd medical explanation, the camera quickly and boldly zooms in to a close-up of a medical diagram of a heart which hangs on the wall, exaggerating the drama of the scene to the point of unintentional humor. This experimental heart transplant takes place in Dr. Krellman's secret laboratory, conveniently located in the basement of Dr. Krellman's home. Cardona depicts the operation via a montage of alternating close-ups of Dr. Krellman, Goyo, and an unconscious Julio; lingering shots of medical equipment set up around the lab; and inserted footage of actual open-heart surgery, which provides both graphic realism and a substantial amount of shock value. In one of the strangest film techniques used by Cardona, the operation suddenly cuts to an out-of-focus close-up of a multi-colored, abstract painting recalling Jackson Pollack, which the camera quickly pans across. A sort of primitive, psychedelic wipe effect is created, and it is used several times throughout the film as a transitional device to either bridge scenes or of depict the passage of time. However, the effect also serves to completely disorientate the viewer and break any filmic continuity.[3] The scene then cuts back to Dr. Krellman, now finished with the operation, closely monitoring Julio's vital signs for a lengthy period, alternating between long takes of Dr. Krellman staring intently and the "electrocardiograph" machine that is supposedly monitoring Julio's heartbeat. Through its protracted nature, the scene serves as a typical example of how mexploitation films tend to alternate between jarring editing (which fragments the film and disorientates the audience) and languid long takes (which last far longer than Hollywood codes of narrative economy would permit). Ultimately, these techniques create a frustrating and challenging relationship between the viewer and the (unintentionally) unorthodox film form as it veers towards a counter-cinema: Godard making a mad scientist movie.

While inevitably the villain in *Bloody Apes,* due to his strange medical experiments (the then-unthinkable idea of using animal organs in human transplants), Dr. Krellman is far different than the cartoonish mad scientists such as Dr. Krupp in the *Aztec Mummy* films or Dr. Wright in *Doctor of Doom.* Dr. Krellman is a rational and respected member of bourgeois society whose motivations are not rooted in criminal gain, world control, or conceitedly creating abominations of nature. His medical experiments are the result of a noble, if misguided, effort to save his dying son. In this respect, he is much closer to Dr. Almada of the *Aztec Mummy* films, or even Santo-as-scientist in *Santo en el tesoro de Drácula,* in that both are dedicated men of science involved in unorthodox experiments which they hope will lead to social progress, but instead inevitably invite social disaster. Interestingly, a profile shot of Dr. Krellman abruptly jump-cuts to a close-up of Lucy in the wrestling ring, the shot virtually identical to the first shot showing her in the ring at the beginning of the first match. This juxtaposition sets up an associative relationship between the two characters: Dr. Krellman, a respected public figure of medical science whose experiments will unknowingly lead to social disorder, and Lucy, the object of public attention as a luchadora who herself is inadvertently bringing disorder to the public world of lucha libre through her own careless wrestling tactics.

In the second match, Lucy's opponent wears black tights and a silver mask bearing a certain similarity to Santo's mask, and one is even tempted to describe her opponent as a "female Santo." Unsurprisingly, Lucy again throws her opponent out of the ring and reacts with horror; Cardona even repeats the shot of Lucy leaning over the ring, her hands clutching the top ropes, looking aghast at her fallen opponent on the concrete floor outside the ring. However, Lucy's opponent is uninjured and quickly recovers, and she defeats the visibly-shaken Lucy by putting her in a painful submission hold. The crowd reacts enthusiastically, and one might infer that this female parody of Santo is the técnico in this particular match: the heroic "Silver-Masked Woman" against the red-devil/panther-woman rudo who nearly (again) mortally injured her opponent. Lucy is depicted as a fallible, even dangerous figure — like Dr. Krellman, a figure who is inadvertently bringing disaster into the public sphere they inhabit.

Following Lucy's defeat, Cardona again uses the jarring "abstract painting insert" as a transition to the next scene. Lucy and Arthur walk into the locker room, and she explains how the potential repetition of the situation with Elena frightened and disturbed her, causing her to lose her concentration and consequently the match. Arthur attempts to console her as he stands behind her (literally), beginning to undo the straps of her mask for her. Once more, Arthur assumes the task of masking and unmasking Lucy and controlling her transition between private and public life. This crucial issue of Arthur's control over Lucy's mask, and public versus private destiny, is explicitly addressed in the next locker room scene when Lucy prepares for the third (and final) match of the film. With Lucy still dwelling on the tragic incident with Elena, Arthur grows impatient and lectures her, telling her she needs to forget about the accident or else leave the ring entirely, a solution he would actually invite: Lucy abandoning her wrestling career in favor of being his wife. Lucy happily agrees and informs Arthur she will retire when her contract expires following "next Monday's free-for-all." The camera provides another long zoom in to a medium close-up of the couple as they lovingly kiss, sealing the agreement on the future course of their relationship. The zoom in also emphasizes and exaggerates the intimacy of the moment, providing an element of melodramatic corniness and unintentional humor; much like the long zoom in on Dr. Krellman seen earlier in the film, the technique hilariously pushes the scene toward pure soap opera. Then, in an utterly disorientating moment, a broadly smiling Lucy turns, faces the camera, and walks directly toward it — the viewer expecting her to run headlong into the camera as her face overwhelms the frame.

This shot cuts to the last lucha libre sequence of *Bloody Apes*, and Lucy, motivated by romantic bliss, quickly and effortlessly defeats her opponent. However, the pleasant romantic mood established between the couple is squashed when Arthur cancels their date: he must instead investigate the mysterious disappearance of the ape from the city zoo. Lucy, who is in the shower when Arthur knocks on the door, walks through the locker room with a towel covering the front of her body, and the film spectator is afforded a gratuitous view of her buttocks (a shot which would have appeared in *Horror y sexo* but obviously not *El horripilante bestia humana*). Needless to say, Lucy is most displeased with the change in plans, especially considering she has just agreed to abandon her entire wrestling career in favor of their relationship. Arthur explains, "But it's my duty, my love," and Lucy hilariously retorts, "My love — *my foot!*" before slamming the door in Arthur's face.

In the first part of *Bloody Apes*, the lucha libre and horror components are not integrated but rather tell parallel and, for the most part, independent stories: Lucy's career crisis and Dr. Krellman's attempts to save his son. Furthermore, the lucha libre aspects of the film do not eventually combine with the horror narrative, so there's no resulting climactic merger of wrestling and horror (as in *Santo vs. the Vampire Women, Doctor of Doom*, etc.). Instead, lucha libre is essentially discarded in the second half of *Bloody Apes*, which focuses on Dr. Krellman unintentionally turning his son into a horrific, savage monster (a theme of crucial importance to the film). In fact, *Lucy* is virtually eliminated from the second half of *Bloody Apes*. The only other substantial scene involving Lucy is another women's locker room moment (coming after an unseen match), a sequence obviously (and only?) included to spotlight a second nude scene by Norma Lazareno; she also briefly surfaces at the end of the film to hastily resolve the problem-plagued romantic relationship between her and Arthur.

Following the heart transplant, the formally frail, sickly Julio transforms into a beefy, muscular man with a Neanderthal face (as noted, yet another ape-man role for Gerardo Zepeda). As Julio transforms into the ape-man and rises from the operating table, the dissonant music from the opening credits blasts forth on the soundtrack, suggesting the film is indeed "starting over" by no longer focusing on the luchadora but instead concentrating on the titular monster: "the blood-curdling human beast." The ape-man escapes from Dr. Krellman's basement laboratory and roams the city streets until it spots a young woman in a window; he immediately scales the wall of the apartment building with steadfast determination. The scene cuts to a young, naked woman leaving the shower, echoing the film's preoccupation with filming Lucy leaving the shower in the locker room. Having invaded her apartment, the monster stands imposingly in front of her, blocking the bathroom door, and grabs her when she faints. Carrying her to bed and then laying beside her, the ape-man begins to clumsily stroke her naked body. This becomes a highly disconcerting moment in the film, as the viewer watches the brutish, subhuman monster fondle the unconscious woman's naked body with its mammoth hands. The ape-man even fumbles to maneuver the woman's body in such a way as to provide the viewer a glimpse of her naked buttocks without disturbing the strategically-placed purple towel necessarily covering her pubic hair.

As the woman regains consciousness, Cardona suddenly inserts an extreme close-up of the monster's eyes, a shot repeated numerous times throughout the remainder of *Bloody Apes*. In one respect, the close-ups seem to be included simply because showing close-ups of a monster's eyes during evil acts is a standard filmic device in mexploitation, specifically the inevitable extreme close-ups of eyes when hypnotic power is employed (the repeatedly recycled shots of Tundra's eyes in *Santo vs. the Vampire Women*, for example). However, the close-ups of the monster's eyes in *Bloody Apes* serve no narrative purpose. Like the sudden inserts of the abstract painting used to bridge scenes, these close-ups do not create dramatic tension, but instead disrupt the flow of the film and produce a disorientating effect on the viewer

153

as the monster stares directly at the camera and the audience. The issue of *sight* itself is being addressed: the monster staring at the viewer, meeting the spectator's gaze and becoming some sort of awful mirror for the male film viewer as he watches the events unfold onscreen. In short, the extreme close-ups do not depict an *act of hypnosis*, but signify the *concept of sadistic voyeurism*: the inherent relationship to sight, sadism, and voyeurism in the horror film genre and the viewer's own status in watching and participating in the violent spectacle of the horror film.[4] When the nude woman screams at the "sight" of the ape-man groping her body, the monster responds by savagely assaulting her in a tightly edited series of close-ups: the woman's bloodied face, hands, and breasts; the monster, shown from behind, on top of the woman; a lamp shattering against the wall; blood copiously splattering the white walls, (which recalls both the dripping blood of the credits and the abstract-painting inserts). It should be stressed that at this point virtually *all* of the footage of this harrowing rape-murder was filmed and inserted by Jerald Intrator, rather than being the work of Cardona, an assumption borne out by the continuity lapses. In the initial scenes where the ape-man carries the woman to bed and fondles her, all the shots are medium-long, full-body shots which clearly depict Zepeda as the ape-man, and the nude woman's vagina is obscured by a one-color *dark* purple towel, indicating these scenes would have appeared in Cardona's *Horror y sexo*. However, when the violence escalates and the rape and murder unfold in graphic detail, the pubic hair of the actress is concealed by a much lighter, *two-tone* purple towel, and it is indeed a different actress than the one who appears in Cardona's footage.

After the vicious attack on the woman, the monster lurks in the shadows of a building as a boy walks down the street cheerfully whistling and carrying some groceries, presumably on an errand for his mother. In a touch of dark comedy, the boy sports a bright, blood-red turtleneck sweater. One initially fears that the poor, unsuspecting child will be the next victim of the ape-man's rampage. However, the monster does not attack the boy, but instead simply watches him walk away down the dark, city street. This suggests another issue the film raises regarding the status of women in Mexican society: while the monster exhibits a sense of moral boundaries even it will not cross (in the form of molesting or killing a child), he has no qualms about raping and killing a naked woman. Fortunately, further violence and more potential disaster are averted by Dr. Krellman and Goyo, who fortuitously manage to locate the monster and fire a tranquilizer dart into its neck, allowing them to return the beast to the safety and confines of the lab. It becomes evident that Dr. Krellman is far more interested in protecting his son, or the abominable creation his son has become, than protecting the Mexican public. In doing so, Dr. Krellman commits the greatest sin science and progress can make in mexploitation cinema: endangering Mexican society rather than promoting social advancement.

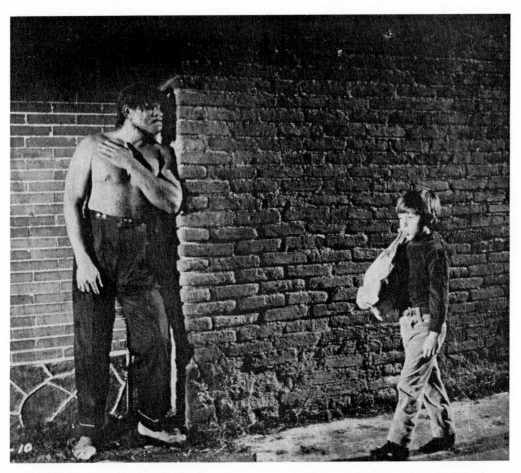

Thinking the unthinkable: horrible human beast (Gerardo Zepeda) encounters a defenseless child on a dark city street in *El horripilante bestia humana* (*Night of the Bloody Apes*).

The scene cuts to a sheet-covered stretcher being removed from the woman's apartment through a crowd of horrified tenants, confirming that the monster indeed killed the woman — a graphic sexual assault added to *Bloody Apes* by Intrator, but one which would have been left to the imagination of its Mexican audiences. Arthur follows the stretcher out of the apartment, and is now properly integrated into the horror film element of *Bloody Apes*. Arthur vainly attempts to question three witnesses, who provide hysterical accounts all at once. Pleading for calm, Arthur asks them to answer "one at a time." There is a brief pause before the three witnesses start speaking simultaneously, interrupting and shouting over each other, at which time the scene abruptly ends. Beyond the narrative importance of integrating

Arthur's character with the horror film proper, the scene provides a moment of comic relief and ill-timed levity, a strategy quite common in mexploitation horror (such as the odd exchanges of dialogue between the detectives in *The Brainiac* or the absurdist-romantic banter between Golden Rubi and Tommy in *Doctor of Doom* and *Wrestling Women*).

Back at Dr. Krellman's laboratory, the monster is now secured to the operating table with ropes. Rivaling his initial absurd medical rationale for the operation, Dr. Krellman dejectedly explains to Goyo, "the heart of a gorilla is too potent for any human," and the resulting increased blood pressure it places on the brain turns a man into an animal(?). Then, without any vocal inflection whatsoever, Dr. Krellman announces: "Suddenly an idea occurs to me before it becomes too late!" (one can practically see the light bulb over his head). Dr. Krellman speculates that a *human* heart transplanted into Julio could reverse the process of de-evolution, and that the donor could be the unfortunate Elena, who lies in a coma at the hospital. Goyo realizes the operation will result in Elena's certain death, which would be tantamount to murder, and reacts to the idea with understandable apprehension. Nonetheless, Dr. Krellman hilariously explains that Elena will probably die anyway, and "if by some miracle she lives, she'll be an *idiot* for the rest of her life!" Allaying Goyo's concerns with this rather cold-blooded justification, Dr. Krellman and Goyo depart in order to bring Elena and her "mindless" body back to the laboratory: as in *Doctor of Doom*, modern science's primary concern for the woman revolves around the utility of her body in its procedures.

However, the monster takes advantage of their absence to escape again, tearing aside the wooden planks that board up the broken window and climbing out in the pursuit of more innocent victims. The scene cuts to Elena's hospital room, where Dr. Krellman and Goyo are climbing *into* her room through the window. The juxtaposition creates an association between the ape-man and Dr. Krellman: both of them are "monsters" and ruthless murderers of women. Again set loose on the Mexican public, the monster's next killing spree is not limited to young women but indiscriminately directed at anyone it encounters. Wandering in a local park, the monster stumbles across a man and a woman (Noelia Noel) necking on a bench. As the music from the opening credits once again blasts forth on the soundtrack, the monster brutally attacks the couple, conveniently ripping the woman's dress to expose her breasts. The woman flees in terror and Cardona provides gratuitous shots of her running directly toward the camera to allow a glimpse of her jiggling breasts. Meanwhile, the monster savagely strangles the man, hands ripping the flesh off the man's throat (a close viewing of the sequence reveals that two very different actors appear in the sequence — the actor in Intrator's inserts is much older than the one in Cardona's original film, and his hair is not only much shorter and straighter, but grey at the temples!).

After killing the man, the monster drops him in a heap and then hunts down the woman, who has conveniently fallen while fleeing from the monster. The ape-man rips her dress to pieces but stops short of actually raping and killing her — another gratuitous moment of female nudity and violent sexual assault. This sequence clearly features both Zepeda and Noel throughout its duration and would have presumably appeared in *Horror y sexo,* demonstrating, if nothing else, that the overtly misogynistic aspects of the film were not simply the result of Intrator's inserts. As the attack builds in unnerving intensity, Cardona suddenly cuts to Dr. Krellman and Goyo parking the station wagon and slowly unloading Elena's body from the back seat. The cross-cutting is one of many instances in Cardona's films where he essentially sabotages any momentum his films might gather by suddenly cutting from intense moments to meandering long takes of other narrative events which easily could have been shown *after* the action sequences had run their dramatic course (or, in the case of Hollywood narrative logic, scenes that *should* have been shown after the action scenes are completed). The scene then abruptly cuts back to the disheveled woman sprawled on the grass as the monster departs. Not only is the dress completely shredded and her underwear pulled halfway around her buttocks, but Noel's long hair extensions have fallen off during the scene and lie next to her, an obvious continuity error which inadvertently implies that the monster brutally pulled a substantial amount of hair out of her head. Nonetheless, she survives the attack and, with her dress and hair now inexplicably and remarkably intact, runs to a butcher shop — another moment of black comedy, considering the "butchering" of human bodies the monster is performing. "A horrible monster is trying to kill my boyfriend! Help him!" she screams. Knife in hand, the butcher sets off in pursuit of the monster, accompanied by the music from the opening credits. Unfortunately, he is almost immediately ambushed by the monster, who wrests the knife from him and brutally stabs him, an attack enhanced by more Intrator gore insets: close-ups of an upraised, bloody knife and the butcher's blood-soaked white shirt. A third victim is quickly dispatched as well, an innocent pedestrian who simply happens to cross the rampaging monster's path. The monster pounces on him, and, in a rather clever (if ghastly) juxtaposition an extreme close-up of the monster's eyes is followed by a close-up of the victim's face as his right eye and brain matter are squeezed out of his eye socket by the monster's powerful hands crushing his victim's skull (presumably another Intrator insert). The images provide a shift from having the eyes of the monster and film viewer meet to a moment where the violence literally has its victim's (and its *audience's*) eyes "popping out of their sockets."[5]

The streets begin to fill with frantic bystanders, witnesses, and police, all baffled and frightened by this sudden explosion of violence; of course, the film itself was made during a period of intense political unrest and violence, culminating in the Tlatelolco massacre. Dr. Krellman and Goyo again locate, subdue, and capture the monster before the police or vigilantes can. After they load the tranquilized monster into the station wagon, a high-angle long shot of the chaotic crowd surveys the area for almost one minute. A police car careens into the shot, nearly colliding with Dr. Krellman's station wagon as it hurriedly flees the scene. Another police car soon enters the frame, almost plowing into the crowd of bystanders. Shortly afterward an ambulance, sirens wailing and lights flashing, drives into the frame, quickly followed by another ambulance. This long take in *Bloody Apes* is markedly different than those in mexploitation films such as *El barón del terror* or *Santo contra las mujeres vampiro*, where the long take is used to establish Gothic atmosphere, exaggerate and parody horror film conventions, and/or dwell on plot exposition, often at the expense of narrative momentum. In *Bloody Apes*, the long take of the crime scene serves to create an unsettling sense of urban violence and disorder. There is a certain grim realism in the long take, as if the viewers were watching actual footage of the chaotic aftermath of an accident or actual crime scene. Unlike the long takes of early mexploitation that introduce the viewer to a fantastic world of horror, in *Bloody Apes*, especially in the context of Tlatelolco, this long take in *Bloody Apes* reveals that the horror has become all too real and the monsters too familiar — no longer consigned to haunted mansions and wrestling rings, but now roaming the bloodied streets of Mexico City.

Having succeeded in abducting Elena and (again) subduing the monster, Dr. Krellman begins the second heart transplant. In a sequence that could be said to sum up *Bloody Apes'* unorthodox film techniques and emphasis on "*horror y sexo*," the surgical procedure begins with Elena laid out on the operating table, with the sheet being pulled down to reveal her naked body. The shot stops just as the sheet reaches her pubic hair, and jump-cuts to a medium close-up of Elena, and specifically her breasts, which are the focal point of the shot. The "abstract painting insert" is then jarringly and incongruously inserted, followed by graphic stock footage of open-heart surgery — the patient's chest is sliced open and the heart can be seen beating. At its most sexist, *Bloody Apes* reduces the woman's body to a set of fetishized tits and eviscerated torso. Indeed, throughout *Bloody Apes* one is struck by how the woman's (nude) body continually becomes a site of male dominance: savage sexual assaults by a subhuman man-monster, the modern procedures of scientific experimentation, or an object of voyeuristic pleasure for the male film audience. The stock footage cuts to an extreme close-up of Dr. Krellman's eyes, which again identifies him as "a monster" by drawing a comparison between his own eyes and those of the ape-man's, seen in close-up throughout the film. The close-up of Dr. Krellman's eyes also suggests he is exercising evil power: the use and abuse of medical science which can — and *will*— only lead to further social disorder and violence.

However, the relentless pace of the film established by its volley of disturbing images during the ape-man's second round of murders and this second gruesome heart transplant is quickly dissipated by two protracted and ponderous expository sequences that grind the film to a complete halt. The first is an interminable scene between Dr. Krellman and the medical staff discussing what to make of Elena's strange and sudden disappearance, and, perhaps more importantly, how to handle the potential public relations debacle that could arise from the hospital misplacing a comatose patient. Overly long and laboriously paced, the scene is completely extraneous in furthering the action or even developing the plot, and eventually only serves to dampen the viewer's growing involvement with the film. This is immediately followed by another conference, this time between Arthur and the other police investigators. Police experts and the coroner put forth their ideas about the strange circumstances surrounding the murders. Summing up the evidence, Arthur posits his own theory, much to the dismay of the derisive police chief:

> ARTHUR: What I am going to say just might sound absurd, and could only happen in this century, but from all of the proof you have just seen and the declaration of the young girl, I have come to this conclusion: that whatever committed these atrocities is a beast, yes, but a horrible half-beast, half human!
> THE CHIEF: I'll say that's absurd — the proofs are circumstantial. It's more probable that of late more and more you're watching on your television many of those pictures of terror!

Certainly, one is first struck by the highly convoluted language of the discussion (which rivals the best of Murray's cumbersome translations and dubbing), arguably the result of translating the dialogue too literally, as well as matching the words to the movements of the actors' mouths. During his analysis of the crimes, the coroner describes the vicious methods of the "assassin," a literal translation of the word *asesino*, which would better translate as "murderer" or "killer" in this context (but "assassin" corresponds better to the movements of the character's mouth). Likewise, the Chief uses the awkward phrase "pictures of terror" instead of "horror movies," since it best correlates to the Spanish phrase *cine del terror* ("cinema of terror"). Indicative of the expository dialogue that often interrupts the narrative flow of mexploitation films, the exchange provides a redundant summary of already-known plot details. Nevertheless, one interesting piece of dialogue is the Chief's comment to Arthur that his preposterous theory about the crimes is the direct result of "watching on your television many of those pictures of terror!" As discussed previously in regards to Cardona's *Las luchadoras contra la momia* and *Santo en el tesoro de Drácula* (as well as Crevenna's *Santo vs. la invasión de los marcianos*), key moments and significant portions of these films are depicted as occurring *on television* (the TV monitor for Prince Fujiyata's hidden camera; Santo's time travel machine's TV monitor; the Martians who deliver their threatening broadcasts on television and watch the film's events unfold on their "panoptic machine"). Such moments become ironic commentaries on the status of the films as low-budget horror movie fare one would view on television. Likewise, events transpiring in *Bloody Apes* are not only described as being out of late-night "pictures of terror," but *are* literally and directly out of a previous "picture of terror," in that the film itself is a loose remake of the popular *Las luchadoras vs. el médico asesino*.

Obligated by his police work to stake out the area where the monster has committed the murders, Arthur is unable to attend Lucy's next wrestling match, but listens to her victory over the car radio and places a phone call to the arena through police headquarters to offer his congratulations. Lucy is in the shower when the phone rings; she exits the shower stall with a towel over her torso, then lies on her stomach on the locker room massage table while she chats with Arthur. The male film viewer is afforded the opportunity to dwell on the sight of her naked body as she stretches out prone on the massage table: the shot could easily be a photograph from a men's magazine or a nudie-cutie sexploitation film. In this way, the film reintroduces of lucha libre not to showcase luchadora matches, but to provide opportunities by which Lucy can be shown naked in the locker room *after* her matches. As seen in the previous *Luchadoras* films, this exclusive, private space of the women's locker room is nevertheless an area which the camera can access or even *trespass into* for the benefit of the male spectator, and the voyeuristic implications of the first two *Luchadoras* films are taken to their logical and now-permissible limits. (However, while Mexican film censorship codes liberally loosened in the late 1960s, it does bear repeating that no nudity would have appeared in the "A" authorized *El horripilante bestia humana* released in Mexico.)

Meanwhile, Dr. Krellman's second operation seems to have been a success, and Julio transforms back into a human. Overjoyed, Dr. Krellman and Goyo carry Julio to his bedroom, where Dr. Krellman gently puts Julio to bed while the soundtrack plays a syrupy, lounge-like version of a children's lullaby: an ironic, darkly-comic accompaniment to Dr. Krellman's devoted, paternal attention to his son, which by now includes brutal scientific experiments and murder. Unfortunately, Dr. Krellman's success with restoring Julio's humanity is short-lived. Returning to the hospital to cover his actions, Dr. Krellman leaves Goyo in charge of Julio, who again transforms into a human beast, albeit a more slender version that now sports fangs. Much like Vendetta in *Doctor of Doom*, Julio is no longer an ape-man, but now an *ape-man-woman*: a monster who is an aberration of nature and society by being both animal and human (ape and man), but also a social and sexual anomaly by being both male and female (man and woman). Whereas Vendetta consists of a male gorilla's brain housed in a woman's body, Julio is a man poisoned by *both* gorilla blood and a woman's heart.

Back in a monstrous form, Julio wanders about the mansion and, as if motivated by animal instinct, eventually locates Goyo in his father's study. Goyo becomes the next victim of the monster when the assistant is violently grabbed and pulled out of a chair by the beast man. Again, like the "girl in the shower" murder, the actual attack on Goyo occurred off-screen in *El horripilante bestia humana*. However, in *Bloody Apes* the murder is depicted in graphic detail courtesy of Intrator. As a way of providing some continuity between Cardona's original film and his inserts, Intrator cross-cuts between shots of Dr. Krellman arriving at his home in his station wagon, the extreme close-ups of the monster's eyes, and the vicious decapitation of Goyo, in which the monster wrenches Goyo's head off his shoulders with his bare hands, replete with the requisite gratuitous and gory close-ups of ripping flesh. However, as with the other added murders footage the gore inserts contain subtle but discernable continuity flaws, particularly regarding the characters' clothing. Whereas Goyo wears an olive shirt, the Goyo dummy wears a lime green jacket and white shirt. Likewise, the ape-man's pajamas, which have white trim around the arm and leg cuffs in Cardona's footage, are a drab, *solid* blue in this scene and the subsequent gore close-ups that appear in the remainder of the film.

Following Goyo's murder, the viewer is bombarded with zoom-ins: when Dr. Krellman walks into the mansion, Cardona slowly and dramatically zooms from a long shot to a medium shot of Dr. Krellman reacting in horror, which is matched by a rapid zoom towards Goyo's disembodied head lying on the floor of the study (inserted by Intrator). The sudden, overly-dramatic zoom both humorously exaggerates and negates the drama and shock effect of the scene, especially in that it is accompanied by a tremolo-tinged electric guitar chord which further renders the scene comical rather than horrifying. The moment certainly echoes Herschell Gordon Lewis and his seminal *Bloodfeast*, which also uses hilarious and highly inappropriate comical musical effects in its most dramatic or horrific moments, such as a belching trombone when a woman histrionically dies screaming in her hospital bed. Frantically, Dr. Krellman searches the house for Julio, whose bare feet are seen in the doorway of the bedroom; the camera then pans upward to reveal the monster nonchalantly carrying Goyo's head (an Intrator insert, in that the white trim around the pants cuffs of Juilo's pajamas is again absent). Attempting to reason with his son the monster ("Julio — *I'm your father!*"), Dr. Krellman stumbles and falls headfirst into a desk, knocking him unconscious. Julio gingerly and thoughtfully picks up his father and places him in bed before embarking on yet another killing spree. Like hurting a child, harming his own father is a crime against society even a monster will not perform.

Arriving at the scene of the stakeout for a romantic rendezvous with Arthur, Lucy immediately witnesses the murder of a policeman by the human beast on the city street. Once again Intrator augments the murder with more graphic inserts showing the monster brutally murdering the cop by tearing off his scalp–a hilarious effect generated by the monster pulling a bloody toupee off the head of the bald actor (again, the effects of Herschell Gordon Lewis spring to mind). Lucy is also promptly and briefly pursued by the monster; she flees in terror before falling helplessly to the ground, but is fortuitously rescued by Arthur. The ape-man's brief attack on Lucy is one of the more important — and disappointing — aspects of *Bloody Apes*. The early luchadoras, Gloria Venus and Golden Rubi, were not only capable of handling themselves *in* the ring, as underscored by their important cultural battle with the Fujiyata sisters in *Wresting Women vs. the Aztec Mummy*, but *out* of the ring as well, specifically when Gloria Venus and Golden Rubi beat up the Mad Doctor's henchmen (three times) and rescued their boyfriends (twice) in *Doctor of Doom*. In *Bloody Apes*, there is a pronounced distinction between the public role of "the luchadora" in the spectacle of the wrestling ring and the private role of "the woman" in Mexican society as a whole. While Gloria Venus and Golden Rubi were capable of great physical prowess and athleticism in or out of the wrestling ring, once Lucy leaves the ring and removes her red devil-cat mask and latex outfit, she adopts the roles of fetishized sex-object and passive, helpless female: an object of male desire and domination.

When Arthur intervenes to rescue Lucy, the monster flees. Dr. Krellman desperately interferes in an attempt to protect his mutated son from the police. After a brief struggle, Arthur subdues the elderly Dr. Krellman and then locates Julio, now transformed back to his human form, barely conscious on the grass in the park. A close-up of the dazed Julio cuts to an out-of-focus shot which refocuses on a close-up profile of Arthur — the camera pulls back to reveal various detectives inside Dr. Krellman's home, and Goyo's dead body being carried out by a stretcher (as with the first murder of the woman, the murder of Goyo would be unseen by Mexican audiences but established by the sheet-covered body on the stretcher). The existence of Dr. Krellman's secret basement laboratory/operating room is also discovered. Informed that both Dr. Krellman and Julio were taken to the local hospital, Arthur's suspicions fall on Julio: "He just might give us the clue to the case!" Indeed, the scene abruptly cuts to the hospital, where a nurse enters Julio's room. Both the nurse and film viewer are greeted by a dizzying montage of zooms and close-ups of an orderly's mangled face as large hands brutally tear at the flesh, intercut with close-ups of blood-soaked, white hospital clothing: Julio, obviously again transformed into the human beast, is savagely mutilating the man (the last of the monster's vicious murders, this entire sequence was probably shot and edited into the film by Intrator, although it certainly would not be out of place in one of Rene Cardona, Jr.'s later exploitation horror films).

The monster then kidnaps a young girl and flees to the roof of the hospital, echoing the ending of *Doctor of Doom* when Dr. Wright and Vendetta seek refuge — and meet their eventual death — atop a water tower. Thematically, the abduction of the child is important in that the monster has now crossed the moral line regarding the fate and safety of Mexico's children. After his first murder of the young woman, Julio, having an *ape* heart and being an *ape-man*, would nevertheless not harm the helpless child in the streets while in his monstrous state. However, by the conclusion of the film, Julio is no longer merely an *ape-man* but an *ape-man-woman*, a being that is not only a monstrous hybrid of animal and human, but man and woman: a crime against nature not only eliminating distinctions between human and animal (civilized verses primitive), but *gender* (man verses woman). At its worst, the scene suggests that while Julio had an *ape* heart, he could not bring himself to harm a child, but now with a *woman*'s heart, the monster has no reservations about endangering a Mexican youth. However, a more sympathetic reading might suggest that the monster's abduction of the girl is not maliciously motivated, but a manifestation of a primitive, instinctual, *maternal* drive brought on by the monster becoming a hybrid of animal-human *and* male-female.

Arthur follows the monster to the roof, once again pursued by Dr. Krellman, who finally realizes the socially destructive consequences of his actions when this innocent *child*, the symbol of Mexico's *future*, is threatened by the scientific, social, and sexual monstrosity he created. Succeeding in reasoning with the human-beast-man-woman he has created out of his son, and perhaps appealing to the monster's "feminine side" (its "heart of a woman"), Dr. Krellman convinces Julio to release the child, at which point the monster is shot by police from the street below. Julio is mortally wounded, and Dr. Krellman pleads for his son to forgive him: "When I knew your sickness was incurable, I acted against the dictates of God trying to save you." The corny lullaby music is again heard on the soundtrack as Julio dies, the young girl standing next to him, providing an ironic contrast between the child saved from the monster, and Julio, the child made into a monster by his father and even unintentionally *killed* by his father through his violation of the laws of science. Importantly, the stock mexploitation character who is both a strong father and respected scientist, the figure signifying both the tenets of *patriarchy* and *modernity*, is rendered a macabre and tragic parody in *Bloody Apes*: Dr. Krellman *fails* to fulfill *either* of his social obligations as family patriarch and modern scientist.

With Julio's death, modern Mexican society is seemingly returned to normality. However, *Bloody Apes*' end presents a far bleaker picture of the myths of modernity and patriarchy. This is not to say that the film questions Mexican patriarchy pertaining to gender constructs and male domination over women — indeed, the film is most conservative in this regard, especially in comparison to the early *Luchadoras* films. Rather, there is a sort of irreconcilable tension in the film that exists between *generations*: fathers and sons. Despite the father's best intentions for his son, to keep him a functioning part of a social order the father turns his son into a violent human beast running wild in the streets, unintentionally causing the death of his son and introducing disaster to society. Conversely, the son is no longer a figure of loyalty and obedience to the father: under the appearance of the son's bourgeois civility lurks an uncontrollable force of disorder and violence. These themes become highly appropriate for a Mexican society whose young people were threatening revolutionary action and being gunned down in the streets at Tlatelolco. Héctor Aguilar Camín and Lorenzo Meyer suggest, "The 1968 rebels were the *sons and daughters of the middle-class* ... the generation that was called on to fulfill that transition and take command of the industrial and cosmopolitan Mexico that was emerging. In this sense ... Tlatelolco *killed the continuity of Mexico's modernization.*"[6] While much of mexploitation's ideological project centered on a valorization of modernity and progress, accomplished by extinguishing the obsolete monsters of the past and their debilitating effect on the present, in *Bloody Apes* the monster is itself a force of the present: a "middle-class son" transformed into horrific, brutal monstrosity of social violence by his scientist father. The monster no longer impedes the drive to modernity; instead, the monster is both the *result* of modernity and the *instrument* of modern society's own destruction. Indeed, the monster is no longer a supernatural monster resurrected from Mexico's past, but a modern middle-class son turned "horrible human beast."

The scene abruptly cuts to Arthur and Lucy seated in his car. They provide a brief summation of the film's narrative and social, moral lesson with all the empathy of one of Jack Webb's *Dragnet* episodes:

> LUCY: How did you discover the disappearance of Elena?
> ARTHUR: Well, Dr. Krellman went out of his mind, but he remained lucid for a moment and confessed everything. Poor fool. The desire to save his son from death was the cause of so many people's suffering.
> LUCY: It's unfortunate — really sad.

Bloody Apes closes with a certain sense of resignation and even lament, literalized by Lucy's blasé summary of the events as "unfortunate — really sad." Dr. Krellman, the devoted father and respected doctor, is left consumed by madness. His scientific knowledge, which violated "the dictates of God" in an attempt to save his son from inevitable death, only succeeded in bring social disorder and violence to society. However, in a seeming attempt to manufacture a "happy ending" for the film, Lucy retires from the ring in favor of domestic bliss with Arthur Martinez. The Amazonian luchadoras of *Doctor of Doom* and *Wrestling Women vs. the Aztec Mummy* are replaced by a nondescript image of the modern Mexican woman whose greatest contribution to Mexican society is not to participate in the public sphere but to accept domestic servitude as a way to heal Mexico's political wounds. In *Bloody Apes*, the onscreen luchadora no longer actively fights for social order within Mexican society, but instead herself becomes a detriment to Mexico's social stability. Whereas the

6. El horripilante bestia humana (Night of the Bloody Apes, *1968*)

family bond between father and son has been hopelessly destroyed, the family bond between husband and wife still provides a semblance of hope.

Ultimately, *Bloody Apes* reflects the violence, disarray, and pessimism of late 1960s Mexican political life. Fittingly, the retirement of the luchadora from the ring closes the book on Cardona's "Wrestling Women" cycle. As Arthur and Lucy drive away into the darkness, perhaps this is also Cardona's concession that the *Luchadoras* film cycle itself has been consigned to the darkness, no longer adequately able to express the simplistic triumph of good over evil within the exploding political tensions of contemporary Mexican society. The car disappears from view in the background, leaving only an abandoned city street and the aftermath of violence. The final shot is recycled from the credits: red liquid forming a pool of blood over which the words "The End" appear. This serves as an ominous warning that the cycle of violence is set to begin again, that more "monsters" born out of the chaos of modernity and progress are yet to appear, that more sons will become monstrous threats to society, that more sons will be destroyed by their fathers, that "the end" for Mexican society is still more bloodshed and violence: that there may be many more Tlatelolcos in Mexico's future.

Conclusion:
The End of Mexploitation

Mexican Horror Cinema After Tlatelolco

The impact of the Tlatelolco massacre on the Mexican national psyche cannot be overstated: it brutally exposed the fragility, inadequacy, and hypocrisy of the myths of Mexican democracy perpetuated by decades of the PRI. As Héctor Aguilar Camín and Lorenzo Meyer observed:

> October 2, 1968, was the starting point of a new crisis in Mexico: on that date, an interval began during which the country lost confidence in its present, ceased celebrating and consolidating its achievements and miracles, and began to confront daily, and for more than a decade, its own previously ignored insufficiencies, failures, and miseries. The crisis of 1968 was not a structural crisis that would place at risk the very survival of the nation; it was, above all, a political, moral, and psychological crisis, a crisis of values and principles, which shook up the triumphant schemes of the governing elite; *it was the bloody announcement that the times had changed, without changing the means to confront them.*[1]

In a bitter political irony, Luis Echeverria succeeded Gustavo Díaz Ordaz as Mexico's president in 1970: Echeverria served as Díaz Ordaz's Minister of the Interior, and is often considered one of the primary instigators of the horrifying events at Tlatelolco. With the nation still reeling from the national trauma of Tlatelolco, the Echeverria presidency of 1970–76 attempted to bring order back to Mexico and, as some would claim, ease its own guilty political conscience. Echeverria's administration spearheaded a populist political agenda which, on the surface, pushed Mexico towards the left, or, perhaps more accurately, brought the country closer to political moderation in the wake of the right-wing excesses of Díaz Ordaz. Echeverria's initiatives included economic reform: luxury taxes targeted at the wealthy, and price freezes on essential goods and services aimed at relieving the burdens of the urban poor. In addition to issuing presidential pardons to student leaders jailed by the Díaz Ordaz administration after Tlatelolco, and improving relationships with the intellectual elite at the universities, Echeverria started the "Democratic Opening," designed to provide channels for oppositional voices in the Mexican public sphere. However, Echeverria's administration did not promote social stability, but instead exacerbated bitter political animosities. Despite Echeverria's progressivism, his presidency "was marked by agricultural downturns and industrial monopolies, land invasions, strikes, and open conflicts between the forces that were growing in society and *those that continued to claim, through the state, the historical roles of judge and father.*"[2] The entrenched political leaders of the PRI party and the Right Wing came to view Echeverria as a sell-out or even a traitor — supposedly one of their own who spinelessly caved in to left-wing malcontents as president. Conversely, the Left saw Echeverria's programs as political damage control rather than social reform, branding his policies as a cynical effort to desperately maintain the *status quo* under the guise of progressive politics. "It was a response to the demands of 'updating' the legacy, in order to preserve what was preservable. The idea of 'letting things change so that everything remains the same' went hand in hand, as an attitude and a perception, with the very anachronism of some the major governmental policy decisions."[3]

Amid the political and cultural tumult of the late 1960s, Mexican horror cinema itself began to experience radical changes. With the advent of less-restrictive censorship policies in the Mexican film industry in the late 1960s, nudity and explicit violence began appearing in mexploitation films, although these nude versions were intended for international rather than domestic release. In Mexico, the films of Santo and other luchadores (and luchadoras) were generally only released under the "A" (all-ages) certification, which necessarily restricted the content and promoted a great deal of self-censorship among film producers and directors. Nevertheless, attempts were made to make lucha libre films more contemporary as early as the mid–1960s, such as the mildly risqué moment in *Atacan las brujas* when the witch Medusa unsuccessfully attempts to seduce the sexually moral countermacho Santo by appearing in his bedroom in a spangled bikini. However, such efforts update the horror-wrestling movies by including actresses in bikinis, incorporating other popular genres at the time (Bond-style spy films), and offering brief scenes of Hammer Studios–inspired bloodshed would inevitably pale in comparison to the scenes of a Mexican army officer being castrated and a battle between two women with whips in Jodorowsy's *El Topo*, let alone the startling and provocative scenes of nuns being sadistically flogged and the crucifixion-murder of a nude woman during a Catholic mass in Juan López Moctezuma's *Alucarda*.

By the 1970s, the lucha libre films which dominated Mexican horror cinema throughout the 1960s began to seem positively old-fashioned in both their comic book–action and view of Mexican morality and society, especially in the wake of the horrors of Tlatelolco. More challenging and confrontational horror films emerged in Mexico in the early 1970s, specifically Juan López Moctezuma's ground-break-ing *La mansión de la locura* (1971) and *Alucarda* (1975). López Moctezuma's hor-ror films combined elements of classic horror (Expressionist silent cinema and the darkly-comic horror films of James Whale), surrealism (López Moctezuma pro-fessed a deep admiration for the work of Luis Buñuel), experimental filmmaking techniques (one can discern a strong affinity between Pier Paolo Pasolini's avant-garde formalism and López Moctezuma's stylized work), and as much sex and vio-lence as could be found in any example of 1970s Eurotrash cinema (*Alucarda*, which recounts the strange, supernatural, and sexually perverse events in a convent, is commonly associated with the Eurotrash "nunspolitation" sub-genre). For López Moctezuma, recognizable horror and exploitation film genre conventions would become a vehicle for experimental films, and in this way López Moctezuma specifically distanced himself from popular Mexican horror cinema. "The Mexican tradition for such films is very simplistic and very conformist, in my opinion, despite their surface delirium. I don't really like them very much.... I think my films much more belong in the surrealist tradition than in the Mexican one."[4] The iconoclastic work of López Moctezuma would radically depart from traditional mexploitation films and demonstrate, as noted Mexican film director Guillermo del Toro observed, "Horror could be done in Mexico in a different way than just masked wrestler movies with tongue in the cheek."[5]

Death of a Genre

By the 1970s the lucha libre films began to show obvious symptoms of genre exhaustion. As Nelson Carro previously noted, lucha libre films were always "a par-asitic genre," freely combining disparate film genres (horror, action-adventure, sci-ence fiction, serials) and elements of Mexican popular culture (melodrama, comic books, and, of course, lucha libre). As the lucha libre genre became standardized, the films became predictable and redundant in their genre clichés, with various luchadores placed in all-too-familiar situations in film after film. Indeed, lucha libre films became virtual remakes of each other, recycling plots, scenes, and even specific lines of dialogue. Clearly waning in popularity by the mid–1970s, lucha libre films proved unable to satisfy audience demands, not only due to their pre-dictable and antiquated genre conventions, but because of their *outmoded social dis-course*. The events of 1968 not only brutally exposed the anachronisms of Mexican politics and its institutions, they also demonstrated that the lucha libre genre itself had also become something of a cultural anachronism. The advent of mexploita-tion films in the 1950s was not simply the sad decline of the Golden Age of Mex-ican cinema into a sorry B-movie Culture Industry, but the emergence of a Mexican cinema which resonated with a young audience and burgeoning popular culture in the 1950s and 1960s, a new audience which the Golden Age films were unable or unwilling to engage. Hardly devoid of "social vision," mexploitation cinema, typified by horror films such as *El barón del terror*, the films of El Santo and other luchadores, and René Cardona's *Luchadoras* films, actively engaged in the primary cultural discourses shaping Mexican society: mexicanidad, modernity, and gender politics. Yet mexploitation's own decline in the 1970s was itself the result of its own increasing inability to reflect the demands and aspirations of a new, radicalized, counter-culture youth audience, especially after the shocking events at Tlatelolco would permanently change the Mexican political landscape.

Even prior to their eventual decline at the box office, the final symptom of a failing genre, lucha libre films themselves began to express an ambivalence regarding the genre's overall ability to adequately express simplistic solutions of "truth and justice" to the growing political problems of Mexico. The inherent contradictions of Mexican political life that reached their violent apex at Tlatelolco began to be expressed in lucha libre films' own textual problematics, as they seemed unable to contain the inadequacy of their idealistic cultural and political solutions. When Aguilar Camín and Meyer suggested that the Tlatelolco massacre became "a bloody announcement that times have changed" for Mexican society, *El horripilante bestia humana* (or, more correctly, what eventually evolved into *Night of the Bloody Apes*) became a sort of "bloody announcement that times have changed" for the Mexican horror film as well, a change that would become far more pronounced with the subsequent films of Juan López Moctezuma. In *Santo y Blue Demon contra Count Drácula and el Hombre Lobo*, Santo is branded "a retrograde man who still believes in truth and justice." Before Tlatelolco, Santo embodied "the countermacho ... a figure of perfect justice"; after Tlatelolco, Santo would come to represent the entrenched powers who desperately "continued to claim, through the state, the historical roles of judge and father." While lucha libre films would occasionally be produced into the 1980s and beyond, they would increasingly appear nostalgic and anachronistic in the wake of the Tlatelolco massacre. At best becoming consciously campy, and at worst unintentional self-parody, by 1977 the lucha libre genre virtually acknowledged its own cultural obsolescence and demise with *Misterio en las Berumdas* (*Mystery in Bermuda*, dir. Gilberto Martínez Solares). The film not only teamed the Big Three of lucha libre cinema — Santo, Blue Demon, and Mil Máscaras — but ended with the legendary trio disappearing forever in the Bermuda Triangle. To put an exclamation point on the death of the genre, the final scene in the film is an insert of an atomic bomb explosion: a closing shot not only signifying apocalyptic destruction but the implosion of the lucha libre genre. It fittingly served as the final image of the mexploitation era.

Selected Filmography

This filmography, *not* a comprehensive list, is intended to provide the reader with a brief reference guide to the more influential, interesting, or infamous mexploitation films of the era discussed in this project. For readers interested in further information and more comprehensive filmographies and biographies, recommended sources are listed in the bibliography.

Only key or well-known cast members are listed. In cases where character names are known to have been changed from the original Mexican version, the name in the English version appears after the original name in quotation marks. In a few instances, a character's name in the original version could not be verified in comparison to an English-dubbed version; in these cases, only the character's name in the English version is listed, again in quotation marks.

Selected Mexican Horror Films Imported by K. Gordon Murray

El vampiro (*The Vampire*, 1957)
Prod: Abel Salazar.
Dir: Fernando Méndez.
Scr: Henrique Rodriguez, Ramón Obón.
Story: Ramón Obón.
Cast: Germán Robles (Duval), Abel Salazar (Dr. Enrique/"Henry"), Ariadna Welter (Marta/ "Martha").
Released in the U.S. as *The Vampire* (1968); English version directed by Paul Nagel.

El ataúd del vampiro (*The Vampire's Coffin*, 1957)
Prod: Abel Salazar.
Dir: Fernando Méndez.
Scr: Ramón Obón, Alfredo Salazar, Javier Mateos.
Story: Raúl Zenteno.
Cast: Germán Robles (Duval/"Lavud"), Abel Salazar (Enrique/"Dr. Henry Heatherford"), Ariadna Welter (Elena/"Martha")
Released in the U.S. as *The Vampire's Coffin* (1965); English version directed by Paul Nagel.

La maldición de la momia azteca (*The Curse of the Aztec Mummy*, 1957)

Prod: Guillermo Calderón Stell.
Dir: Rafael Portillo.
Scr: Alfredo Salazar, Guillermo Calderón Stell.
Cast: Ramón Gay (Dr. Eduardo Almada/ "Dr. Edward Almaden"), Luis Aceves Castañeda (Dr. Krupp), Rosita Arenas (dual-role: Flor/"Flora" and Xóchtil), Crox Alvarado ("Peacock").
Note: Alvarado is revealed to be El Ángel at the film's end, but El Ángel is obviously played by a much younger and more muscular stand-in in the action sequences.
Released in the U.S. as *The Curse of the Aztec Mummy* (1962); English version directed by Paul Nagel.

La momia azteca contra el robot humano (*The Aztec Mummy vs. the Human Robot*, 1957)

Prod: Guillermo Calderón Stell.
Dir: Rafael Portillo.
Scr: Alfredo Salazar.
Story: Alfredo Salazar, Guillermo Calderón Stell.
Cast: Ramón Gay (Dr. Almada), Luis Aceves Castañeda (Dr. Krupp), Rosita Arenas (dual role: Flor/"Flora" and Xóchitl), Crox Alvarado ("Pincate").
Released in the U.S. as *The Robot vs. the Aztec Mummy* (1965); English version directed by Manuel San Fernando.

El espejo de la bruja (*The Witch's Mirror*, 1960)

Prod: Abel Salazar.
Dir: Chano Urueta.
Scr: Alfredo Ruavano, Carlos Enrique Taboado.
Story: Alfredo Ruavano.
Cast: Isabela Corona (Sara), Armando Calvo (Eduardo Ramos/"Edward Handly"), Rosita Arenas (Deborah Ramos/"Deborah Handly"), Dina de Marco (Elena Ramos/"Helen Handly"), Alfredo Wally Barron (police inspector).
Released in the U.S. as *The Witch's Mirror* (1969); English version directed by Paul Nagel.

El mundo de los vampiros (*The World of the Vampires*, 1960)

Prod: Abel Salazar.
Dir: Alfonso Corona Blake.
Scr: Raúl Zenteno, Ramón Obón.
Story: Raúl Zenteno, Jesús "Murciélago" Velázquez.
Cast: Guillermo Murray (Count Subotai), Erna Martha Baumann (Leonor Kolman/"Leonore Coleman"), Mauricio Garcés (Rodolfo Sabre/"Rudolph Summers"), Silvia Fournier (Mitra Kolman/"Martha Coleman").
Released in the U.S. as *The World of the Vampires* (1964); English version directed by Paul Nagel.

Muñecos Infernales (*Infernal Dolls*, 1960)

Prod: Gulilermo Calderón Stell, Pedro A. Calderón.
Dir: Benito Alazraki.
Scr: Alfredo Salazar.
Cast: Elvira Quintana (Karina/"Karen"), Ramón Gay (Valdés/"Dr. Baldwin"), Quintin Bulnes (Zandor/"Bokos"), Roberto G. Rodríguez (Police Inspector Molinar/"Robert"), Jorge Mondragón

(Luis), Xavier Loyá (Juan/"John"), Luis Aragón (Daniel), Salvador Lozano (Gilberto/"Albert").

Released in the U.S. as *The Curse of the Doll People* (1968); English version directed by Paul Nagel.

El barón del terror (*The Baron of Terror*, 1961)

Prod: Abel Salazar.
Dir: Chano Urueta.
Scr: Federico Curiel, Antonio Orellana, Adolfo López Portillo.
Cast: Abel Salazar (Baron Vitelius), Rubén Rojo (dual role: Marcus/"Marcos" and Reynaldo/ "Ronnie" Miranda), Rosa María Gallardo (Victoria/"Vicki" Contreras), Luis Aragón (Professor Milan), David Silva ("Chief," the head detective), Federico Curiel ("Bennie"), Germán Robles (Indalecio de Pantoja), René Cardona (Luis Meneses), Ofelia Guilmaín (Mrs. Meneses), Ariadna Welter (woman in bar), Mauricio Garcés (medical examiner).
Released in the U.S. as *The Brainiac* (1969); English version directed by Paul Nagel.

La cabenza viviente (*The Living Head*, 1961)

Prod: Abel Salazar.
Dir: Chano Urueta.
Scr: Federico Curiel, Aldofo López Portillo.
Cast: Germán Robles (Professor Mueller), Ana Luisa Peluffo (dual role: Xochiquétzal and Marta Mueller/"Martha Mueller"), Mauricio Garcés (dual role: Ácatl [the Living Head] and Roberto), Guillermo Cramer (Xiu), Abel Salazar ("Inspector Halliday").
Released in the U.S. as *The Living Head* (1969); English version directed by Manuel San Fernando.

La maldición de La Llorona (*The Curse of the Crying Woman*, 1961)

Prod: Abel Salazar.
Dir: Rafael Baledón.
Scr: Rafael Baledón.
Story: Fernando Galiana.
Cast: Rosita Arenas (Amalia/"Emily"), Abel Salazar (Jamie/"Herbert"), Rita Macedo (Selma/ "Thelma"), Carlos López Moctezuma (Juan/"Fred"), Domingo Soler (Daniel).
Released in the U.S. as *The Curse of the Crying Woman* for television syndication in 1964, later released theatrically as a double feature with *The Brainiac* in 1969; English version directed by Stim Segar.

Selected Santo Films

Santo contra los zombies (*Santo vs. the Zombies*, 1961)

Prod: Alberto López.
Dir: Benito Alazraki.
Scr: Benito Alazraki, Antonio Orellana.
Story: Antonio Orellana, Fernando Osés.
Cast: Santo (Santo/"the Saint"), Armando Silvestre (Sanmartin/"Savage"), Lorena Velázquez (Gloria Sandoval/"Gloria Rutherford"), Jamie Fernández (Rodríguez), Dagoberto Rodriguez (Chief Detective Almada), Carlos Agosti (Denero/"Herbert").
Released in the U.S. as *Invasion of the Zombies*.

Santo contra las mujeres vampiro (Santo vs. the Vampire Women, 1962)

Prod: Alberto López.
Dir: Alfonso Corona Blake.
Scr: Rafael García Travesí, Alfonso Corona Blake.
Story: Antonio Orellana, Fernando Osés, Rafael García Travesí.
Cast: Santo (Santo/"Sampson"), Lorena Velázquez (Zorina), María Duval (Diana), Ofelia Montesco (Tundra), Agusto Benedico (Professor Orlof/"Professor Rolof"), Xavier Loyá (Jorge/"George"), Fernando Osés (Igor), Guillermo Hernández "Lobo Negro" (Marcus), Nathanael León "Frankenstein" (Taras).
Released in the U.S. by K. Gordon Murray as *Samson vs. the Vampire Women* (1963); English version directed by Manuel San Fernando.

Santo en el museo de cera (Santo in the Wax Museum, 1963)

Prod: Alberto López.
Dir: Alfonso Corona Blake.
Scr: Fernando Galiana, Julio Porter.
Cast: Santo (Santo/ "Sampson"), Claudio Brook (Dr. Karol), Rubén Rojo (Ricardo/"Charles Humphrey"), Roxanna Bellini (Susana/"Susan Madison"), Norma Mora (Gloria).
Released in the U.S. by K. Gordon Murray as *Samson in the Wax Museum* (1965); English version directed by Manuel San Fernando.

Atacan las brujas (The Witches Attack, 1964)

Prod: Luis Enrique Vergara.
Dir: José Díaz Morales.
Scr: Rafael García Travesí.
Story: Rafael García Travesí, Fernando Osés.
Cast: Santo (Santo), Lorena Velazquez (Mayra, alias Elisa Cárdenas), María Eugenia San Martín (Ofelia), Edanea Ruiz (Medusa), Ramón Bugarini (Arturo), Fernando Osés (witch henchman), Guillermo Hernandez "Lobo Negro" (witch henchman).

Santo, el Enmascarado de Plata vs. los invasión de los marcianos (Santo, the Sliver-Masked Man vs. the Invasion of the Martians, 1966)

Prod: Alfonso Rosas Priego.
Dir: Alfredo B. Crevenna.
Scr: Rafael García Travesí.
Cast: Santo (Santo), Wolf Ruvinskis (Argos), Manuel Zozoya (Professor Odorica), Nicolós Rodríguez (Father Fuentes), Maura Monti (Afrodita), El Nazi (Kronos), Beni Galán (Hercules), Ham Lee (Morfeo), Eva Norvind (Selena), Gilda Mirós (Artemisa), Belinda Corell (Diana).

Santo en el tesoro de Drácula (Santo in the Treasure of Dracula, 1968)

Prod: Guillermo Calderón Stell.
Dir: René Cardona.
Scr: Alfredo Salazar.
Cast: Santo (Santo), Aldo Monti (Count Dracula), Noelia Noel (Luisa Sepulveda), Carlos Agosti (Dr. César Sepulveda), Alberto Rojas (Perico), Roberto G. Rivera (Dr. Kur, alias the Black Hood).
Alternate Spanish version with female nudity released internationally as *El vampire y el sexo* (*The Vampire and Sex*).

Santo contra los jinetes del terror (*Santo vs. the Riders of Terror*, 1970)

Prod: Guillermo Calderón Stell.
Dir: René Cardona.
Scr: René Cardona, Jesús "Murciélago" Velázquez.
Story: Jesús "Murciélago" Velázquez.
Cast: Santo (Santo), Armando Silvestre (Dario), Gregorio Casals (José), Julio Almada (Camerino), Mary Montiel (Carmen), Ivonne Govea (Lupe), Carlos Agosti (Dr. Ramos).
Alternate Spanish version with female nudity reportedly released internationally as *Los leprosos y el sexo* (*The Lepers and Sex*).

Santo contra la hija de Frankenstein (*Santo vs. Frankenstein's Daughter*, 1971)

Prod: Guillermo Calderón Stell, Santo.
Dir: Miguel M. Delgado.
Scr: Fernando Osés.
Cast: Santo (Santo), Gina Romand (Dr. Freda Frankenstein), Roberto Cañedo (Dr. Yanco), Anel (Norma), Sonia Fuentes (Elsa), Gerardo Zepeda (dual role: Truxon [ape-man] and Urses [Frankenstein's monster]), Carlos Suárez (Tuerto).

Santo y Blue Demon contra Dracula y el Hombre Lobo (*Santo and Blue Demon vs. Dracula and the Wolf Man*, 1972)

Prod: Guillermo Calderón Stell, Santo.
Dir: Miguel M. Delgado.
Scr: Alfredo Salazar.
Cast: Santo (Santo), Blue Demon (Blue Demon), Aldo Monti (Count Dracula), Agustín Martínez Solares, Jr. (Rufus Rex, the Wolf Man), Nubia Martí (Lina), Wally Barron (Eric), María Eugenia San Martín (Laura Cristaldi), Jorge Mondragón (Prof. Luis Cristaldi), Lourdes Batista (Josefina, the maid).

Santo y Blue Demon contra el Dr. Frankenstein (*Santo and Blue Demon vs. Dr. Frankenstein*, 1973)

Prod: Guillermo Calderon Stell, Santo.
Dir: Miguel M. Delgado.
Scr: Lic. Francisco Cavazos, Alfredo Salazar.
Story: Alfredo Salazar.
Cast: Santo (Santo), Blue Demon (Blue Demon), Jorge Russek (Dr. Irving Frankenstein), Sasha Montenegro (Alicia), Jorge Mondragón (Professor Ruiz), Ruben Aguirre (Dr. Molina), Ivonne Govea (Marta), Sonia Aguilar (Carmen), Carlos Nieto (Chief of Police Gutiérrez).

Selected Luchadoras Films

All films listed produced by Guillermo Calderón Stell and directed by René Cardona.

Las luchadoras vs. el médico asesino (*Wrestling Women vs. the Killer Doctor*, 1962)

Scr: Alfredo Salazar.

Cast: Lorena Velázquez (Gloria Venus), Elizabeth Campbell (Golden Rubi), Armando Silvestre (Armando Campos/"Mike Henderson"), Chucho Salinas (Chema/"Tommy Johnson"), Roberto Cañedo (Professor Ruiz/"Professor Wright"), Sonia Infante (Alicia/"Alice"), Jesús "Murciélago" Velázquez (Marcado/"Harry"), Jorge Mondragón (Boris), Chabela Romero ("Vendetta"), Gerardo Zepeda (Gomar), Armando Acosta (police chief).

Released in the U.S. by K. Gordon Murray as *Doctor of Doom* (1965); English version directed by Manuel San Fernando.

Las luchadoras contra la momia (*Wrestling Women vs. the Mummy*, 1964)

Scr: Alfredo Salazar.

Story: Alfredo Salazar, Guillermo Calderón Stell.

Cast: Lorena Velázquez (Loreta Venus), Elizabeth Campbell (Golden Rubi), Armando Silvestre (Armando Rios/"Mike Henderson"), Chucho Salinas (Chucho Gómez/"Tommy Johnson"), Ramón Bugarini (Prince Fujiyata), Victor Velázquez (Dr. Luis Trelles/"Dr. Lewis Tracy"), María Eugenia San Martín (Chela Van Dine/"Charlotte Van Dine"), Jesús "Murciélago" Velázquez (Mao).

Released in the U.S. by K. Gordon Murray as *Wrestling Women vs. the Aztec Mummy* (1965); English version directed by Manuel San Fernando.

El horripilante bestia humana (*The Horrible Human Beast*, 1968)

Scr: René Cardona, René Cardona, Jr.

Cast: Armando Silvestre ("Arthur Martinez"), Norma Lazareno ("Lucy Ossorio"), José Elias Moreno ("Dr. Krellman"), Carlos López Moctezuma ("Goyo"), Agustin Martínez Solares, Jr. ("Julio"), Gerardo Zepeda (the ape-man), Noelia Noel (woman in park).

Alternate Spanish version with female nudity released internationally as *Horror y sexo*. Dubbed and re-edited version released in the U.S. as *Night of the Bloody Apes* (1972), with additional scenes directed by Jerald Intrator.

Chapter Notes

Chapter 1

1. Carlos Monsiváis, *Mexican Postcards*, trans. John Kraniauskas (New York: Verso, 1997), 20. Emphasis added.

2. Carl J. Mora, *Mexican Cinema: Reflections of a Society, 1896–1980* (Berkeley: University of California Press, 1982), 101. Emphasis added.

3. Carl J. Mora, *Mexican Cinema: Reflections of a Society, 1896–1982*, 99. Emphasis added. For further discussion of the film industry in this era, see also: Frank Brandenberg, *The Making of Modern Mexico* (Englewood Cliffs, NJ: Prentice Hall, 1964), 304–5; Paulo Antonio Paranaguá, "Ten Reasons to Love or Hate Mexican Cinema," in *Mexican Cinema*, ed. Paulo Antonio Paranaguá, trans. Ana M. López (London: BFI, 1995), 8; Tómas Pérez Turrent, "The Studios," in *Mexican Cinema*, ed. Paranaguá, 140–1; Eric Zolov, *Refried Elvis: The Rise of the Mexican Counterculture* (Berkeley: University of California Press, 1999), 30–31.

4. *Mexican Cinema: Reflections of a Society, 1896–1980*, 102. See also Turrent, 140–2.

5. The concept of "Culture Industry" is taken from Max Horkheimer and Theodor W. Adorno, *Dialectic of Enlightenment*, trans. John Cumming (New York: Verso, 1997). In the chapter "The Culture Industry," Horkheimer and Adorno offer a seminal and often virulent critique of American popular culture (Hollywood film, pop music, popular literature), arguing it is entirely both product and producer of capitalist ideology and interests. In the grasp of the Culture Industry, culture is purged of any meaningful social or cultural critique, and reified strictly into an entertainment commodity. The workings of Hollywood — the creation of cultic stars as fetish-commodities, formulaic film products, a studio system derived from modern, industrial mass production — epitomize the Culture Industry. While Horkheimer and Adorno are providing a specific critique of Hollywood, it can be suggested that their concept of the Culture Industry resonates with Mora's own analysis of the downfall of the Mexican film industry.

6. *Refried Elvis*, 30–31.

7. See "Fantasmas del Cine Mexicano," in *Fear Without Frontiers: Horror Cinema Across the Globe*, ed. Stephen Jay Schneider (Surrey: FAB Press, 2004).

8. Information from personal correspondence with David Wilt.

9. Heather Levi, "Masked Media: The Adventures of Lucha Libre on the Small Screen," in *Fragments of a Golden Age: The Politics of Culture in Mexico Since 1940*, eds. Gilbert Joseph, Anne Rubenstein, and Eric Zolov (Durham: Duke University Press, 2001), 337–8.

Chapter 2

1. Susan Sontag, *Against Interpretation* (New York: Doubleday Books, 1967), 283.

2. Annalee Newitz, "What Makes Things Cheesy?: Satire, Multinationalism, and B-Movies," *Social Text* 18.2 (2000): 58.

3. *Against Interpretation*, 282.

4. Newitz's article devotes a substantial amount of discussion to *From Dusk Till Dawn* (1996), a collaborative effort written by and starring Tarantino, and directed by Robert Rodriguez (*El Mariachi*, *Desperado*). *From Dusk Till Dawn*, whose second half takes place in a Mexican truck-stop/strip-club operated by vampires, "borrows" quite liberally from mexploitation conventions, such as the casting of Salma Hayek as a sexy vampire-stripper (perhaps a sort of postmodern Lorena Velázquez). This is an aspect of *From Dusk Till Dawn* that Newitz applauds — the parodic use of "trash cinema" iconography to make an intentionally "cheesy" film that satirically critiques gender politics, masculinity, race, and other cultural issues. However, the chief failure of Tarantino's work is that the original sources from which Tarantino derives his inspiration (Asian cult cinema, blaxploitation, grindhouse films) are infinitely more interesting in their original forms than his own dilettante appropriations, which often fall under the category of what Fredric Jameson referred to as "blank parody" — homage, references, and parodies that simply borrow (or steal) from other artistic sources without engaging in the cultural criticism of the original sources. See Jameson's *Postmodernism, or, the Cultural Logic of Late Capitalism* (Durham: Duke University Press, 1990), Chapter 1. For instance, in Bruce Lee's unfinished film *Game of Death*, Lee wears a yellow track

suit instead of traditional martial arts attire in order to signify that he is not beholden to one specific, rigid style and instead reflects the eclectic, athletic, pragmatic, and functional philosophy of Lee's own martial-arts fighting system, *jeet kun do*. The tracksuit is especially significant as Lee's iconoclasm proved to be a source of heated controversy between him and traditional martial-arts instructors throughout his life. In Tarantino's *Kill Bill*, Uma Thurman wears a yellow tracksuit for no purpose other than to provide an in-joke for those aware of the reference to Bruce Lee.

5. Jeffrey Sconce, "'Trashing' the Academy," *Screen* 36: 4 (Winter 1995): 374. Emphasis added.

6. Ilan Stavans, *The Riddle of Cantinflas: Essays on Hispanic Popular Culture* (Albuquerque: University of New Mexico Press, 1998), 31, 34. Emphasis added.

7. Andrew Syder and Dolores Tierney, "Importation/Mexploitation, or, How a Crime-Fighting, Vampire-Slaying Mexican Wrestler Almost Found Himself in an Italian Sword and Sandal Epic," forthcoming in *Horror International*, ed. Steve Schnieder and Tony Williams (Detroit: Wayne State University Press, 2004), page 5 of 20. Page numbers and citations are taken from a copy of the essay provided by Kathleen Newman *ca.* Spring 2002.

8. As quoted in Levi, "Masked Media," 337. Emphasis added.

9. As Alison Greene noted, "Latin American media scholars are in general agreement about the tremendous importance of the melodramatic genre ... [but] melodrama is produced, broadcast, and consumed in specific social and historical contexts." From "Cablevision(nation) in Rural Yucatán: Performing Modernity and *Mexicanidad* in the Early 1990s," in *Fragments of a Golden Age*, 446–7. Thus, while melodrama can be considered an essential part of Mexican popular culture, melodrama should be assessed not as a monolithic form, but rather in how it is applied to various forms of popular culture (mexploitation, comic books, popular music) and for various audiences (middle-class, urban poor, rural poor).

10. Probably the most popular example of this treatment of bad films was *Mystery Science Theater 3000*, which began as a series for an independent station in Minneapolis in 1988 before becoming a national show running weekly on the cable–TV networks Comedy Central (1989–96) and the Sci-Fi Channel (1997–9).

11. John Soister, "The Vampire," page 5 of 14. Available at "The Wonder World of K. Gordon Murray" website.

12. Elissa J. Rashkin, *Women Filmmakers in Mexican Cinema: The Country of Which We Dream* (Austin: University of Texas Press, 2001), 8.

13. "Cablevision(nation) in Rural Yucatán," 419. Emphasis added.

14. Héctor Aguilar Camín and Lorenzo Meyer, *In the Shadow of the Mexican Revolution: Contemporary Mexican History, 1910–1989*, trans. Luis Alberto Fierro (Austin: University of Texas Press, 1993), 165.

15. See Greene, "Cablevision(nation) in Rural Yucatán," 418, 420. This intertwined, dual perpetuation of modernity and mexicanidad that Greene describes occurring in Mexican television of the 1990s can be traced back to the mexploitation era as well.

16. "Importation/Mexploitation," page 4 of 20.

17. Carlos Monsiváis, "All the People Came and Did Not Fit Onto the Screen," in *Mexican Cinema*, ed. Paranaguá, 150.

18. My appreciation goes to David Wilt for information about this film. See also his *Mexican Filmography, 1919–2001* (Jefferson, NC: McFarland, 2004), 312.

19. See Anne Rubenstein, *Bad Language, Naked Ladies, and Other Threats to the Nation: A Political History of Comic Books in Mexico* (Durham: Duke University Press, 1998), 42, 176.

20. "Cablevision(nation) in Rural Yucatán," 420.

21. "All the People Came and Did Not Fit on the Screen," in *Mexican Cinema*, ed. Paranaguá, 150. Alison Greene also cites Monsiváis' work on melodrama and the Golden Age of Mexican cinema, in which melodrama served a specific political function for urban and rural poor Mexican audiences: melodrama "'became a secular form of catechism: modernity condensed, made simple and consumable'" (Monsiváis as quoted in Greene, "Cablevision (nation) in Rural Yucatán," 420).

22. *Bad Language, Naked Ladies, and Other Threats to the Nation*, 42. Emphasis added.

23. Observations taken from an interview with Wilt in the short documentary "Juan López Moctezuma — A Cultured Maverick," available on a highly-recommended DVD issue of *Alucarda* (Mondo Macabro).

24. *Bad Language, Naked Ladies, and Other Threats to the Nation*, 79–80. Emphasis added. Of course, Luis Buñuel's strongest cinematic attacks on Catholicism — specifically *Viridiana* (1961, shot in Spain) and *El ángel exterminador* (*The Exterminating Angel*, 1962) — were made while Buñuel lived in Mexico.

25. *Bad Language, Naked Ladies, and Other Threats to the Nation*, 46. Emphasis added.

26. Rob Craig, "The World of the Vampires," page 8 of 15. Available at "The Wonder World of K. Gordon Murray" website.

27. *Bad Language, Naked Ladies, and Other Threats to the Nation*, 46. Emphasis added.

28. *Bad Language, Naked Ladies, and Other Threats to the Nation*, 9.

29. *Bad Language, Naked Ladies, and Other Threats to the Nation*, 46.

30. Like a number of René Cardona–directed Santo films of the era, a version of *Blue Demon y las invasoras* containing nudity for foreign consumption was released as *Blue Demon y las seductoras* (*Blue Demon and the Seductresses*). See David Wilt, *The Mexican Filmography, 1916–2001*, 385.

31. The movie poster for *Santo contra la hija de Frankenstein* spotlights this particular moment by employing a drawing of the bare-chested, chained Santo as its central image.

32. Anne Rubenstein, "Bodies, Cities, Cinema: Pedro Infante's Death as Political Spectacle," in *Fragments of a Golden Age*, 226. Emphasis added.

33. Steven J. Stern, *The Secret History of Gender: Men, Women, and Power in Late Colonial Mexico* (Chapel Hill: University of North Carolina Press, 1995), 324.

34. Rubenstein, "Bodies, Cities, Cinema," 227. Emphasis added.

Chapter 3

1. Indeed, perhaps the most famous of Goya's *caprichios* is *caprichio* no. 43, *El sueño de la razon produce monstruos* (*The Sleep of Reason Produces Monsters*). It depicts a person asleep in a study, surrounded by menacing owls. As the image and very title obviously suggests, Goya warns that the loss of intellectual reason can only produce irrational fear.

2. However, as David Wilt pointed out, this interpretation is highly problematic in that in *El barón del terror* "Astera" is actually "D'Estera," with "Astera" being an inaccurate English translation. In this sense, the allusions that can be drawn between "Astera" and "Asteria" are the product of the English dubbed version, and probably unintended.

3. Alberto Rojas, making his film debut in *Santo en el tesoro de Drácula*, enjoyed a successful career as a comedic actor in Mexican cinema and television.

4. This theme of a "brain-eating vampire" would soon reappear in a two-film series from 1962 directed by Alfredo B. Crevenna which certainly seems "inspired" by *El barón del terror*: *Rostro infernal* (*Infernal Face*, U.S. title: *The Incredible Face of Dr. B.*) and *La huella macabra* (*The Macabre Mark*). These films feature the evil "Count Brankovan" (played by Eric del Castillo in *Rostro infernal* and Guillermo Murray in *La huella macabra)* who sustains his existence by vampirically consuming the brains of his victims, allowing him to absorb their skills and intelligence. See David Wilt, *The Mexican Filmography: 1916–2001*, 310, 313.

5. Rubenstein, 9–10.

Chapter 4

1. Much of this biographical sketch of Santo is derived from an excellent and highly informative commentary by Professor Juan Carlos Vargas included on the DVD edition of *Santo, el Enmascarado de Plata vs. la invasión de los Marcianos* (available through Kit Parker Films and VCI Entertainment). Another essential source on Santo is David Wilt, "Masked Men and Monsters," in *Mondo Macabro: Weird and Wonderful Cinema from Around the World*, ed. Pete Tombs (New York: St. Martin's Griffin, 1997). Additionally, Wilt's Santo website, "The Films of El Santo," is an essential source for the entire film oeuvre of Santo and also provides numerous links to several other Santo, *lucha libre*, and Mexican cinema websites. As a whole, this chapter owes a tremendous debt to Wilt. Also recommended is the "La (Nueva) Arena de Lucha Libre" website, which contains numerous biographies of former and current lucha libre stars, and the "Santo and Friends" website: www.santoandfriends.com, which contains biographies and filmographies of Santo, Blue Demon, and Mil Máscaras, as well as an informative general filmography of Mexican horror and wrestling cinema. However, it must be noted that in reviewing and utilizing these various sources, there does tend to be some discrepancies and inconsistencies regarding details of Santo's career, specifically the exact nature of Guzmán Hureta's pre–Santo identities; my own account is primarily an attempt to correlate this sometimes divergent material.

2. According the "La (Nueva) Arena de Lucha Libre" website, Velázquez wrestled as *El Murciélago Enmascarado*, a notorious masked rudo, from 1938 to 1940. In 1940, Velázquez lost a "mask vs. hair" match against técnico Octavio Gaona, and continued his career minus mask as "Murciélago" Velázquez. In 1943, Velázquez wrestled Santo in two famous matches: a "mask vs. hair" match in January, followed by a championship match in March — both won by Santo. Velázquez, who over the course of his career perfected the rudo role of inspiring audience hatred, received a lifetime ban in 1955 after one of his matches resulted in a near-riot situation. Following his wrestling career, like many luchadores, Velázquez found worked in mexploitation films, and collaborated frequently with René Cardona.

3. The binary melodramatic conflict between heroic técnicos and villainous rudos is quite similar to professional wrestling in America, where wrestlers are primarily divided into *faces* (or *baby-faces*), the popular "good" wrestlers who win through their skills, and *heels*, the arrogant villains of the ring who usually win by brute force, cheating or outside interference. As Barthes notes, many times the heel in American wrestling serves as an obvious political metaphor. For instance, in the aftermath of the Iranian hostage crisis, a famous WWE (then WWF) heel was "the Iron Sheik" from Iran, a symbol of America's foremost international enemy at the time. To further ensure audience displeasure, The Iron Sheik would enter the arena proudly waving an Iranian flag and generally bad-mouthing America in his promos. Ironically, the wrestler known as "the Iron Sheik," Kazrow Vaziri, wrestled for Iran at the 1968 Olympics and served as a personal bodyguard for the Shah of Iran in the 1970s. While not averse to being a highly unpopular heel, Vaziri reportedly detested being perceived as a supporter of Kohmeni's Iran.

4. See Wilt, "Masked Men and Monsters"; Levi, "Masked Media," 336.

5. "Un rudo bajado del ceilo" ("A Rudo Fell from the Heavens"), *Somos* magazine (October, 1999): 43. My thanks to David Wilt for providing this reference source. "La (Nueva) Arena de Lucha Lire" website also dates Santo's conversion from rudo to técnico as occurring in 1962.

6. These approximate dates are provided due to the discrepancies regarding the exact dates of the publishing history of the Santo comic books. According to Anne Rubenstein, the Santo comic book series began in 1949 and ended in 1976 when Santo sued publisher José G. Cruz over unpaid royalties and the unauthorized use of his name and image. See *Bad Language, Naked Ladies, and Other Threats to the Nation*, 174. Elsewhere in Rubenstein's book, she dates the Santo comic books from "1953 to at least 1974" (134). Juan Carlos Vega dates the publication of the Santo comic books from 1951 to 1980; see the DVD edition of *Santo vs. la invasión de los marcianos, op. cit.* Mauricio Matamores Duran also dates the Santo comic books from 1951 to 1980 ("El Santo en las historietas," *Somos, op. cit.*). However, what is ultimately much more important is not the particulars of dates, but the general consensus that the Santo comic books were both highly popular and instrumental in developing Santo's heroic status in Mexican popular culture.

7. The construction of Hurácan Ramírez into a luchador was itself a highly convoluted process. According to "La (Nueva) Arena de Lucha Libre" website, several promoters created their own versions of Hurácan Ramírez, resulting in the appearance of a number of luchadores named Hurácan Ramírez wrestling simultaneously on the lucha libre circuit in the 1950s. Eventually, the wrestling commission intervened to sort out the confusion, and Daniel Garcia Arteaga was awarded sole possession of the name and persona.

8. Levi argued Médico Asesino was little more than a blatant attempt to create a popular rival for Santo and other luchadores through the mass media, rather than through the often grueling wrestling circuit of live arena events. See "Masked Media," 340.

9. In this regard, I refer to Rob Craig's comments in his review of "*The Curse of the Aztec Mummy*," available on his "The Wonder World of K. Gordon Murray" website.

10. As David Wilt noted, the U.S. title *Neutron vs. the Black Mask* is highly inaccurate in that Neutron wears the *black* mask, while the villain, Dr. Caronte, wears a *white* mask. See *The Mexican Filmography, 1916–2001*, 289.

11. Ruvinskis would reprise his role as Neutrón in two films from 1964 directed by Alfredo B. Crevenna: *Neutrón contra el criminal sádico* (*Neutrón vs. the Sadistic Criminal*; U.S. title: *Neutron the Atomic Superman vs. the Maniac*) and *Neutrón contra los asesinos de karate* (*Neutrón vs. the Karate Assassins*; U.S. title: *Neutron Battles the Karate Killers*).Also in 1964, René Cardona directed *El asesino invisible* (*The Invisible Killer*), featuring a masked superhero called El Enmascarado de Oro ("The Gold-Masked Man," played by Jorge Rivero). The film was dubbed into English and passed off in America as a *Neutrón* film under the title *Neutron Traps the Invisible Killer*. See Wilt, *The Mexican Filmography, 1916–2001*, 330.

12. Roland Barthes, *Mythologies*, trans. Annette Lavers (New York: Hill and Wang, 1972), 23. Of course, this leads to the age-old question of whether professional wrestling is "real," an issue seemingly settled when WWE (World Wrestling Entertainment), in order to avoid local taxes on sporting events, announced that its matches were staged events and the outcome prearranged, and thus pro-wrestling was not "a sport" but "sports entertainment." However, Heather Levi has noted that those personally involved in lucha libre consider it very much a "sport" that has been bastardized by the mass media into a form of popular "entertainment" (see "Masked Media," 330–1). Levi argues that lucha libre is "both a sporting event and a melodrama" (334) and that "endings are, in fact, predetermined, even though much of what happens during the match is improvised" (365).

13. Syder and Tierney, page 7.

14. Dan Murphy, "Mexican Wrestlers Give the Smackdown to Vice," *Christian Science Monitor*, 8/22/20001, vol. 93, no. 188: 7. The legacy of lucha libre as spectator event and political metaphor also carried over to the Mexican political sphere proper. In an example of life imitating art, Murphy cites the case of political activist Marco Rascón Bandas, who in 1987 adopted the persona of Superbarrio Gómez, a masked figure who led a popular movement on behalf of the urban homeless in the aftermath of the 1985 earthquake in Mexico City. Eventually, Rascón Bandas was elected to the Mexican Congress in 1997. Levi also discusses the Superbarrio Gómez phenomenon in "Masked Media," 346–7.

15. "Masked Media," 344.

16. See "Masked Media," 338–44. Another important aspect of the television ban was that lucha libre developed outside the influence of television broadcast and instead focused on live events, resulting in long, theatrical, athletic matches between luchadores instead of the "promo"—the on-camera, pre-match or post-match interview segment (343). This emphasis on the promo clearly can be seen in WWE Monday night "Raw" and Thursday night "Smackdown" broadcasts. A typical two-hour WWE telecast contains approximately forty-five minutes of actual wrestling, with the remainder of television time devoted to interminable interviews, monologues, and verbal confrontations occurring in or out of the ring, as well as obligatory and often dismal locker room and other "behind-then-scenes" vignettes either played for comic-relief or as soap-operatic subplots.

17. "Importation/Mexploitation," page 7 of 20. While mexploitation films share Hollywood horror and science fiction films' concerns about "atomic energy," they also seem as concerned with "European infiltration" as with "Communist infiltration."

18. "Masked Media," 368.

19. Fredric Jameson, "Third-World Literature in the Era of Multinational Capitalism," *Social Text 5:3* (1986): 69.

20. "Masked Men and Monsters," 138–9. Emphasis added.

21. According to David Wilt's "Films of El Santo" website, *Santo contra los zombies* (*Invasion of the Zombies*) is rumored to have been dubbed at K. Gordon Murray's Sound Labs studio, but not released by Murray. The other Santo film dubbed into English was *Santo contra Dr. Muerte* (*Santo vs. Dr. Death*, 1973), which was retitled *Masked Man Strikes Again*. Wilt notes that the post-production and dubbing of *Santo contra Dr. Muerte* is suspected of having been done in Canada, and it is uncertain whether the film was ever legally released in America.

22. While four writers are credited on *Santo contra las mujeres vampiro* (Antonio Orellana, Fernando Osés, Rafael Garcia Travesi, and Alfonso Corona Blake), none of *El mundo de los vampiros'* writers are credited (Raúl Zenteno, Ramón Óbón, Jesús "Murciélago" Velázquez).

23. The shot is possibly included as an homage to *The Bride of Frankenstein*, in which a similar close-up of an owl is inserted: the owl "witnesses" the monster's resurrection and murder of a villager in the flooded caverns of the burned windmill early in the film.

24. It is possible the name "Orlof" in *Santo contra las mujeres vampio* is a reference to Spanish director Jess Franco's horror film *The Awful Dr. Orloff*, released the previous year.

25. Carlos Monsiváis, "All the People Came and Did Not Fit on the Screen," 149–150.

26. Carlos Monsiváis, "All the People Came and Did Not Fit on the Screen," 150.

27. "Importation/Mexploitation," page 5 of 20.

28. See Syder and Tierney, page 6 of 20. Here one can see a vast difference between "audience participation" and "bad movies," in which the bemused spectator engages in a running commentary regarding the film. Also comparable is an intentionally camp film such as *The Rocky Horror Picture Show*, in which audience participation is highly ritualized and orchestrated (throwing rice at the screen during the wedding, joining in the dance numbers in the theater aisles).

29. See Syder and Tierney, page 5 of 20.

30. The potential, and even paradoxical, thrill and disaster of Santo being unmasked is self-consciously incorporated in the publicity material of *Santo contra las mujeres vampiro*. In the film's best-known poster, a large question mark appears over a drawing of Santo, perhaps posing the question that this will be the moment when Santo is unmasked. In the Santo film prior to *Santo contra las mujeres vampiro*, *Santo contra los zombies*, the movie poster similarly depicts Santo with a huge question mark over his body.

31. See Wilt's overview of the *Estrangulador* films, available at his "Films of El Santo" website.

32. While *Santo vs. la invasión de los marcianos* is the best-known of Crevenna's Santo films, Crevenna also directed the crime drama *Santo, el Enmascarado de Plata contra los villanos del ring* (*Santo, the Silver-*

Masked Man vs. the Villains of the Ring, 1966), the *rancheras* melodrama *El águila real* (*The Royal Eagle*, 1971), the crime-adventure saga *La bestias del terror* (*The Beasts of Terror*, 1972), the horror-mystery *Santo contra la magia negra* (*Santo vs. Black Magic*, 1972), and the martial-arts inspired adventures *El puño de la muerte* (*The Fist of Death*) and *Furia de los karatecas* (*Fury of the Karate Experts*, both 1981). For further information, see Wilt's "Films of El Santo" website.

33. See *"Santo, el Enmascarado de Plata vs. 'la invasion de los Marcianos,'"* at Wilt's "Films of El Santo" website.

34. The dubious nature of the encounter aside, Adamski's accounts of the experience were widely published (some of which were actually rejected science-fiction stories Adamski had written which were reworked into documents of his extraterrestrial "encounter").

35. Aguilar Camín and Meyer, 191.

36. Elissa J. Rashkin, *Women Filmmakers in Mexican Cinema*, 8. Emphasis added.

37. "Argos" could also be derived from two other figures of Greek mythology as well: "Arges," the one-eyed cyclops, as well as "Argus," the all-seeing watchman of the Greek gods who had 100 eyes. Both references would compliment the Martian Argos and the powerful "Astral Eye" in his forehead (Arges), and the Martian's "panoptic" ability to see any place on earth at any time (Argus).

38. As observed by David Wilt, the "disintegration" murders of women and children are depicted rather tamely, presumably to keep the film within the parameters of an "A" (all-ages) certification. See *"Santo el Enmascarado de Plata vs. 'la invasion de los marinas,'"* available on Wilt's "Films of El Santo" website.

39. See Michel Foucault, *Discipline and Punish: The Birth of the Prison*, trans. Alan Sheridan (New York: Vintage, 1995), 195–230, especially 200.

40. *Discipline and Punish*, 217. Emphasis added.

41. Foucault does not deny the existence of the society of the spectacle, but rather postulates that the old societies of Greece, Rome, or the European monarchies and their manifestations of power (public punishment, executions) gave way to the modern world's mechanisms of power defined by surveillance (prisons, asylums, hospitals). "The necessarily spectacular manifestations of power were extinguished one by one in the daily exercise of surveillance" (*Discipline and Punish*, 217). However, several responses to Foucault insisted the replacement of spectacle with surveillance in modernity is far too simplistic, most notably Guy deBord's aptly-titled *The Society of the Spectacle*.

42. David Wilt, *"Santo el Enmascarado de Plata vs. la invasion de los marcianos,"* at the "Films of El Santo" website.

43. During this era, Capulina made other horror-comedies, such as *Capulina contra los vampiros* (*Capulina vs. the Vampires*, 1970; also directed by René Cardona), *Capulina contra las momias* (*Capulina vs. the*

Mummies, 1972, dir. Alfredo Zacarias, who also wrote and produced *Santo contra Capulina*), and *Capulina contra los monstruos* (*Capulina vs. the Monsters*, 1973, dir. Miguel Morayta).

44. See Wilt's review of *Santo contra los cazadores de cabezas* at his "Films of El Santo" website.

45. See David Wilt, *The Mexican Filmography, 1916–2001*, 423.

46. For further and more detailed discussion of these Cardona-Santo films, Wilt's "Films of El Santo" website is indispensable.

47. Both Blue Demon and Black Shadow wrestled under the English translations of their respective ring names (*Demonio Azul* and *Sombra Negra*): they felt the English names had more panache. For further biographical material on Blue Demon, both "La (Nueva) Arena de Lucha Libre" and the "Santo and Friends" websites are highly recommended.

48. Four of Gory Guerrero's sons (Mando, Chavo, Héctor and Eddie) and a grandson (Chavo, Jr.) also became successful pro-wrestlers. Certainly the most famous is Gory's youngest son Eddie Guerrero of WCW and WWE fame.

49. Much of the information on these Santo–Blue Demon films came from David Wilt's "Films of El Santo" website.

50. Carrión provided the music for countless mexploitation films, including most of Abel Salazar's productions (*El vampiro*, *El mundo de los vampiros*, *El barón del terror*); his work is at once bombastic, melodramatic, cliché-ridden and challenging. Besides the music for *Santo y Blue Demon contra Drácula and el Hombre Lobo*, his work on the other Delgado-Santo films also bears mention. The opening theme to *Santo y Blue Demon contra el Dr. Frankenstein* is a breezy cocktail jazz piece appropriate to an evening of restaurant dining but thoroughly incongruent with a horror film. The opening theme to *Santo contra la hija de Frankenstein* is, simply put, one of the most fascinating pieces of music ever written: an utterly bizarre pastiche blending musical styles, much in the same way the *lucha libre* films merge disparate genres, featuring blasts of generic horror-film organ, bouncy surf-rock guitar, meandering free-jazz drumming, and avant-garde electronic music.

51. In Delgado's subsequent *Santo y Blue Demon contra el Dr. Frankenstein*, the same set and dubbed crowd noises are used to film the wrestling scenes, but Delgado also inserts footage of Santo's girlfriend Alicia (Sasha Montenegro) and extras watching the match inside the arena, although the ring and the audience never appear in the same shot.

52. David Wilt, "Biographical Dictionary of Mexican Film Performers," available on Wilt's "Mexican Film Resource Page": www.umd.edu/~dwilt/mfb.html.

53. The massacre would later be depicted in Jorge Fons' harrowing account of Tlatelolco, *Rojo amanecer* (*Red Dawn*, 1989).

54. An observation gathered from Wilt's discussion of *Santo vs. las mujeres vampiro*, available on his "Films of El Santo" website. The romantic life of the superhero is also a vitally important issue in Hollywood's depiction of comic book characters. In *Batman* (1986), Bruce Wayne reveals his secret identity to the woman he has fallen in love with, and one might suggest this construction of a female love interest for Batman was also a conscious effort to refute the issue of Batman and Robin's homosexual relationship as alleged in Fredric Wertham's famous 1954 anti-comic book polemic *Seduction of the Innocent*—(of course, Robin does not appear at all in the first *Batman* film). Similarly, in *Superman II* (1980), Superman and Lois Lane consummate a sexual relationship long hinted at in the comic books.

55. See "*Santo y Blue Demon vs. Dracula y el Hombre Lobo*," at Wilt's "Films of El Santo" website.

56. "See "*Santo y Blue Demon vs. Drácula y el Hombre Lobo*" at Wilt's "Films of El Santo" website.

57. Again I refer to Wilt's comments regarding the film at his "Films of El Santo" website.

Chapter 5

1. Rob Craig, "*Santa Claus*," at "The Wonder World of K. Gordon Murray" website.

2. Rhino Video re-edited and re-released the two films in the 1980s on home video under the respective titles *Rock and Roll Wrestling Women vs. the Aztec Ape* and *Rock and Roll Wrestling Women vs. the Aztec Mummy*. Eliminating some of the more ponderous scenes, adding a retro-rock soundtrack, and dubbing in some additional "intentionally humorous" dialogue, the overt attempts to make the *Wrestling Women* films intentionally "campy" only succeeded in greatly diminishing the surreal and avant-garde qualities of the original films, serving as an excellent example of Sontag's assessment that "camp which knows itself to be camp is less satisfying."

3. Less than enamored with *The Wild World of Batwoman*, DC comics sued Warren for copyright infringement, and Warren changed the title to *She Was a Hippie Vampire*, although the film's original title was eventually used for its home video release. Apparently DC comics never took legal action against *La Mujer Murciélago*.

4. I must admit that I have only personally seen the three *Luchadoras* films that I will discuss in detail in this and the following chapter. The information on these other three *Luchadoras* films comes from David Wilt and his "Elizabeth Campbell Filmography" website: www.wma.umd.edu/~dwilt/campbell.htm.

5. See "*Las luchadoras vs. el médico asesino*" and "*Las luchadoras contra la momia*," available at Wilt's "Elizabeth Campbell Filmography" website.

6. Heather Levi, "Masked Media," 335. Not only was the world of lucha libre hospitable to women spectators, but women were actively encouraged to attend wrestling events through such promotions as monthly "ladies nights," at which women received free admission (see "Masked Media," 335).

7. See Laura Mulvey, "Visual Pleasure and Narrative Cinema," reprinted in *Film Theory and Criticism: Introductory Readings*, 4th ed., eds. Gerald Mast, Marshall Cohen, and Leo Braudy (New York: Oxford University Press, 1992), 753.

8. This reduction of women wrestlers to idealized and fetishized sex-objects of both male lust and adolescent derision in American pro wrestling is most evident in the WWE's depiction of its own stable of women wrestlers ("Divas"), epitomized by announcer Jerry "the King" Lawler's predictable, incessant, and offensive yelping of the word "Puppies!" in referring to wrestler Trish Stratus' breasts.

9. In *Doctor of Doom*, the woman's body becomes a site for various regimes of male control, specifically the law and medicine. By the 1970s, issues of who controls a woman's body became central in Mexican feminism: not simply by confronting paradigms of patriarchy and machismo, but by addressing issues of how abortion was (and still is) restricted, how rape and wife-beating were tacitly accepted, and how sexual harassment in the streets was commonplace. See Eli Barta, "Neofeminism in Mexico" (Working Paper #33), pages 5–7 of 31. Copy available at www.duke.edu/web/las/workingpapers/neofeminism.pdf.

10. Wilt notes that the title of the first *Luchadora* film, *Las luchadoras vs. el médico asesino*, is also a bit misleading in that Médico Asesino was the popular luchador who starred in *El Enmascarado de Plata*, the film vehicle originally designed for Santo. Médico Asesino appears nowhere in *Las luchadoras vs. el médico asesino*, and Wilt suggests that the usage of Médico Asesino in the title may have indeed been designed to take advantage of Médico Asesino's notoriety, with a more accurate title for the film being *Las luchadoras contra el sabio loco* (*Wrestling Women vs. the Mad Genius*), or even *Las luchadoras contra el médico loco* (*Wrestling Women vs. the Mad Doctor*). See Wilt's "Elizabeth Campbell Filmography" website.

11. *The Mask of Fu Manchu* itself is a highly racist film, pitting noble Anglo archeologists against the "Oriental trickery" of Fu Manchu at a time when the U.S. and Japan were heading towards an inevitable war. From 1964 to 1969, a historical era highly influenced by the growth of Maoism, Christopher Lee starred in a series of five *Fu Manchu* films.

12. An observation owed to David Wilt; see "*Las Luchadoras contra la momia*" at his "Elizabeth Campbell Filmography" website.

13. In *Santo contra los cazadores de cabezas* the obligatory scientist character is named "Dr. Castro." However, in Curiel's *Santo contra la Mafia de vicio*, the head of the criminal syndicate is named "Fidel."

14. See *In the Shadow of the Revolution*, 190–1.

15. See Brandenberg, 115–8.

16. David Wilt, "*Las luchadoras contra la momia*," at Wilt's "Elizabeth Campbell Filmography" website.

17. In *Doctor of Doom*, there is a scene early in the film where Tommy calls his grandmother, who "can't hear," on the phone to warn her about the Mad Doctor and that she should not go out at night. Cupping the phone with his hand, he screams into the receiver, "GRANDMA, DEAR! DON'T GO OUT TO-NIGHT!"

18. In response to the growing left-wing sentiment in Mexico fostered by progressive political leader Lázaro Cárdenas and Fidel Castro's victory in Cuba, the López Mateos administration actively promoted economic development and reform, although it is less clear whether this was prompted by a desire to help the poor and down-trodden or to stem a potential "radical-left" movement in Mexico (i.e. Cuba), especially considering the strong anti–Communist measures taken by the López Mateos presidency. See Donald Hodges and Ross Gandry, *Mexico 1910–1976: Reform or Revolution?* (London: Zed Books, 1979), 101.

19. There is a similar, even more interminable sequence in Cardona's *Santo en el tesoro de Drácula*, where Santo and his entourage spend several minutes exploring the underground caverns of Dracula's lair; to further exacerbate the tedium, the Black Hood and his henchmen follow Santo through the passages, and they must literally duplicate Santo's path shot by shot, *doubling* the amount of film time the already ponderous sequence consumes.

20. This specific shot prompted a degree of aggravation in David Wilt's comments on the film, with Wilt noting that apparently "the producers were too damn cheap" to shoot the bat actually flying out the window. See "*Las luchadoras contra la momia*," available at the "Elizabeth Campbell Filmography" website.

21. Also in 1964, *Atacan las brujas* begins with a surreal dream sequence in which San Martín, the actress portraying Chela (Charlotte), is similarly shown chained to a slab in a crypt and threatened with human sacrifice by evil monsters — in this case witches. Indeed, San Martín spends most of *Atacan las brujas* chained to a slab either awaiting an untimely death or a timely rescue by Santo.

Chapter 6

1. Observations owed to personal correspondence with David Wilt.

2. Rene Cardona, Jr. himself would eventually become a legend in cult cinema, directing such exploitation classics as *Tintorera!* (*Tiger Shark*, 1976), a low-budget, blatant copy of *Jaws* with nudity and copious gore; *Ciclón* (*Cyclone*, 1977), a version of Hitchcock's *Lifeboat* stressing cannibalism; *Guyana, el crimen del siglo* (*Guyana, Crime of the Century*, 1979; U.S. title: *Guyana, Cult of the Damned*), in which "Reverend Jim

Johnson" leads his religious cult to mass suicide at "Johnsontown"; *Ataque de los pájaros* (*Attack of the Birds*, 1986; U.S. titles: *Beaks* and *Birds of Prey*), a shameless copy of Hitchcock's *The Birds* with some gratuitous, full-frontal female nudity and graphic close-ups of pigeons mangling humans; and *Los placeres ocultos* (*Hidden Pleasures*; 1988; U.S. title: *Playback*), a Brian DiPalma–influenced, and rather explicit, sex and violence psychodrama starring Sonia Infante.

3. Cardona also uses this "painting-insert" to bridge scenes in *Santo contra los jinites del terror*; while in *Santo en el tesoro de Drácula* he employs both the "painting-insert" as well as the "dripping blood" opening credit sequence (however, in that *Santo en el tesoro de Drácula* is only readily available in a black and white version, the effects are not nearly as striking).

4. Many horror films offer an internal critique of voyeurism and its relationship, a theme pioneered in Michael Powell's vastly underrated *Peeping Tom* (1959) and, of course, Alfred Hitchcock's *Psycho* (1960).

5. In René Cardona, Jr.'s *Ataque de los pájaros*, two early scenes feature grisly close-ups of a bird attacking and pecking out the respective victim's eyes, suggesting that this shot, even if filmed by Intrator, would not be inconsistent with the work of the Cardona, Jr., co-screenwriter on *Bloody Apes*.

6. Héctor Aguilar Camín and Lorenzo Meyer, *In the Shadow of the Mexican Revolution*, 201. Emphasis added.

Conclusion

1. Héctor Aguilar Camín and Lorenzo Meyer, *In the Shadow of the Mexican Revolution*, 201. Emphasis added.

2. Aguilar Camín and Meyer, 203. Emphasis added.

3. Aguilar Camín and Meyer, 207.

4. As quoted in an interview with J.P. Bouyxou and Gilbert Verschooten published in *Cine Girl* (1977). The text of the interview is included on the Mondo Macabro DVD reissue of *Alucarda* (Mondo Macabro).

5. As quoted in the interview with Del Toro included on the DVD edition of *Alucarda* (Mondo Macabro).

Bibliography

Aguilar Camín, Hèctor, and Lorenzo Meyer. *In the Shadow of the Revolution: Contemporary Mexican History, 1910–1989*. Translated by Luis Alberto Fierro. Austin: University of Texas Press, 1993.

Barta, Eli. "Neofeminism in Mexico." Available at www.duke/edu/web/las/workingpapers/neofeminism.pdf.

Barthes, Roland. *Mythologies*. Translated by Annette Lavers. New York: Hill and Wang, 1972.

Bouyxou, J.P., and Gilbert Verschooten. Interview with Juan López Moctezuma. Originally published in *Cine Girl* (1977). Text of interview included on the DVD edition of *Alucarda* (Mondo Macabro).

Brandenberg, Frank. *The Making of Modern Mexico*. Englewood Cliff: Prentice-Hall, 1964.

Craig, Rob. "The Wonder World of K. Gordon Murray" website: www.kgordonmuarry.com. Comprehensive filmography and reviews of Murray's Mexican horror imports, children's films, and exploitation films.

del Toro, Guillermo. Interview with Pete Tombs. Included on the DVD edition of *Alucarda* (Mondo Macabro).

Foucault, Michel. *Discipline and Punish: The Birth of the Prison*. Translated by Alan Sheridan. New York: Vintage Books, 1995.

Greene, Alison. "Cablevision(nation) in Rural Yacatán: Performing Modernity and *Mexicanidad* in the Early 1990s." In *Fragments of a Golden Age*, 415–51.

Hodges, Donald, and Ross Gandry. *Mexico 1910–1976: Reform or Revolution?* London: Zed Books, 1979.

Horkheimer, Max, and Theodor W. Adorno. *Dialectic of Enlightenment*. New York: Verso, 1997.

Jameson, Fredric. "Third World Literature in the Era of Multinational Capitalism." *Social Text* 5:3 (1986).

_____. *Postmodernism, or, the Cultural Logic of Late Capitalism*. Durham: Duke University Press, 1990.

Joseph, Gilbert, Anne Rubenstein, and Eric Zolov, eds. *Fragments of a Golden Age: The Politics of Culture in Mexico Since 1940*. Durham: Duke University Press, 2001.

"Juan Lopez Moctezuma — A Cultured Maverick." Included on the DVD edition of *Alucarda* (Mondo Macabro)

Kurtz, Frank. "The Weird World and Wanderings of the Aztec Mummy." Available at www.monstershindig.com.

"La (Nueva) Arena de Lucha Libre" website: www.highspots.com/arena/profiles.htm. Features numerous biographies of former and current luchadores.

Levi, Heather. "Masked Media: The Adventures of Lucha Libre on the Small Screen." In *Fragments of a Golden Age*, 330–72.

Monsiváis, Carlos. "All the People Came and Did Not Fit on the Screen." In *Mexican Cinema*, ed. Paranaguá, 145–51.

_____. *Mexican Postcards*. Translated by John Kraniauskas. New York: Verso, 1997.

Mora, Carl J. *Mexican Cinema: Reflections of a Society, 1896–1980*. Berkeley: University of California Press, 1982.

Mulvey, Laura. "Visual Pleasure and Narrative Cinema." In *Film Theory and Criticism: Introductory*

Readings, 4th ed, ed. Gerald Mast, Marshall Cohen, and Leo Braudy, 746–57. New York: Oxford University Press, 1992.

Murphy, Dan. "Mexican Wrestling Heroes Give the Smackdown to Vice." *Christian Science Monitor*, 8/22/2001, vol. 93, no. 188: 7.

Newitz. Annalee. "What Makes Things Cheesy? Satire, Multinationalism, and B-Movies." *Social Text*, 18:2 (2000): 59–82.

Paranaguá, Paulo Antonio, ed. *Mexican Cinema*. Translated by Ana López. London: BFI, 1995.

_____. "Ten Reasons to Love or Hate Mexican Cinema." In *Mexican Cinema*, ed. Paranaguà, 1–13.

Raskin, Elissa J. *Women Filmmakers in Mexico: The Country in Which We Dream*. Austin: University of Texas Press, 2001.

Rhodes, Gary D. "Fantasmas del Cine Mexicano." In *Fear Without Frontiers*, ed. Steven Jay Schnieder. Surrey: FAB Press, 2004.

Rubenstein. Anne. *Bad Language, Naked Ladies, and Other Threats to the Nation: A Political History of Comic Books in Mexico*. Durham: Duke University Press, 1998.

_____. "Bodies, Cities, Cinema: Pedro Infante's Death as Public Spectacle." In *Fragments of a Golden Age*, 199–233.

"Santo and Friends" website: www.santoandfriends.com. Features biographies and filmographies of Santo, Blue Demon, and Mil Máscaras, as well as an overall filmography of Mexican horror and wrestling films.

Sconce, Jeffery. "'Trashing' the Academy." *Screen* 36:4, Winter 1995: 373–91.

Sontag, Susan. *Against Interpretation*. New York: Doubleday Books, 1967.

Stavans, Ilan. *The Riddle of Cantinflas: Essays on Hispanic Popular Culture*. Albuquerque: University of New Mexico Press, 1998.

Stern, Steven J. *The Secret History of Gender: Women, Men, and Power in Late Colonial Mexico*. Chapel Hill: University of North Carolina Press, 1995.

Syder, Andrew, and Dolores Tierney. "Importation/Mexploitation, or, How a Crime-Fighting, Monster-Slaying Wrestler Almost Found Himself in an Italian Sword-and-Sandal Epic." In *Horror International*, ed. Steven Jay Schnieder and Tony Williams. Detroit: Wayne State University, forthcoming. Page numbers and citations taken from a copy of the essay provided courtesy of Kathleen Newman in Spring 2002.

Tombs, Pete. *Mondo Macabro: Weird and Wonderful Cinema from Around the World*. New York: St. Martin's Griffin, 1997.

Turrent, Tómas Pérez. "The Studios." In *Mexican Cinema*, ed. Paranaguá, 133–44.

Wilt, David E. *The Mexican Filmography: 1916–2001*. Jefferson, NC: McFarland, 2004. The definitive guide to Mexican cinema.

_____. "Masked Men and Monsters." In *Mondo Macabro*, 137–47.

_____. "The Films of El Santo" website: www.wam.umd.edu/~dwilt/santo.html. Comprehensive filmography and reviews of Santo's entire film career.

_____. "Elizabeth Campbell Filmography" website: www.wam.umd.edu/~dwilt/campbell.htm.

_____. "Biographical Dictionary of Mexican Film Performers" at "The Mexican Film Resource Page" website: www.wam.umd.edu/~dwilt/mfb.html.

Zolov, Eric. *Refried Elvis: The Rise of the Mexican Counterculture*. Berkeley: University of California Press, 1998.

Index

Numbers in **_bold italics_** refer to pages with illustrations.

Index

Index

Index